Also by Suzanne O'Malley

How to Avoid Love and Marriage
(with Dan Greenburg)

Suzanne O'Malley

"*Are You*

There Alone?"

The Unspeakable Crime
of Andrea Yates

Simon & Schuster

NEW YORK   LONDON

TORONTO   SYDNEY

SIMON & SCHUSTER
Rockefeller Center
1230 Avenue of the Americas
New York, NY 10020

For information regarding special discounts for bulk purchases,
please contact Simon & Schuster Special Sales:
1-800-456-6798 or business@simonandschuster.com.

Designed by C. Linda Dingler

Manufactured in the United States of America

10   9   8   7   6   5   4   3   2   1

Library of Congress Cataloging-in-Publication Data
O'Malley, Suzanne, date.
    Are you there alone? : the unspeakable crime of Andrea Yates / Suzanne O'Malley.
        p.   cm.
    Includes index.
    1. Yates, Andrea.   2. Infanticide—Texas—Houston.   3. Filicide—Texas—
Houston.   4. Women murderers—Texas—Houston.   5. Trials (Murder)—Texas—
Harris County.   6. Postpartum psychiatric disorders—Texas—Houston.   I. Title.
HV6541.U62H68   2004
364.152'3'092—dc22   2003067248

ISBN 0-7432-4485-0

Some passages of this book originally appeared in the following publications:

O, the Oprah Magazine, February 2002, "A Cry in the Dark"
The New York Times, March 3, 2002, "Standing by His Woman"
Salon.com, March 13, 2002, "Worst-Case Scenario"

For Barbara Ida Haag and Mary Catherine Heenan

I see, the thing I do;
It's love not ignorance leads me astray.
My help shall save you; only—saved—fulfil,
Fulfil your promise.

—Euripedes, *The Medea*

CONTENTS

AS AN INVESTIGATIVE REPORTER, I began covering the murders of Noah, John, Paul, Luke, and Mary Yates hours after their mother, Andrea Yates, then 36, drowned them in their suburban Houston, Texas, home on June 20, 2001.

A transplant to New York City, I was visiting my hometown, Richardson, Texas, in suburban Dallas when regional news of the drownings broke live from the crime scene. Each of the people and places in those early broadcasts became intimately known to me as I pursued the story first for *O, the Oprah Magazine,* and later for the *New York Times Magazine, Salon.com,* and the television newsmagazine *Dateline NBC* (for whom I broke the story of an itinerant preacher who had influenced Andrea Yates).

On March 12, 2002, Andrea Yates was found guilty of the murders of three of her five children. Harris County reserves the right to prosecute the murders of Paul and Luke at another time.

One day after the guilty verdict, my reporting regarding the mistaken testimony of a key prosecution witness, Dr. Park Dietz, contributed to a motion for mistrial and grounds for an appeal of Andrea Yates's conviction. Dietz's testimony fueled the argument that Yates planned the murders based on an alleged episode of an NBC television series, in which a mother kills her children and uses a postpartum defense to set herself free. Dietz, a consultant to *Law & Order,* testified that the episode had aired shortly before the murders. I had worked as a script writer for *Law & Order* on several occasions and did not recall that episode. Overnight, I confirmed that no such episode had ever been written or produced. The next day, network attorneys began discussions with the defense and prosecution. Dietz recanted that portion of his testimony, but the jury had already reached its guilty verdict. The judge did instruct jurors to consider the impact of the mistestimony in determining whether to choose death or life in prison as Yates's punishment. The *New York Post* reported on March 22, 2002, that I "saved Yates" from the death penalty.

Andrea Yates is currently serving life in the Skyview Unit of Rusk Penitentiary in Rusk, Texas. She will not be eligible for parole until the year 2041 when she will be nearly 77.

More than a year after the children's murders, I knew that the real story of Andrea Yates had not been adequately told. I also understood that correlation and analysis of interviews, information, and the public record would take at least a year and could only be adequately reported in book form. Much of what I have written has not been previously reported.

I divided my research into twenty areas of investigation:

Andrea Pia Kennedy Yates
The Yates family
The Kennedy family
Andrea Yates's attorneys
Office of Harris County District Attorney
Harris County Police Department
Staff of Harris County Jail
Office of Judge Belinda Hill
Mental Health and Mental Retardation Administration of Texas
Andrea Yates's psychiatrists
Religious influences on Andrea Yates
Medical staff of Ben Taub Hospital
Medical staff of Memorial Spring Shadows Glen Hospital
Medical staff of Devereux Texas Treatment Network, League City
Expert witnesses
Independent experts
Jurors
Friends and colleagues of Andrea Yates
Others who talked with or visited Andrea Yates

The public record: sworn testimony; trial transcripts; books; newspaper, magazine, and television stories; public statements; video-
and audiotapes; public documents

From these sources, I constructed a list of more than one hundred
people whose sworn testimony I had witnessed or whom I had interviewed at the time of the Yates trial or whom I had yet to interview.
Over twenty-four months, I interviewed many of them. *"Are You There
Alone?"* is based largely on these interviews; my notes and observations of more than five weeks of trial testimony and court proceedings;
portions of transcribed trial testimony; nearly 2,000 pages of Andrea
Yates's medical records; autopsy reports; and Texas Department of
Health records. I attempted wherever possible to verify one person's
recollection of an event with another's, and where recollections di-
verged I chose what I believed to be the most reliable account. I have
not changed any names or identities of characters. As is customary, my
sources understood from the beginning that they did not have the right
to read or revise the manuscript before publication.

Some sources spent dozens of hours with me and offered information freely; others spent less than an hour. I interviewed Andrea Yates's
husband, Rusty Yates, more than thirty times. My correspondence with
Andrea Yates began in 2002 and continues today, totaling more than
30,000 words. Her frame of mind and whereabouts at certain times
were confirmed by correlating many types of police, jail, and hospital
records, including admission and discharge reports, health assess-
ments, consultations, patient progress notes, physician's orders, nursing
reports, medication dispensation records, nutritional intake reports,
and special intervention and precautions charts.

I interviewed Michael Woroniecki and his family in person on two
occasions and have corresponded with him and his family for more
than a year. His correspondence with me exceeds the length of this
book. Some sources provided me with diaries, time lines, medical
records, letters, notes, and calendars. Others gave information in response to facts or information obtained elsewhere. And there is original
material gleaned from living in Houston, Texas, for two years as well as
from trips to Michigan, New Orleans, and Galveston.

All of my notes were written by hand or on computer and/or transcribed from tape and indexed under the appropriate area of investigation. Subject areas were further divided chronologically into each of the days and years leading up to the deaths of the Yates children.

The feelings and thoughts of people described in the narrative are based on what they told me they felt and thought, or what they described as their thoughts and feelings in trial testimony. The trial testimony quoted is true to the substance of the official trial transcript and in some cases has been edited to assist in the narrative flow. In several instances I relied on my trial testimony notes alone, including instances of obvious trial transcription errors. I relied chiefly on two versions of the Bible, *New American Bible* (a Catholic Bible consistent with the early Catholicism of Andrea Yates and Michael Woroniecki) and *New American Standard Bible* (the Bible Michael Woroniecki prefers now).

Suzanne O'Malley
October 2003

- April 17, 1993—Russell Edison Yates and Andrea Pia Kennedy married.
- February 26, 1994—Noah Jack Yates born.
- December 15, 1995—John Samuel Yates born.
- November 1996—Miscarriage.
- September 13, 1997—Paul Abraham Yates born.
- February 15, 1999—Luke David Yates born.
- June 17, 1999—Andrea Yates took overdose of Trazodone.
- June 17–24, 1999—Andrea Yates's first hospitalization (The Methodist Hospital–Texas Medical Center); diagnosis: "major depressive disorder, single episode, severe."
- July 20, 1999—Andrea Yates attempted to kill herself with a knife.
- July 21–August 8, 1999—Andrea Yates's second hospitalization (Memorial Spring Shadows Glen Hospital); diagnosis "major depressive disorder, severe, recurrent, with psychotic features. Rule out schizophrenia, catatonic type."
- August 9–20, 1999—Andrea Yates continued hospital care as a day patient.
- October 1999—Andrea Yates's Haldol/Decanoate injections discontinued.
- January 2000—Andrea Yates's last monthly visit with psychiatrist Eileen Starbranch.
- March 2000—Andrea Yates became pregnant with Mary.
- November 30, 2000—Mary Deborah Yates born.
- March 12, 2001—Andrea Yates's father died.
- March 31–April 12, 2001—Andrea Yates's third hospitalization (Dev-

ereux Texas Treatment Network, League City); diagnosis: "Postpartum depression. Major depression, recurrent. Rule out psychotic features."

- April 2, 2001—Andrea Yates's Devereux psychiatrist, Mohammad Saeed, MD, requested her court-ordered commitment to Austin State Hospital; diagnosis: "Major depression, with psychotic features."
- April 13, 2001—Andrea Yates admitted as a day patient at Devereux Texas Treatment Network, League City, Partial Hospitalization Program, one day.
- April 19, 2001—Dora Yates arrived to visit her grandchildren.
- May 3, 2001—Andrea Yates filled bathtub with water.
- May 4–14, 2001—Andrea Yates's fourth hospitalization (readmitted to Devereux); diagnosis: "Postpartum depression" and "Major Depression recurrent severe (postpartum)." Haldol prescribed for second time in Yates's medical history.
- May 15–22, 2001—Andrea Yates continued care at Devereux, League City, as day patient in the Partial Hospitalization Program.
- June 4, 2001—Psychiatrist Mohammad Saeed ordered Andrea Yates to discontinue Haldol; did not prescribe another antipsychotic medication.
- June 2001—Tropical Storm Allison flooded downtown Houston.
- June 18, 2001—Andrea Yates's last appointment with psychiatrist Mohammad Saeed.
- **June 20, 2001—Andrea Yates drowned her children.**
- July 30, 2001—Andrea Yates's attorneys filed Notice of Intent to offer insanity defense.
- August 9, 2001—State of Texas filed motion to seek the death penalty.
- September 12, 2001—Andrea Yates's sanity hearing postponed because of 9/11 attack on World Trade Center and Pentagon.
- September 18, 2001—Competency hearing began.
- September 22, 2001—Andrea Yates found mentally competent to stand trial after the jury deliberated more than eight hours.
- February 18, 2002—Andrea Yates's murder trial began.
- March 12, 2002—Andrea Yates found guilty of two counts of capital murder after the jury deliberated less than four hours.
- March 15, 2002—Andrea Yates sentenced to life in prison after jury deliberated for thirty-five minutes.

PROLOGUE

I CAN TELL YOU with certainty that on June 18, 1999, at precisely 1:30 in the afternoon, Andrea Yates had been quietly sitting in the dayroom of the Methodist Hospital and fifteen minutes earlier she had been sleeping in her hospital bed. That on August 5, 1999, she sat with her consulting doctor at Memorial Spring Shadows Glen Hospital and said no to electroconvulsive therapy (ECT). I can tell you that on April 4, 2001, at 1:00 in the afternoon, she was drinking Carnation Instant Breakfast mixed with chocolate milk through a straw. That nurses watched every day as her husband came to the hospital and tried to feed her the same drink. I can tell you that on May 5, 2001, she went to group therapy and said nothing. When she got a little better, she introduced herself in group as "Andrea, Depression." At 9:00 AM on June 20, 2001, she was sitting at her kitchen table in suburban Houston uncharacteristically eating Corn Pops out of the box while her children watched morning cartoons. Between 9:00 AM and 9:45 AM the same day, she went into her guest bathroom and, calling her children to her one at a time, drowned them.

I can trace the steps of her body in exacting detail; knowing the mind of Andrea Yates was the challenge.

CHAPTER 1

The Prophecy

A little before 10:00 AM—9:56, to be exact—Russell "Rusty" Yates's cell phone rang in the sixth-floor Shuttle Vehicle Engineering Office he shared with three other National Aeronautics and Space Administration (NASA) employees. It was his wife, Andrea, calling. Not even an hour had passed since he had left her at home with the kids. She'd been sitting at the kitchen table eating Corn Pops out of the box. He'd given her a 300-milligram morning dose of the antidepressant Effexor and, the previous night, a 45-milligram dose of the antidepressant Remeron with a 15-milligram dissolvable Remeron SolTab booster. His mother was due at the house to watch the kids at any minute. He had a 10:30 AM presentation to give to the Space Shuttle Program manager on the progress of the space vehicle's instrumentation systems upgrade.

"You need to come home," Andrea said, in a "firm, sober" voice Rusty had heard only once before—and dreaded. Not long after the birth of their fourth son, Luke, two years earlier, she'd had a sort of nervous breakdown. That time, she had *asked* Rusty to come home from work; now she wasn't asking him, she was telling him.

"What's wrong?" he asked.

"It's time," Andrea said.

"What do you mean?"

"It's time," she repeated, later recalling that she hadn't "said it well."

Rusty Yates didn't need to hear any more. When his wife's father had died three months before, she'd gotten sick again. And there was a new baby at home, 6-month-old Mary. He left his office, stopping only to tell a colleague he had a "family emergency." On the elevator he wished for the days before Andrea had become sick, when he didn't have to communicate with her through a filter of mental disease, wondering whether she was really well or might try to kill herself as she had twice before. Wondering whether he'd micromanaged life well enough to be there to stop her if she did.

He raced through the lobby and out the front doors of NASA Building One, dialing his mother on the way. Dora Yates had come from her home in Hermitage, Tennessee, to help out when Andrea became ill. A couple of weeks had stretched into a couple of months. Her daughter-in-law had been hospitalized twice, but she hadn't improved much. They were all running on fumes.

"Mom, are you there yet?" Rusty asked.

"No," Dora Yates answered. She hadn't left the Extended Stay America Hotel on NASA Road 1 yet.

"Hurry," he told her. "Something's wrong at the house."

He was ten minutes away. He sprinted across the employee parking lot to his SUV and dialed Andrea from behind the wheel. Thank God she answered.

"Is anybody hurt?" he asked.

"Yes," Andrea answered.

"Who?"

"The kids."

The kids? What did she mean? "Which ones?" Rusty asked.

"All of them" was her unfathomable answer.

AT 9:48 AM on Wednesday, June 20, 2001, eight minutes before she called her husband, Andrea Yates had dialed 911. "I need a police officer," she said, her breath heaving unsteadily into the phone.

"What's the problem?" police telecommunicator Dorene Stubblefield asked with a whiff of attitude.

"I just need him to come," Yates said.

"I need to know why they are coming," Stubblefield persisted. "Is your husband there?"

"No."

"What's the problem?"

"I need him to come."

"I need to know *why* they are coming," Stubblefield repeated.

No answer. Nothing but Andrea Yates breathing irregularly, as if an intruder might be holding a gun to her head.

"Is he standing next to you?"

Yates fumbled the phone.

"Are you having a disturbance?" Stubblefield asked, thinking this might be a domestic problem. No answer. She had to determine whether she was sending officers into a dangerous situation. "Are you ill, or what?"

"Yes, I'm ill."

"What kind of medical problems?"

Valuable seconds ticked by. Who could explain this to a stranger on the phone?

"You need an ambulance?" Stubblefield suggested.

"No, I need a police officer," Yates said.

"Do you need an ambulance?" Stubblefield repeated.

"No . . . Yes, send an ambulance . . ." Yates's breath became even more labored. Then nothing but static.

"Hello?" Stubblefield asked, urgency finally mounting in her voice. Still no answer. "Is someone burglarizing your house?" she asked.

"No."

"What is it?" asked Stubblefield, frustrated.

Silence.

"What kind of medical problems are you having?"

More time slipped away. At length, Yates once more asked Stubblefield for a police officer.

"Are you at 942 Beachcomber?"

"Yes."

"Are you there alone?"

"Yes," Yates said. Suddenly there was more static, then another long silence. Stubblefield wondered if she'd lost her. The sound of panicked breathing returned.

"Andrea Yates?"

"Yes."

"Is your husband there?"

"No. I'm sick."

"How are you sick?" Stubblefield asked. Yates's answer was unintelligible.

"Andrea Yates, is your husband there?"

"No."

"Why do you need a policeman, ma'am?"

"I just need him to be here."

"For what?"

"I just need him to come."

A long silence ensued, followed by static.

"You're *sure* you're alone?" By now Stubblefield knew something was wrong, but was Yates refusing to answer her questions or was someone stopping her from answering? After eight years on the job, Stubblefield thought she knew how to recognize a battered wife when she heard one.

"No," Yates said finally, she was not alone. "My kids are here." But her rasping breaths continued.

"How old are the children?"

"Seven, 5, 3, 2, and 6 months."

"You have five children?"

"Yes."

She might not know exactly what was wrong, but five children were enough to satisfy Stubblefield. "Okay. We'll send an officer."

"Thank you," Yates said politely and hung up.

OFFICER DAVID KNAPP was patrolling alone in his marked police car. He was a "uni"—a uniformed police officer—doing the 6:00 AM to 2:00 PM shift in south Houston. At 9:52 AM his radio announced a dispatch to Beachcomber Lane, a 911 call. He needed to do a "welfare check." Welfare checks made him glad he'd done crisis intervention training in his spare time. What was up this morning?

A wet, white female with long, dark hair met him at the front door to the single-level brick home. She was wide-eyed and breathing heavily.

"What do you need a police officer for, ma'am?" he asked.

"I just killed my kids," she said, looking him straight in the eye.

Okay, he hadn't been prepared for that. All he could think to ask was "Why?"

"I killed my kids," she repeated flatly.

"Where are they?"

"They're in the bed." Andrea Yates motioned Officer Knapp into the house, past the dog barking from her kennel in the family room, down the hallway lined with framed family photos and carpeted in beige plush, and into the master bedroom. A king-size mattress and box springs sat on the floor. The first thing Knapp noticed was a small child's arm sticking out from under the deep burgundy cotton sheets, the arm was porcelain white, and Knapp later learned it belonged to 2-year-old Luke Yates. There were "what appeared to be four lumps in the bed." When he pulled back the covers, he had "the impression the children were all in bed resting peacefully. It appeared the children were tucked in. Mary's head was lying on her older brother's arm."

Methodically, Knapp checked each of the children for signs of life. He noticed a frothy substance under three of the children's noses—it was the sign that their lungs had "more or less burst." There was no way Knapp or Emergency Medical Services could revive them now. He was too late.

He wished the dog would stop barking.

TWENTY-ONE YEARS in the Houston Police Department specializing in narcotics and hostage negotiation had done little to erase Officer Frank Stumpo's New York City accent, or his hard-edged cop prose. Like Knapp, Stumpo had been called to the scene on a welfare check. He pulled up in his blue-and-white, approached with caution, knocked, and opened the door. He found Officer Knapp in the family room with Andrea Yates.

Stumpo retraced Knapp's steps down the hallway to the left. "I saw a sparsely furnished room with a mattress on the floor, and I saw a little head on the mattress," he said. "I thought it was a doll. The closer I got, the more [it] came into focus and when I got close enough, I realized it was the head of a child. . . . I touched the child's head. . . . It was warm to the touch." In the guest bathroom tub he discovered a fifth child, 7-year-old Noah, floating face down with no pulse. He wanted to hurl.

Andrea Yates sat on a blue love seat. Knapp sat beside her. He asked for her driver's license, which she gave him, and permission to use the telephone in the adjacent kitchen to call his supervisor.

FOR JOHN TREADGOLD, it was a slow news day. Treadgold was a roaming cameraman for KPRC, Houston's NBC Television affiliate. Ten public safety radios cluttered the dash of his well-worn, white Ford Explorer. His radios were tuned to the ambulance chasers' "Top Ten" favorites: Houston's Fire Department; Emergency Medical Services; Police Department; Coast Guard; Sheriff's Department; Life Flight Helicopter; Pasadena, Texas, Fire and Police Departments; and area VHF and UHF Volunteer Fire Departments. He used his "go to" radio when he keyed in on a story. Camera gear crowded the back of his van. He stored his $20,000, broadcast-quality Beta Cam SP in a camera safe. The safe, along with tripods, light stands, weight bags, videotape, and other equipment were stowed behind a locked cage purchased at a police supply store.

One had to have an ear for filtering through the shrill radio static to catch one code word that might be tonight's lead story. That, and an unusual tolerance for noise. Treadgold was dodging the crisscross of downtown Houston streets, every one of them, it seemed, perpetually under construction. He'd spent enough time hanging outside the front doors of the old Criminal Courts building with his video camera weighing on his shoulder to notice a quotation etched in the sidewalk: "I think I'll like Houston if they ever get it finished." Oveta Culp Hobby, a matriarch of contemporary Houston, had said that in 1946. Houston still wasn't finished.

Somebody had a kitchen fire. An elderly Houstonian had died of natural causes. The police band droned on like the rest, requesting an officer to this address or that, a supervisor for . . . what was that? He spun the volume dial on the police radio. Automatically, his brain searched his audio memory for a sentence fragment. He couldn't have heard right. "Multiple pediatric DOAs?" That was something he'd *never* heard. The dispatcher must have said GOAs: Gone on Arrival. Crackling on another channel he recognized the ambulance number of a southeast Houston EMS unit in service for something major.

Treadgold called his assignment editor back at KPRC and asked her to check for a police computer dispatch record. There it was at 10:00 AM. The editor double-checked the listing with Fire Dispatch. It was a respiratory problem, "unconscious," with a tag note indicating "possible children," the editor told him, intersection of Beachcomber and Sealark in Clear Lake. A twenty-minute drive southeast—with no traffic. He headed for the Gulf Coast Freeway.

NINE MINUTES AFTER Officer Knapp entered the house on Beachcomber, Sergeant David Svahn, a patrol supervisor with sixteen years on the force, arrived in answer to the "code one" call from his men. Knapp remained with Yates on the love seat, while Stumpo met his sergeant at the front door. "She killed her kids," he told him.

Svahn authorized Stumpo to arrest and handcuff Yates, then did a walk-through of the home that was now a crime scene. He saw a typical suburban residence with family photos on the refrigerator door, cereal bowls on the kitchen table, and toys on the floor. He noticed a child's wet gray-and-white sock lying on the hallway carpet. Outside, additional officers were already putting crime-scene tape around the house.

Svahn stationed himself in the entryway to the Yates house. He heard a scream outside and ran out the front door. An athletic man in his mid-thirties ducked under the yellow tape. He was "visibly upset and hollering some things," Svahn said. The man was Rusty Yates, Andrea's husband, the father of all five children.

"What did she do to my kids? What did she do to my kids?" Svahn remembered Rusty Yates pleading. "He said, his wife had called him at work and told him it was time to come home. His wife told him she had hurt all five of the kids and that she finally did it."

"I told him all five of his children had passed away," Svahn said. "He fell to the ground and pounded the ground and began screaming." Hell, after seeing the child in the bathtub floating in fecal matter, Svahn felt like doing the same thing. He could be another sixteen years on the force and never get used to a crime like this one. At length, Yates got up off the ground and, in his pain, grabbed a plastic yard chair and threw it at nothing in particular. Then he fell to the ground again and coiled into a fetal position, still screaming.

Rusty Yates wanted to see his kids. Wanted to hold them, talk to his wife, be told that this was a bad dream. Instead, Svahn explained that the Yates home was off-limits. Perhaps the backyard of the L-shaped corner lot would be a more private place to wait out the crime-scene investigation.

At the rear of the cedar-fenced house, through a slit in the curtain fashioned from a white pin-striped bedsheet, Rusty Yates could just see his wife sitting on the couch. He yelled through the glass, through the depth of the house, through the shell of his wife. "How could you do this? I don't understand," he yelled again and again. He was sinking to his knees. And then he was just sinking. For a second, Andrea's eyes rested on the sliver of her husband's face. "Rusty is crying," she thought. "He wants to come in but the police officer won't let him."

Stumpo walked to the French doors and shut the curtain tight, then turned to Andrea Yates. "Do you realize what you've done?" he asked.

"Yes," she answered.

> Who? . . . Whoever . . . whoever causes one of these little ones to stumble . . . I'll tell you what he has explained to me . . . I'm looking for the scripture, something like . . . it would be better to tie a mill-stone around their necks . . . hang on.[1]

Shut out, Rusty heard sobbing from the front of the house. He thought it was Andrea, but it was his mother. An officer had just told her that her grandchildren were dead.

Rusty turned and banged his fists against the side of his house. He was a NASA engineer; his life mission was to anticipate consequences. He had baby-proofed every electrical outlet in the house, put plastic corners on every table, installed keyed locks on cabinet doors where the bleach and cleaning products were stored. But he had not anticipated this. He had failed. He had not protected his wife, he had not protected his children, and he had not protected himself. "I was crying

---

1. *Letter of Andrea Yates to author, postmarked January 6, 2003; Dr. Phillip Resnick, interview with A. Yates, July 14, 2001.*

for the kids and crying for Andrea and crying because I knew I could never trust her again. It broke my heart. Andrea's the only person I met that I ever wanted to marry," he remembered later.

The only person he'd ever wanted to marry had done *this*. What did that say about him? With or without his wife he wasn't safe: he'd chosen her. Even before his wife was arrested, Rusty Yates had been sentenced to life. His mother patted his back, sobbing and trying to console her son at the same time. He turned and cried in her arms.

John Treadgold pulled out of the tight camera shot of Rusty and Dora Yates. No other news crew had made it through before police locked down the street. He warned the KPRC news helicopter not to shoot footage of street signs to prevent competing stations from intercepting the microwave signals and pinpointing the scene from the air. Treadgold had an exclusive. That night his videotaped footage led the *NBC Evening News* with Tom Brokaw. He was a father himself. He wished there were no exclusive.

Stumpo went outside and took a break, leaving Andrea Yates with Knapp. He noticed that Rusty Yates briefly recovered his composure, then became distraught again. To say that this day sucked didn't begin to cover it. Stumpo offered the guy and his mom some water—it was their house. Yates replied that Stumpo would be lucky to find a clean glass: five kids had just eaten breakfast in front of the TV. Stumpo searched the kitchen. "The guy was right," he muttered, "there aren't any clean glasses."

"There are glasses in here," Andrea Yates said, helpfully pointing to the china cupboard. The stuff suspects say never ceased to amaze Stumpo. He thought "stoic" was a good word to describe Andrea Yates's demeanor.

Outside, in the 90-degree heat, Rusty and his mother sat in yard chairs talking as crime-scene personnel filtered in and out of the house. Between bouts of crying, they pieced together their new reality. "It was hard enough to comprehend she had killed one of the kids—much less all of them," Rusty said. Before his mother arrived, he'd babbled something about how maybe Noah was with his grandmother. "I knew Noah had been in the house when I left for work, but my mind wanted to believe one of my kids had somehow survived." Dora Yates's grandsons sometimes took turns going back to her motel room at Extended

Stay America for an overnight—a coveted treat for kids with four siblings. "I remember holding out hope Noah had been spending the night with Mom," Rusty said. "Then the press wrote I didn't know whether my own son was in the house."

"One to two hours after we'd found out they were dead, and we were crying the whole time, we were thinking about when Andrea filled the tub in May. 'I guess she finally did it,'" Rusty Yates said offhandedly to his mother, still bewildered and grasping for answers. According to Rusty, Sergeant Svahn overheard the conversation and reported it to his colleagues inside the house. Later that day, it appeared in the media. Speculation took on the force of fact, treated as concrete evidence of premeditation in the drownings.

There was actually no connection between that incident and the children's drownings. When she'd filled the bathtub on May 3, 2001, Andrea Yates was acting on a different delusion. She'd just been discharged from Devereux Texas Treatment Network in League City following her third inpatient hospitalization and had had two follow-up sessions with her psychiatrist there, Mohammad Saeed, MD. She was on a regimen of 4 milligrams of the antipsychotic drug Risperdal, plus 300 milligrams of the antidepressant Wellbutrin SR and 150 milligrams of the antidepressant Effexor XR. According to witnesses, she had seen a water truck on the street and began to imagine her family's bills were unpaid and the utility workmen were going to cut off water to her house. When Dora asked her daughter-in-law why she was filling the tub, Andrea said, "I might need it." Filling one's bathtub with water for washing dishes and flushing toilets was prudent. Wasn't that what one did as a precaution before losing running water in a Gulf Coast tropical storm like the one that had just flooded Houston?

The next day, May 4, 2001, Andrea's husband put her back in the hospital. Andrea was "sad, tearful, depressed, not talking," according to Devereux records. On May 7, Saeed wrote that her "husband was gravely concerned." Andrea had refused to eat "anything even on his [Rusty's] request—which was unusual for patient. We discussed the options including ECT [electroconvulsive therapy]. They remain reluctant and want to try exactly the same treatment that got her better last time." Andrea was discharged as an inpatient after ten days in Devereux, on May 14.

She spent eight more consecutive days at Devereux's daytime Partial Hospitalization Program, mostly in substance abuse groups. Lacking a program for postpartum disorders, Devereux drug counselors instead taught Andrea how to avoid chemical and alcohol dependency and how damaging these substances were to the brain. By the time of her discharge on May 22, 2001, she was once again able to speak in complete sentences.

AT 11:00 AM, Officer Bob King and his partner, Officer Douglas Bacon, both homicide investigators, arrived at the crime scene to begin collecting evidence along with Sergeant Boyd Smith, who interviewed Dora Yates outside.

King took one look at Andrea Yates and asked that her handcuffs be removed. He pulled a worn card from his pocket and read Yates her rights "one at a time from the card verbatim." She "gave him her yeses."

"You have the right to remain silent and not make any statement at all. Do you understand that?" he asked her.

Yates nodded.

"Any statement you make may be used—and probably will be used—as evidence against you in court," King continued. "Do you understand that?"

"Yes."

"You have the right to have a lawyer present to advise you prior to and during any questioning. Do you understand that?"

"Yes."

"If you are unable to employ a lawyer you have the right to have a lawyer appointed to advise you prior to and during any questioning. Do you understand that?"

"Yes."

"And finally, you have the right to stop this interview at any time. Do you understand that?"

"Yes."

"Are you willing to give up your right to remain silent and to have an attorney present?" he asked.

"Yes," Yates replied.

Then he asked for Yates's consent to search the house, handing her a Voluntary Consent for Search and Seizure. She spent thirty seconds reading the form and signed it.

King selected some dry clothes from the master bedroom closet: some underwear, a purple short-sleeved T-shirt, white socks, blue jeans, and tan shoes. He asked Yates whether that clothing would be all right; she nodded. King handed the dry clothing to Stumpo. Without a female officer present, Andrea Yates would have to change back at the jail.

Stumpo wanted to take Andrea to his squad car through the back of the house to avoid the media activity in front. Another officer was taking a statement from Rusty Yates at the cedar picnic table in the backyard. Stumpo tried the knob on the side door to the garage with no luck. "Great, it's locked," he said out loud.

"The keys are there," Andrea volunteered, pointing to a cork bulletin board in the kitchen. Wherever Andrea Yates's mind had gone, Stumpo thought, she damn sure knew where things were.

Stumpo drove Andrea Yates to police headquarters at 1200 Travis for interrogation and later to the Mykawa police facility. He tuned the car radio to a talk show reporting on the Yates homicides. It was "harsh," he recalled. Andrea Yates was already "the Medea" of Houston. Already the stuff of which myths were made. The "Rub-a-dub-dub, five dead kids in a tub murderer," one shock jock called her. Stumpo "noticed her reacting to the words the gentleman was saying on the radio show." She was "quivering" and began to look "sullen." "Honestly," he recalled, "she seemed very embarrassed." He later told Yates's lawyer that he didn't recall purposely turning up the radio. "I may have," he said. "I was on the freeway." But Andrea Yates heard the volume rising, or thought she did.

Stumpo exited onto Airport Boulevard, turned right onto Mykawa, then made a left into the driveway. There were hordes of cameramen. Even a seen-it-all guy like Stumpo was impressed.

"You're a celebrity," he told Andrea Yates.

ANDREA YATES LOOKED across the table at the man who had brought her the Diet Coke. Her eyes were dead black.

"If you could, just go ahead and, and name your children and give their ages," Sergeant Eric Mehl said as the audiotape whirred on in Interview Room 6 of the Harris County Police Headquarters at 1200 Travis in Houston. Mehl, a twelve-year veteran homicide detective, never used videotape to interview a subject. It wasn't his habit.

"Noah, 7 years old. John, 5 years old. Paul, 3 years old. Luke, 2 years old. Mary, 6 months old," Yates replied. She had no attorney. There was a readiness in her answers that didn't match the lethargy of her speech. Mehl had been over these questions with her already, taking notes before interviewing her on tape. She was the only one left alive who'd been in the house during the drownings, and she was about to tell exactly what had happened in her own words.

"Okay, and we also talked about earlier—you've been treated for depression," Mehl said, consulting the interview notes he would destroy the next day. "Is that right?"

"Yes."

"And who's your current doctor?"

"Dr. Saeed."

"And the last time you saw him?"

"Two . . . two days ago."

"Okay, and what time does Rusty leave for work?"

"He left about 9."

"And, by the time Rusty left, were all of your children awake at that time?"

"Yes."

"Okay. What was going on in the household at that time? Were they eating breakfast . . . ?"

"Yes."

"What were they having?"

"Cereal."

"After Rusty left, you filled the bathtub with water, is that correct?"

"Yes."

"How many bathtubs in your home?"

"One." There was a stall shower in the bathroom off the master bedroom.

"Okay, so it's just the—the master bath, I guess you would call it?"

"Yes," Yates replied, incorrectly. The shallow white enamel tub was in the blue-walled guest bathroom.

"Okay, is it a regular-sized bathtub or is it a big one?"

"Regular-sized."

"How far did you fill it?"

"About three inches from the top."

"About three inches from the top—after you drew the bath water, what was your intent?" Mehl asked, hoping to steer the questioning toward motive. "What were you about to do?"

"Drown the children," Yates said in the same monotone in which she had answered all of Mehl's other questions. No wailing, no moaning, no facial expression, he recalled. "Okay. Why were you going to drown your children?"

As if her script had come to a sudden dead end, for fifteen seconds Andrea Yates said nothing. "She was staring directly at me," Mehl recalled. "She was within two feet of me, and she just sits there and stares. Her lips maybe quivered like she wanted to say something, but it wasn't coming out."

How long would he have to wait for an answer if he didn't prompt her? Mehl had no idea. It was important to try to establish motive. "Was it, was it in reference to, or was it because the children had done something?" he asked.

"No," she said, simply.

"You were not mad at the children?"

"No." He'd struck out there.

"Okay, you had thought of this prior to this day?"

"Yes."

Bingo. "How long have you been having thoughts about wanting— or not wanting to—but, drowning your children?"

"Probably since I realized I have not been a good mother to them."

Better to . . . to . . . I'm looking for it . . . tie a millstone around his neck and be thrown . . . have I lost you? Wake up . . . thrown into the sea . . .[2]

"What makes you say that?" Mehl asked, searching for the premeditation that is the difference between manslaughter and murder.

---

2. *Letter of A. Yates to author, postmarked January 6, 2003; Dr. Phillip Resnick, interview with A. Yates, July 14, 2001.*

"They weren't developing correctly."

"Behavioral problems?" Mehl suggested.

"Yes," Yates agreed.

"Learning problems?" Mehl continued.

"Yes" again.

"So after you drew the bath water, what happened?"

"I put Paul in," Yates answered. "Perfect Paul" was the best behaved and most compliant of all the children.

"And how old is Paul?" Mehl asked. The children had died so
recently, they lingered in the present tense for both Mehl and their
mother.

"Paul is 3."

"Okay, and when you put Paul in the bath water, was he face down
or face up?"

"He was face down."

"And did he struggle with you?"

"Yes."

"How long do you think that struggle happened?"

"A couple of minutes."

"And you were able to forcibly hold him under the water?"

"Yes," Yates said, agreeing to Mehl's description.

"By the time you brought him out of the water, had he stopped
struggling?"

"Yes."

"There was no more movement?" Mehl asked.

"No."

"And after you brought him out of the water, what did you do?"

"I laid him on the bed."

"Face up or face down?"

"Face up."

"Did you cover him?"

"Yes."

"Did you cover his entire body?"

"Yes."

"With what?"

"A sheet."

Mehl didn't ask why. The confession to the first drowning was complete. "Okay, so after you put Paul on the bed and covered him, then what happened?"

"I put Luke in," Yates answered wrongly. In fact, she had drowned John, her most rambunctious boy, second, not Luke, but it would be months before anyone knew that.[3]

"Okay, how old is Luke?" Mehl began again, as he would for each child.

"He's 2."

"Okay, and was he face down in the water or face up?"

"Face down."

"Did he struggle?"

"Yes."

"How long do you think that struggle lasted?"

"Just a couple minutes."

"Okay, and when you brought Luke out of the water, was he—any movement at all?"

"No."

"What happened to Luke then?"

"I put him on the bed."

"Did you cover him with the same sheet that you'd used to cover Paul?"

"Yes."

"Okay, so Paul and Luke are on the bed, then what happens?"

"I put John in."

"Okay, and how old is John?"

"John is 5."

"Okay. How did you get John to come into the bathroom?"

"I called him in."

"Okay, and, and he came in—"

"Yes," Yates replied, her yeses beginning to come with such robotic quickness that Mehl couldn't finish the question before she answered.

"Did you say anything to him?"

"I told him to get in the tub," she answered.

"Okay, and did he?"

"No."

---

3. *Letter of A. Yates to author, postmarked January 6, 2003.*

"What did he do?"

Yates gave no description of what John did. She responded automatically, "I put him in the tub."

"Did you pick him up?" Mehl asked. "How? Under the arms?" he suggested.

"Yes."

"And did he go into the water face down or face up?"

"Face down."

"Okay. Did he struggle with you violently?"

"Yes," she said, again agreeing with Mehl's description.

"Did that struggle last longer than with the younger children?"

"A little bit, yeah," Yates said.

"Okay, but still you were able to hold John under the water? And eventually he stopped struggling?"

"Yes."

"Okay, when you brought John out of the water, was there any movement at all from him?"

"No."

"Okay, and then what happened?" Two more deaths to document, and then it would be over.

"I put Mary in."

"Did you actually have to go out into the other room to get Mary?" Sergeant Mehl asked, apparently noticing he'd skipped a question.

"No, she was in there already."

"Was Mary in the bathroom with you when Paul, Luke, and John all went in the water?"

"Yes."

"Okay, what was she doing?"

"She was crying."

"Okay, was she, was she sitting in a chair, one of those—" What was the word he wanted? Infant seat?

"She was sitting down," Yates said.

"On the floor?"

"Uh-huh."

"Okay, so you picked Mary up?"

"Uh-huh."

"She go into the water face down or face up?"

"Face down."

"Okay, she was able to struggle with you?"

"Yes."

"Because she's only 6 months old, right?" Mehl pressed on, not stopping over Yates's affirmative answer.

"Uh-huh," she responded.

"But she struggled, and how, how long do you think she was able to struggle for?"

"A couple of minutes."

"Okay, and after Mary had died, what did you do with her body?"

"I left it in there and called Noah in." Noah, namesake of the last good man left on earth, spared from death in an Old Testament flood, came immediately when his mother called.

"When Noah walked in the bathroom, did he see Mary in the tub?"

"Yes."

"What did he say?"

"He said, 'What happened to Mary?' "

"And what did you say?"

"I didn't say anything. I just put him in."

"Did he try to run from you?"

"Yes."

"Did he get out of the bathroom or were you able to catch him?"

"I got him." Andrea Yates would later say she had not chased her eldest son around the house as detectives and prosecutors later alleged and *Time* magazine reported in lurid detail.[4]

"Okay, and Noah is 7, is that correct?"

"Yes."

"Did Noah put up the biggest struggle of all?" Establishing a drowning order from younger to older might be helpful to prosecutors, Mehl thought.

"Yes." Yates nodded.

"Okay, did he go in the water face down or face up?"

"He was face down."

"When you were struggling with Noah, did you have to, did he try to flip over and come up for air at any time?"

"Yes."

---

4. *Letter of A. Yates to author, November 1, 2002.*

"Did he ever make it out of the water long enough to get a gasp of air or anything?" Without his descriptive questions, Mehl thought, Andrea Yates's confession would be little more than a series of lifeless yeses and nos.

"Yes."

"How many times?"

"A couple times."

"But you forced him back down into the water."

"Yes."

"How long do you think that struggle lasted?"

"Maybe three minutes."

"Okay, and after Noah was dead, when you brought him out of the water, was there any sign of life from him?"

"No."

"What did you do with his body?"

"I left it there."

"Okay, so Mary and Noah were left in the bathtub?"

"I took Mary out," Yates said.

"After John, excuse me, after Noah was dead?"

"Yes."

"Okay, what did you do with Mary's body?"

"Put her on the bed."

"Did you cover her?"

"Yes."

"And you left Noah's body in the tub?"

"Yes," Yates said.

A string of the words yes and no, facedown, a couple of times, and a couple minutes, and what would become Andrea Yates's iron-clad confession was over.

"Okay, you had told me earlier that, that you'd been having these thoughts about hurting your children for up to two years. Is that, is that about right?"

"Yes."

"Okay, is there anything that happened two years ago that, that made you believe—led you to have these thoughts?"

"I realized that it was time to be punished," she answered.

"And what do you need to be punished for?"

"For not being a good mother."

"How did you see drowning your five children as a way to be punished?"

No answer. Mehl had to encourage her.

"Did you want the criminal justice system to punish you or did you—"

"Yes," Yates answered, cutting off the end of his question.

"Okay, we were also talking earlier and there was one other time when you filled the tub with water and were going to do this and did not do it," Mehl reminded her. "Is that correct?"

"Yes," Yates again agreed in monotone.

"How long ago was that?"

"It was two months ago," she said.

"Okay, were all the children at home at that time?"

"Yes. Rusty was there, too."

"Rusty was there, too? Do you think Rusty would have stopped you?"

"Yes."

"So you filled the tub with water that time. What is it within yourself that stopped you from, from doing it that time?"

"Just didn't do it that time."

"Okay, Noah, what's his date of birth?"

"February 26, 1994." She ticked off each birthday in turn as Mehl prompted her: John, December 15, 1995; Paul, September 13, 1997; Luke, February 15, 1999; Mary, November 30, 2000. She remembered dates with a precision that disappeared rapidly within the next twenty-four hours.

"Okay, after all your children were dead, did you let the water out of the tub or did you . . ."

"I left it in."

"Okay, so when the first officer got there, Noah was still in the tub?"

"Yes."

"And the other children were on the bed?"

"Yes."

"Were they still covered?"

"Yes."

"Okay, it's now 1:23 in the afternoon and I'm going to stop the tape."

It had been three hours and thirty-five minutes since Andrea Yates had dialed 911. Mehl took three Polaroids of her. She had only one question, he later recalled. "She wanted to know when her trial would be."

BACK AT THE crime scene, Officer King and his partner remained in the house identifying evidence for the crime-scene unit. King searched the three bedrooms. Bacon took responsibility for the hall bathroom, where Noah's body still floated facedown in the tub, and the rest of the house, including the family room, kitchen, and living room (used as a homeschooling classroom). On the stackable drawers in a corner of the master bedroom, King found a Post-it note referring to a doctor's appointment two days earlier on June 18, at 5:30 PM, and the business card of Dr. Mohammad Saeed, "Board Certified in Adult, Child, Adolescent and Addiction Psychiatry," noting a future appointment on June 26, Tuesday, at 6:00 PM. The only prescription drugs the officers found in the Yates home were the psychiatric medications in the kitchen cabinet prescribed by Dr. Saeed. Bacon called Saeed's office. He and the other detectives speculated about the mental status of Yates that day. "Something like this, you just got to wonder," King said, shaking his head.

Outside, Rusty Yates and his mother waited—and waited—for Noah, John, Paul, Luke, and Mary to be brought out of the house. The police wouldn't let the father and grandmother in, and Rusty and Dora wouldn't leave without seeing the children. It took maybe thirty minutes to drive from the medical examiner's office to the house on Beachcomber. It bothered Rusty that one of his sons was still floating facedown in bathtub water. It had been at least three hours since the tragedy. He and his mother had spent some of that time with the Schultzes, neighbors across the street.

CSU photographer Glenn West arrived and drew a diagram of the crime scene while he awaited the arrival of Senior Deputy Chief Medical Examiner Jesus Sanchez, MD, Assistant ME Patricia Moore, MD, and Investigator Harold Jordan. It was after lunchtime when Sanchez arrived and personally lifted Noah, dressed in shorts and a T-shirt, out of the nine-inch-deep bathwater. He rested the child on his back on the bathroom floor. West videotaped and photographed Noah's water-logged body. Noah's arms were raised over his head, his fists were clenched, knees bent. Rigor mortis had begun to set in as a result of the boy's struggle at death. Sanchez maneuvered Noah's body into a white body bag, zipped it shut, and tagged it #1.

Next, West photographed the gruesome tableau of the four slain children lying in bed. He shot other subjects as well: a close-up of the refrigerator door, family repository of children's drawings, color-ful magnets, and photographs; cereal bowls; the boys' bunk beds; the ceramic-tiled middle bedroom earmarked to be Mary's big-girl room; Mary's portable crib in the master bedroom; close-ups of the frothy substance beneath the noses of Paul and John and Mary; close-ups of the OshKosh B'Gosh and Carter's clothing the children wore; Luke's foot with one sock missing. A tech had attached a "toe tag" marked #2 around the big toe of Luke's bare left foot. Until he got to the bed in the master bedroom and the bathtub, "it looked like a pretty normal house to me," West said. "Weren't those five bodies in absolute stark contrast to everything else in the house?" one of Yates's attorneys, Wen-dell Odom, later asked him. "I have to say yes, sir."

By 4:00 PM the police cleared out. "The media people watched us go back inside the house," Rusty Yates remembered. "They were call-ing us. Nonstop. One after another. And I'd answer the phone. I re-member they asked me to bring some pictures out."

Thoughts of what he usually saw when he returned home from work careened inside Rusty Yates's head. The homeschooling room was empty. The family room, also empty. No shouts, no cries, no whispers, no hyper hellos or cries for watching *Johnny Bravo* on Cartoon Network. Even the familiar havoc of Blackie's barking was missing—the police had taken her out of the family room and penned her up in the backyard.

Rusty Yates looked up the hallway to his left and inhaled sharply. The water in which his children had drowned still spilled out of the bathroom, watermarking the hallway carpet. He wanted to retreat to the Extended Stay America Hotel, but he needed clothes and toiletries. To get them, he had to pass by the bathroom and enter the master bed-room, where the burgundy sheets were still damp with the shapes of his children. "It was really hard," he said. Rusty talked the NASA speak of "the right stuff." "Concerned" was how you felt when *Apollo 13* was stuck on the far side of the moon with no way back to Earth. "Hard" was walking twenty paces past the spot your children had died.

Rusty Yates would have difficulty remembering the details of that evening. He spent the night at the Extended Stay America Hotel with his mother and his only sibling, Randall "Randy" Yates, 35, whose co-workers at Tech Data had pitched in to buy him a plane ticket from Tampa.

It was like old times, his mother in one room, Rusty and his brother sharing another—*not in a good way* like old times. It was as if the past eight years of his life, including the existence of his wife and kids, had been erased.

Later that night, Dr. Saeed called Rusty on his cell phone. Rusty had never received a phone call from Saeed over the twelve weeks he had been his wife's psychiatrist. "Is this happening?" the former Pakistani native asked worriedly.

"Yes."

"I asked her about suicide, but not this. Wasn't your mother there?"

"She was on her way," Rusty said.

"Is there anything I can do for you?" Dr. Saeed asked.

"It's a little late for that now," Yates answered. If Saeed had put Andrea on the proper medication sooner and hadn't taken her off too soon, Yates thought, his kids might be alive. Thirty minutes later his cell phone rang again. It was Magellan calling.

"Magellan?" he asked, unable to place the name. A representative explained that Magellan Health Services handled psychiatric claims for Blue Cross/Blue Shield, the Yateses' health insurance provider. The rep wondered whether there was anything the company could do. Yates thought the concern would have been nice when his sick wife needed longer hospital coverage and their children were still playing in the backyard.

Rusty struggled with his thoughts all night. As the reality of his loss soaked in, he wondered, was there something, *anything*, he could have done differently? Stunned family members would be arriving in Houston. There was so much to do. When he finally fell asleep, he dreamed that only three of his children had been killed. His nightmares were better than his reality.

• • •

MELISSA FERGUSON, MD, was the Mental Health and Mental
Retardation Administration psychiatrist on call that first night. Over
the phone, she prescribed 2 milligrams of Ativan every six hours and
approved Andrea Yates's admission to the third-floor psychiatric unit
of the jail. Ativan is a common medication used for calming patients
down, milder than Valium, but similar. It is also used to treat patients
who stop speaking. Like alcohol, Ativan has a disinhibiting effect. Ferguson was unaware of the antidepressant medications—Remeron and
Effexor—Yates was taking, or the antipsychotic medication her doctor had previously prescribed. So Ferguson did not prescribe them.
Andrea Yates went cold turkey into the night.

At 1:30 AM on June 21, 2001, Andrea Yates appeared before Magis-
trate Carol Carris, who found "probable cause for further detention"
and ordered her held with no bond. Defendant Yates was returned
naked—a precaution against her using her clothing to kill herself—to
isolation cell 2H6. Her cell lights remained on throughout the night,
another antisuicide precaution. At 3:00 AM and again at 4:00 AM, she
asked for a phone. She remained awake, alternately lying in a fetal position or sitting with her knees drawn up to her chest.

Dr. Ferguson saw Yates in person for the first time at 9:00 Thursday morning. "Client [Andrea Yates] had requested to her [psychiatrist]
that she be allowed to attend her children's memorial service," Registered Nurse John Bayliss reported in that day's progress notes. "She
also requested that her doctor cut the consumer's [patient/inmate's]
hair in the shape of a crown." She wanted to see whether the "mark of
the beast," the number 666, was still there. She asked for her husband
and wanted to see a religious person. Ferguson inquired whether she
preferred Catholic. "Yes," she replied.

Ferguson saw Yates again at 11:40 AM. "Mrs. Yates, how could this
have happened?" the doctor asked.

Yates talked guardedly about a "prophecy" but couldn't explain
what she meant.

"I'm so stupid," Yates wailed, hitting herself in the head with her
fist. "Couldn't I have killed just one to fulfill the prophecy? Couldn't I
have just offered Mary?"

"Mrs. Yates, could I tell you the truth about what's going on here?" Dr. Ferguson asked. "Your mind is playing tricks."

"No, it's not. I'm not mentally ill. It's real. . . . The state will impose the death penalty on Satan. . . . The drowning was the way, . . . Are they in heaven?"

Dr. Ferguson had treated more than six thousand patients since becoming a psychiatrist. When she saw Andrea Yates on June 21, 2001, "she was one of the sickest patients" she'd ever seen. To date, not a single doctor has disagreed with that characterization. Ferguson terminated the interview when Yates disintegrated into moaning and crying. She prescribed an additional dose of Ativan to calm her.

CHAPTER 2

Rocket Fuel

Rusty Yates would never forget the day he met his future wife. He had gone downstairs to the swimming pool at the Sunscape Apartments where he lived on Farm Road 1959, carrying his boom box tuned to a rock station. He didn't visit the pool often, but it was Houston in midsummer, and hot. What he saw laid out before him was a vision. A woman, whose slender and perfectly formed body was interrupted only by a bikini, lay motionless on the surface of the water. Her long, dark hair floated about her face. Her arms were outstretched. She was absolutely still. Her only contact with the nonaquatic world was the spot where the tips of her toes touched the glossy-tiled edge of the pool. Because her eyes were closed, he was free to contemplate her beauty undetected. A girl this lovely, he thought, could never fall for him. He was not in her league. He said a few words to her anyway. He had been voted "Mr. DuPont," the ideal student representative of DuPont High School, after all. He told her it was remarkable how she could float like that. She thanked him sweetly but seemed unapproachable.

On September 6, 1989, his twenty-fifth birthday, his buddies at NASA took Rusty out drinking. For every tequila shot they drank, they bought him a giant shot. He never remembered being as sick as he was the next day. He finally went to the doctor and was diagnosed with mononucleosis.

One night in early October during his recuperation, he was on the phone when there was a knock at his apartment door. A young woman introduced herself and mentioned that someone had dinged her car in the parking lot the night before. She wondered if he might have seen anything. She was, he realized, the water nymph. He told his friend on the phone he couldn't believe that this gorgeous woman had just shown up out of nowhere.

Andrea Yates didn't socialize much outside of work. She was a registered nurse at the University of Texas M. D. Anderson Cancer Center of Houston. That night she'd decided to get dressed up and take herself to a nice restaurant. Watching the other couples there, she was inspired to knock on Rusty Yates's door on her way back to her apartment. She was shy, and the ding on her car was as good a reason as she was ever going to find to say hi.

Later that month, she left a note on a scrap of paper on Rusty's car window asking if he wanted to stop over after work sometime. He went, giving up watching *Monday Night Football*. He enjoyed their conversation—not about trivial things, but about interesting and challenging things. He still had the scrap of paper with her note.

The two began dating. She'd heard about his birthday bender. After a date in November, she said, "Rusty, I've got something important to tell you and I'll understand if you don't want to see me anymore."

He gulped. How bad could this be?

"I don't drink," she said.

If you shake any family tree long and hard enough, you'll find alcohol problems somewhere. The Yates and Kennedy families were no exception. Rusty's father had been a drinker, and Andrea described a brother and sister who had drinking problems in the past. The fact that Andrea didn't drink made Rusty trust her more. He stopped drinking aside from an occasional beer. "I wanted her to trust me, too," he said. "Most of the stuff I'd done that I ever regretted was when I'd been drinking.

"We get along well, we always have," Rusty said. "Andrea says the doctors in jail kept saying, 'Tell me about when you fought.' And she'd say, 'We didn't fight.' And the doctor would say, 'Oh, come on, everybody fights.' And she'd say, 'No, we didn't fight.' And it's true. We just get along." One of the reasons may be that Rusty Yates had no qualms about identifying or expressing his needs. "That's the way it was in my family. If someone needs something, then speak up," he said. "Andrea was not allowed to have any needs [in her family]. She can't even *identify* her needs. And that's odd to me."

The youngest of five children, a competitive swimmer, and a high school valedictorian, Andrea Pia Kennedy had graduated from the University of Texas School of Nursing at Houston with a BSN degree. Her mother grew up in Nazi Germany and met her father during the British occupation, when he was an Air Force B-24 navigator and she an interpreter. After the war, her dad worked as a technician for Ford Motor Company in Houston and later as a schoolteacher. When he lost his job and times got tough, Andrea's mom went to work as a floor manager at JCPenney. She remained there twenty years before retiring. The family attended St. Christopher's Catholic Church. The boys went to Catholic school. "I don't have one of them that's Catholic now," said Mrs. Kennedy, who converted to Catholicism when she married. "We don't know why. Maybe we were too strict. I go every morning to Mass." Andrea was studious and shy, and didn't date seriously until she was 23. One of her first experiences of depression followed a failed relationship when she was 24. The issue was sex before marriage. Andrea Yates's virginity was becoming a heavy burden to her.

Raised near Nashville, Russell Edison Yates played football and was active in the Fellowship of Christian Athletes at DuPont Senior High School. He graduated third in his class and went to Auburn University on a Navy ROTC scholarship. He dropped out of the program after four quarters and a six-week summer cruise, realizing the Navy wasn't for him. His gridiron career, like that of many high school athletes, ended at college. "I tutored athletes there." He laughed. He still had a buff physique and dressed almost exclusively in blue jeans, polo shirts, and black Doc Martens–style shoes. Rusty introduced Andrea to his friends and religious mentors, Michael and Rachel (formerly Leslie Jean Ochalek) Woroniecki, not long after he'd begun dating Andrea.[1] He had listened to Woroniecki preaching on the concourse near the Auburn Tiger's good-luck war eagle cage and was intrigued because the man didn't sound like a hypocrite. Yates, the president of the Methodist youth group, had been raised Nazarene (his father's father was a Nazarene preacher) and Methodist. He took some of Woroniecki's lit-

---

1. *Marriage license, Wayne County, MI, August 7, 1979.*

erature. Over time, the two men struck up a correspondence that led to friendship and religious kinship.

Woroniecki and his wife and six children traveled the United States in a motor home, visiting college campuses, preaching hellfire and brimstone wherever anyone would listen. They were hard people to find, unless they wanted to be found. And then they were difficult to miss. "I don't care if you don't like me yelling and preaching at you like this today," Penn State's *Daily Collegian* (October 1, 1998) quoted Woroniecki as saying. "What I care about is saving you because you are going to answer to God." Students often found his diatribes disturbing. "All I keep hearing are the words 'Satan' and 'Hell,' " one student told the *Collegian*.[2] Woroniecki's wife told the *Indiana Student Daily*, "Seek Jesus not in the church or religion and not in Christianity and not in the system. The system cannot save you because it is based in Satan."[3] Was there any place the Woronieckis did recommend seeking Jesus? Yes, in the New Testament at home—or at least not in a church.

The Woronieckis continued their peripatetic lifestyle by home-schooling their children. "I can't fathom sending them off to strangers, and strange spirits 8 hours a day," Rachel wrote in the Woroniecki publication, *Perilous Times*. "A woman is created to be a 'helper,' " according to Woroniecki's interpretation of the Bible. "This does not mean a wife. It means a servant, single or married."[4]

"Rusty told me he had met the girl of his dreams," said Michael Woroniecki. "He knew she was the one. And he was really impressed with her. She was a nurse. And he wanted us to meet her, you know, real bad."

Their meeting took place at the home of a mutual friend in southwest Houston. Andrea seemed "a little intimidated," Woroniecki remembered. "You're coming into a situation. You're gonna maybe get married to this guy. And you want to impress somebody that he likes, you know?

"My heart kinda went out to her," Woroniecki said. "Andrea, to me,

2. Katie O'Hara, "Oregon Family Delivers Fire and Brimstone Sermon at Penn State Campus," Daily Collegian, October 1, 1998.

3. Olivia Clarke, "Family of Preachers Spreads Word of the Gospel," Indiana Daily Student, October 21, 1997.

4. Rachel Woroniecki, "The Truth," Perilous Times, January 2000.

wasn't somebody that you would feel intimidated by. She was just somebody you could sit down and talk with . . . very, I don't know, just real. I did caution Rusty not to get married, as I do most young people, for the simple reason that, for myself when I came to Christ, I realized I was not mature enough to be able to love a woman and take care of her needs as well as children. I needed to have some real character and some real wisdom and things that I knew I could only get from the Lord."

Woroniecki was 20 and Rachel 18 when they fell in love. "Michael was telling Rusty that you need to have a foundation in Jesus before you involve yourself deeply in the life of another person," explained Rachel, who waited five years before marrying Michael.

Early in 1992, Andrea Kennedy and Rusty Yates began living together; Andrea had difficulty with her guilt about not being married. Rusty proposed at Christmastime, and the couple was married not long after, on April 17, 1993, by a nondenominational minister named Ronald L. Collins in a chapel at Clear Lake Park. Though her new husband was the only man she'd ever slept with, when her father escorted her up the aisle, she wouldn't wear her wedding veil over her face because she wasn't a virgin. Andrea's brother Andrew Kennedy, 47, took videos of the couple's wedding, which a hundred friends and family attended. He said he'd never forget how happy his little sister was that day. Andrea made Rusty promise he'd marry her again on their twentieth wedding anniversary. He said he would—if she could still fit into her wedding dress.

A few weeks before the wedding, Rusty bought a brand-new four-bedroom $95,000 house in Friendswood, Texas. A little under 2,000 square feet, it was among the less expensive brick homes in the suburban Houston neighborhood, but there was more than enough room for two plus a baby.

Unlike her mother and father, who had been surprised when they conceived their firstborn after five years of seeming infertility, Andrea was pregnant within two months of being married. She'd stopped using the birth control pill; she and Rusty had agreed they would accept as many children as God sent their way, whether the number was zero or ten. She continued her nursing job at M. D. Anderson Hospital until Noah was born on February 26, 1994. Rusty said she was still pushing stretchers there until the day before Noah's birth.

Andrea became a stay-at-home mother and quickly had another son, John. "Andrea is two months older than I am," Rusty liked to recall. "When she turned 30, I'd introduce her and say, 'This is my wife, Andrea. She's in her thirties and I'm in my twenties.' " He would laugh. "I'm going to do the same thing when she turns 40."

When Rusty's NASA job required a six-month stint in Tampa, Florida, the family rented out their home, put most of their belongings in storage, and accompanied him, living in a trailer home. Back in Houston, Rusty said, they'd forgotten why they ever needed half the things they'd stored. They rented a plum spot for their 38-foot Jayco 376FB travel trailer at the edge of Lazy Days RV Campground in Hitchcock, Texas, an exurb halfway between Houston and Galveston. The site overlooked acres of bucolic grasslands where wild milkweed grew and butterflies emerged from cocoons in profusion. There was a swimming pool, Laundromat, playground, bath facilities, and plenty of full-time residents, like the Greens and the Ahlbergs, who quickly adopted the Yateses as their friends. Eventually, they sold their Friendswood home to the people to whom they had rented it. Andrea's parents were disappointed. They thought their daughter and grandchildren deserved better than a trailer-park lifestyle. So did some of her friends.

In the spring of 1998, the Yateses learned that the Woronieckis wanted to sell their 350-square-foot customized GMC motor home and replace it with a sailboat. They made a trip to Miami to explore whether they might be interested in buying the bus.

The trip amounted to a weeklong marriage encounter, with disastrous consequences. The Woronieckis saw Rusty as a workaholic. Others would consider him a typical middle-class family man, uninterested in giving up his worldly possessions to spend his life traveling in a bus preaching the gospel. "I believe Rusty was willing to sacrifice his wife and his children for the sake of his job," Michael Woroniecki said. It is also possible that Rusty Yates's having $37,000 in his bank account to pay for a motor home Woroniecki wanted badly to sell raised issues surrounding the older man's own material success, or lack of it.

"She was desperately lonely," Woroniecki said of Andrea. "She had the responsibility for all those children and she was all alone in that, you know? And she didn't know how to handle it. You can buy a person a house, but unless you fill that house with love, it's a tomb, baby. I mean it's a tomb."

Some of their conversation focused around a simple book called *Hope for the Flowers,* used by the Woronieckis as a teaching tool. "I bought *Hope for the Flowers* for Andrea before we ever married, when we were dating," Rusty Yates explained. Michael Woroniecki had recommended the book when Rusty was a student at Auburn. "The thing I like about that book is it shows how futile it is to make work your life's mission. Once you're on top, it's 'What's the point of that?' The guys underneath will just throw you over."

Andrea seemed to like the idea of the motor home. Noah was hardly an impartial voter: only 4, he'd fallen in love with the bus's secret play space hideaway in a converted baggage compartment, which the six Woroniecki children had dubbed "the hole." Rusty was more concerned with the five leaks he found in the roof when he spent the night alone on the bus after he'd taken his family back to Houston and returned to Tampa to finalize the bus's purchase. The GMC might have a bigger and better engine than their SUV-trailer combination, but it didn't have the same high-end finishing or safety features.

Rachel, who cried when Rusty drove her longtime home away, corresponded with Andrea in July 1998. "The window of opportunity that God has opened up for you at this time through us will only stay open for a certain time," she wrote, referencing Paul's 2 Corinthians 6:2 and Letters to the Hebrews 3:7. "All the rebuke, confrontation and sharing that went on between us was intended to effect your souls for salvation. If you allow Satan to come in and 'steal the understanding' the consequences will be tragic," she predicted, citing Matthew 13:19. There Matthew had written, "The seed sown on the path is the one who hears the word of the kingdom without understanding it, and the evil one comes and steals away what was sown in his heart."

Somehow Andrea found time to write to Rachel and tell her that Luke, conceived during the visit with the Woronieckis, had been born. "So that's four boys!" Rachel wrote back cheerfully. "Wow. I know you were probably wishing for a girl." She had a more serious message for the new mother as well: "It is so very crucial for you to do whatever you have to RIGHT NOW before you are overwhelmed by things. I have seen many women just continually put off their salvation in Jesus. Then as the years slowly slip by so does any hope for them to be truly saved. They keep waiting for their husbands to 'get right' [with the Lord] and they slowly hunker down in a worldly mentality. Oh that's just so terrible, Andrea. Don't let this happen to you!

"I know you're frustrated Andrea. I know things are not the way you would like them to be. But you can change them. There will be a day when it is too late," Rachel predicted, "but we don't believe that day has happened yet. There is still hope."

Andrea began reading the Bible with renewed intensity.

WITH LUKE'S BIRTH, Andrea, like many new mothers, was breast-feeding every three hours and sleeping only a few hours a night. "On June 16, 1999, Andrea called me at work, crying, and asked me to come home," Rusty later wrote in a journal. "At the time we were living in our bus conversion motor home in Hitchcock, Texas. I dropped what I was doing at work and just drove," he recalled. "I was worried because she sounded like she needed me. I found Andrea in the back room of the bus in a chair, bent over, shaking her legs and—to a lesser degree—hands, uncontrollably." She had difficulty speaking. "I need help," she managed to stammer.

"I tried to comfort her," Rusty said. "I wasn't sure what was happening; I guessed it was a nervous breakdown. In '99 when she called me home I didn't know anything about depression."

Rusty Yates had no useful data in his brain for "nervous breakdown." Systems had failed. He had no contingency plan and no time for a "root cause" analysis. The first creative thought he had was "fresh air." He got the boys and the strollers and Andrea, put them all in the Suburban and drove half an hour to Galveston. Andrea didn't say anything. They strolled along the sidewalk on the Galveston seawall, built along the Gulf Coast in the early 1900s after the city had been flooded by a hurricane. It was a peaceful, relaxing place, one of their favorite spots. Still, there was no relief for Andrea. Rusty drove her and the boys to Andrea's mother's house for help.

At NASA he was in charge of replacing old space shuttle parts. If someone held a blowtorch to one side of a shuttle tile, while he held his hand on the other, he wouldn't feel a thing. Perhaps a wall of those tiles insulated a husband from the reality of his wife's raging psychosis. But like the *Columbia* shuttle flight STS-107, the Yates family was headed for disaster.

The next afternoon, while the family napped, Andrea took forty to fifty 50-milligram Trazodone tablets—a medication with a strong sedative quality—that had been prescribed for her father. The dose could have killed her, but her mother found her in time to rush her to Houston's Ben Taub Hospital Emergency Room. The date was June 17, 1999. Rusty had returned to his in-laws' house after doing errands and discovered an ambulance in the driveway. It might have been there for his ailing father-in-law. "I remember that all the kids were crying, especially Paul, as the attendants pushed Andrea out of the house on a stretcher," Rusty said. "I rode in the ambulance with Andrea. The driver asked me which hospital I wanted to take her to, and I asked if he could take her to the Medical Center. He agreed."

At Ben Taub Emergency Room, doctors assessed Andrea, lavaged her, and gave her liquefied charcoal to drink. "After they were sure she was stable," Rusty said, "a couple of officers escorted her to the Methodist Hospital down the street. This was just before midnight. They wouldn't let me ride with them, I had to run from Ben Taub to Methodist."

Intake Nurse Anita Lopez described Andrea's reason for admission as "overdose. Doesn't want to die but wants for [sic] the misery to go away." Lopez noted that Mrs. Yates had lost ten pounds in less than three weeks. She had poor eye contact, poor concentration, low energy, and fatigue. Still breast-feeding four-month-old Luke, she was negative for menstrual periods and negative for sexual contact with her husband. She was, however, positive for hopelessness. "Very guarded responses when given by patient," Nurse Lopez noted.

By the time Andrea made her way through the admissions morass to James Flack, MD, the psychiatrist on call, her chief complaint had morphed into "I guess there has been turmoil." Although mostly nonverbal, "She does nod her head and then confirms that she thought the medication she was taking would end her life," Flack wrote. "She just wanted to sleep forever." His medical history of Andrea Yates is a glossary of neuropsychological buzz words: minimal speech, retarded psychomotor activity, paucity of thought, depressed mood, affect extremely constricted and shallow, attention poor. Most interesting, Flack raised the question of whether Andrea suffered from "some delusional guilt," but learned no details from his patient. "She thought she was a bad mother. That's delusional right there," her husband later commented.

Flack's preliminary and final diagnoses were major depression, single episode, severe. He marked his new admission as "high risk for suicide/self harm," placed her on one-to-one suicide observation every fifteen minutes, and prescribed 0.5 milligrams of Ativan for sleep. Flack took his monosyllabic patient's word that she had been well until her fourth child's birth.

On June 18, 1999, Flack prescribed a starter dose of 50 milligrams per day of the antidepressant Zoloft. His orders specified that "patient may go off the unit with family during visiting hours to see her children, accompanied by husband or family." She slept only three hours the night following her overdose, eight hours the next night, and intermittently thereafter.

Andrea was tearful and ashamed after trying to commit suicide, but she also felt worthless—a nurse who couldn't even kill herself successfully. "I have my family to live for," she told Nurse Bridget Fenton, who recorded their conversation in her progress notes of June 18, 1999. She worried to another nurse that the Trazodone overdose would make it unsafe to continue breast-feeding Luke. But she couldn't discuss her hopelessness. "She was only able to ask if she had done any permanent damage to her body," Flack reported.

In her notes from a joint counseling session with Andrea and Rusty Yates that week, social worker Norma Tauriac, LMSW, described Andrea as "unwilling" or "unable" to "identify any recent life stressors." Rusty was "aware and accepting" of his wife's disease and was more comfortable calling it postpartum depression than major depression. Tauriac carefully noted that all the children were born naturally—"no meds"—and that "the second child, John, then 3½, had difficulty focusing and staying with one thing very long." She described Andrea Yates as someone who made friends easily and had several close friends, from whom she'd drifted apart over the years.

Rusty Yates, Tauriac reported, "saw the marriage as close, with four beautiful kids." He described Andrea's increasing reliance on him to make decisions. "Sometimes I feel like she lost her identity," he confided in Tauriac. "Now all her energy is focused on [the] children." To Rusty, their strong points as a couple were "similar values, honesty, and trust." Andrea was nearly mute, advancing to a disorder called catatonia: loss of voluntary movement, notably speech.

Tauriac was the single health-care professional who sensed something was dangerously wrong, but since she wasn't a doctor, she was unequipped to identify or treat the problem. The prospect of such a sick patient's being released from the hospital, though, spurred her to action. She focused her concern on the Yateses' living arrangements. "As a rule, the patient and her husband and the four children live in a converted bus," she wrote in her session notes. Tauriac called Houston's Child Protective Services Abuse and Neglect Hotline on June 23, 1999, to report the family's "unusual living arrangements and the fact that patient's husband allows the 3½ year-old son to use a power drill."

Seven days after Tauriac's complaint, Dan Willbur, CPS Supervisor II, wrote thanking Tauriac for her concern for the Yates children. However, "because the situation does not appear to involve the occurrence and/or substantial risk of abuse or neglect . . . we plan no further inquiries," his letter read. CPS suggested directing further concerns to the Houston Police Department because "they do appear to have jurisdiction in such matters." Tauriac jotted a note on the bottom of the CPS letter: "*Important.* Please place in the chart of Andrea Yates." The letter lay dormant in Andrea's file until the murders.

ON JUNE 20, 1999—two years to the day before Andrea Yates would drown her five children—Dr. Flack raised her dose of Zoloft to 100 milligrams every morning. Realizing her depression was not abating, on June 21, he wrote instructions to "push Zoloft dose as fast as possible. Patient will probably need to remain inpatient the week."

That day, Nurse Fenton found her patient more "withdrawn, vague, and guarded" as well as "worried about paying the hospital bill." Money shortage became a constant companion of Andrea Yates's delusional reality.

"Interviewed patient again this am" Flack's patient progress notes for June 23 read. "She seems emotionally detached, withdrawn and minimally verbal. Depression remains severe." He raised the Zoloft dose to 150 milligrams and he wrote on June 24 that neither group nor individual therapy seemed to make any difference in Andrea's depression. He concluded that "her home and children may be more therapeutic" than a psychiatric wing of a hospital. The patient's "husband thinks the patient may be struggling with the concept of Salvation and that she put a burden on herself," he added.

Flack interviewed Andrea again the morning of June 24. He also spoke with her husband "at length." "They are requesting that she be discharged to the family's care. They have agreed to watch her around the clock and are aware that she is at risk of harming herself again," he reported in the patient progress notes. Tellingly, Flack's Discharge Summary also revealed that Andrea was being discharged because of insurance restrictions after seven days in the hospital. In any case, that day Flack discharged Andrea in "stable" condition with a month's supply of Zoloft, a list of follow-up care providers, and a recommendation to visit psychiatrist Eileen Starbranch. Andrea Yates was described on discharge as "quite depressed," but denied wanting to commit suicide again. Her true condition was written between every line of her medical records.[5]

"Anyone who worships the beast or its image, or accepts its mark on forehead or hand will also drink of the wine of God's fury," . . . I heard a voice from heaven say, "Write this: Blessed are the dead who die in the Lord from now on."[6]

THREE WEEKS LATER, on July 21, 1999, Andrea tried to slit her throat in the bathroom of her parents' home. "Please let me do it," she implored her husband. Rusty Yates drove his wife to the emergency room. This time she was admitted to Memorial Spring Shadows Glen Hospital, where her new psychiatrist, Dr. Starbranch, practiced. She'd been uneasy about seeing a psychiatrist, but Rusty had made an appointment and taken her to see Starbranch anyway, on July 1, for an evaluation. Though she'd been holding baby Luke all the time, she was

---

5. *Discharge from Methodist Hospital, June 24, 1999.*
6. *A. Yates, Bible study, Revelation 14:9 and 14:13, per R. Yates interview.*

reluctant to feed him. If he cried, she paced with him, swung him, gave him a pacifier, but didn't feed him. Usually, her mom, her brother Brian, or Rusty fed Luke. If they encouraged Andrea long enough, eventually she fed him. She didn't interact much with her other children but was concerned that they were eating too much. She'd begun scratching her head and often retreated to the bedroom. She'd been taking inconsistently the Zoloft Flack had prescribed. She had flushed the Zyprexa Starbranch prescribed down the toilet when she realized the drug was an antipsychotic. Her illness had clearly progressed since being released from Memorial Hospital.

"She put a steak knife to her neck," Rusty Yates told Gail Pechacek, RNC. "I had to force it out of her hand." Pechacek sketched "self-mutilation behavior" on a diagram and placed it in Andrea's chart. She indicated "deep scratches two weeks old in four places on her scalp," "deep scratches in her nose," and self-inflicted scratches on her arms and legs. Starbranch evaluated her patient at 3:00 PM that day and easily determined she was mute, suicidal, and psychotic. Apparently, "the sign of the beast was already there," psychiatrist Deborah Sichel noted years later.

In a follow-up consultation with hospital psychologist James P. Thompson, PhD, Yates was able to describe thoughts that included audio and visual hallucinations. "I had a fear I would hurt somebody. . . . I thought it better to end my own life and prevent it [from happening]." Two years before she murdered her children, Yates's distorted thinking already excluded any hope that psychiatric medication might cure or manage her fears. "There was a voice, then an image of the knife. . . . I had a vision in my mind—get a knife, get a knife. I had a vision of this person being stabbed . . . the aftereffects." The vision occurred "about ten times" over several days. She revealed to Thompson that she'd had her first "vision" when Noah was a newborn. She remembered the time was early in the morning. When the vision stopped, she gladly "blew it off." She didn't say whom she was afraid of harming and changed the subject.

The knife was:
1. *Dull*
2. *Thin*

3. *Long, like a slicer*
4. *Wood handle*[7]

At the time of Andrea Yates's first breakdown, she suffered from a "poverty of thought." She appeared to Dr. Thompson "to block and constrict her thought production and emotional expression" in order to avoid symptoms of psychosis.

Yates also acknowledged obsessive thoughts "over our children and how they'll turn out." She grew nervous about "the kids, trying to train them up right, being so young. [It's a] big responsibility. . . . I don't want to fail." She no longer shared her thoughts about Salvation with her husband, because a rift had developed between Michael Woroniecki and Rusty Yates over the sale of the motor home. According to Woroniecki, "Andrea did not make mention of Rusty. When I did try to reestablish contact with Rusty, she wrote thanking me."[8] Asked by a caregiver to write a sentence spontaneously, she scribbled, "I love my husband and kids."

With the advent of visual hallucinations, schizophrenia became a diagnosis to rule out. Andrea's major depressive disorder with psychotic features advanced beyond a "single episode" to "recurrent." She certainly suffered from postpartum psychosis (PPP), a "poor prognosis psychosis," as well, but that was now only a small piece of a larger medical puzzle. PPP, which affects only one in one thousand mothers, is a medical emergency that endangers both the mother's and the child's lives. Postpartum depression (PPD), which is not accompanied by psychosis, affects about one in ten new mothers. The more common "baby blues" gives 75 percent of new mothers mild emotional symptoms. Though all three disorders are thought to be triggered by hormonal changes in the brain, neither PPD nor "baby blues" is considered a medical emergency.

About . . . the code "1E" [patient's room, yelling/screaming]: I was in
bed, trying to take a nap. I started to hear a rumbling voice coming

---

7. *Letter of A. Yates to author, June 13, 2003.*
8. *Letter of M. Woroniecki to author, February 2002.*

from the wall behind me. It got louder and louder and turned into more of a guttural sound. I heard what I thought was "Andrea, come here!" (Later, I believed it was Satan.) I sat up in bed and shouted, "What do you want?!!" I can't remember what happened then. No one came to check on me—I didn't know it was documented.[9]

Starbranch ordered a consultation for her patient with Arturo Rios, MD, a psychiatrist who specializes in ECT. He recommended the treatment for Andrea, but both Yateses were against it. Instead, Starbranch prescribed an antipsychotic drug mixture described in medical records as an "injectable cocktail including Haldol and Cogentin." Haldol is the dinosaur and also the workhorse of neuroleptic medications. How it works is unknown; apparently, it blocks certain brain cell activities, primarily those involved with the neurotransmitter dopamine. Psychiatrists prefer Haldol's newer and less toxic equivalents, Risperdal and Zyprexa (which also has some mood-stabilizing effects), but those drugs seemed not to work for Andrea Yates. And, as Starbranch pointed out, they are not available in injectable form, with which a physician could monitor Yates's compliance. Cogentin is prescribed to eliminate some of Haldol's more unpleasant symptoms: tremors, twitching, stiffened limbs, blurred vision, and a masklike face. Haldol Decanoate, the drug's injectable form, was ultimately given to Yates— 100 milligrams every three weeks—to ensure she took her medication. Starbranch also prescribed a combo of the antidepressants Effexor XR and Wellbutrin.

To hear Rusty Yates describe it, the drug combination was miraculous. Within twenty-four hours, he felt he had his wife back. They sat up late in Andrea's hospital room having one of the best conversations of their lives.

Rusty visited his wife diligently in the psych ward. Nurses' reports describe him as "supportive and caring." He brought flowers, complained when Andrea hadn't been bathed in three days, and worried over the effects of her medications. "Most of visit, patient was lying on sofa with husband sitting next to her stroking her head," one nurse

---

9. *Letter of A. Yates to author, August 4, 2003.*

wrote. "Rusty really tries the best he possibly can," Starbranch later recalled. "He really is a good person. . . . When I had her hospitalized, he would come and see her every day. And that was a long trip. And he would bring the kids with him so she could see the kids. He worked with her to try to get her to take the medicine. He really tried hard."

Nineteen days into this second hospital stay, Andrea was again discharged to a Partial Hospitalization Program. She continued PHP for eleven days but slept at home, now a three-bedroom house in Clear Lake, Texas.

"I bought the house when Andrea was sick the first time," Rusty said. "She never complained about the bus, I just thought the house might be better for her. I didn't even know if she liked the house until one day she told me, 'I'm glad you bought it.' " Rusty described how he built bunk beds for his sons in one of the bedrooms. Another was used for storage.

At Andrea's first posthospital appointment, Dr. Starbranch told her that even though she was feeling better, she should "remain compliant with [her] medications." In the past, Andrea often took half doses or skipped her medication altogether. She feared drugs and addictions. Depending on drugs made her "feel like she's weak," she told her PHP therapy group.

By the next visit, August 16, 1999, Starbranch reported in disbelief that Andrea "is talking of wanting off medications!" She "wants to get p.g. [pregnant] and have more kids. Wants to home school the children." On August 18, Starbranch wrote, "Apparently patient and husband plan to have as many babies as nature will allow! This will surely guarantee future psychotic depression."

She was right.

CHAPTER 3

The Apocalypse

Within seven months—by March 2000—Andrea Yates was pregnant again. She was homeschooling Noah at the kindergarten level and caring for three toddlers in their Beachcomber home. Rusty Yates babysat one night a week to give his wife a mom's night out. For a time, Andrea continued monthly visits to her psychiatrist, Dr. Starbranch, whose notes of their December 1999 session quoted Andrea as saying she was "doing great—baking cookies and getting ready for Xmas." Rusty accompanied his wife to her January 12, 2000, appointment. Starbranch wrote that Andrea "admits she's off all meds since 11/99: Husband says he didn't like her doing this but [she] seems to be doing okay. . . . [Patient] wants to be off meds unless symptomatic. Husband agrees." There are no records of further visits to Starbranch.

That winter, Andrea was finally well enough to talk to her close friend of seventeen years, Debbie Holmes, about why she had tried to kill herself twice. The two women had been nursing colleagues at M. D. Anderson Cancer Center. Holmes still worked there part time. She had a daughter Noah's age and a 10-year-old son. When Andrea was sick, "All she saw was darkness—even when the lights were on," Holmes said. When Andrea tried to kill herself with the serrated kitchen knife, she looked in the mirror of her parents' pink-and-green tiled bathroom and saw a face, not her own, looking out at her from the blackness. With her first attempt, she said she was sobbing as she pushed the pills in her mouth, some falling out unswallowed. She didn't want to kill herself.

Andrea confided a terrible secret to Debbie: she felt she was possessed. Satan had either influenced her or possessed her and was the source of her breakdown. She talked about not being able to wear the crucifix her family had given her, and she had thoughts about hurting someone or something harmful being done to the children.

Andrea asked Debbie, an evangelical Presbyterian and vacation Bible school teacher, to check with her pastor about whether Satan could read minds. The pastor said no, Satan could not read thoughts, but he could hear the spoken word. The information relieved Andrea.

> Michael Woroniecki told us that, but he never gave scripture to back it up.[1]

She had a twofold problem: Satan and a hormonal imbalance. Dr. Starbranch had cured the postpartum hormonal imbalance; it was Satan she had to work harder against in the future. Debbie and Andrea consulted the Bible. Luke, Andrea pointed out, wrote that "When a strong man, fully armed, guards his own house, his possessions are undisturbed." "I need to be stronger," Andrea said. "I just need to be stronger."

The two friends read further in Luke about "demon-oppression." "When the unclean spirit goes out of a man," he wrote, "it passes through waterless places seeking rest, and not finding any, it says, 'I will return to the house from which I came' . . . and takes along seven other spirits more evil than itself, . . . and the last state of that man becomes worse than the first."

Holmes remembered Andrea struggling through that first Christmas season after the suicide attempts, trying to make people think she was okay and concerned about the stigma of having been mentally ill. She was also considering getting pregnant again. Holmes encouraged her friend not to overdo and certainly not to become pregnant again.

"I've had a long enough vacation," she told Holmes.

"Honey, you've tried to kill yourself twice. You've been in the hospital more than you've been out," Holmes said. "If you truly believe

---

1. *Letter of A. Yates to author, received July 13, 2003.*

Luke, then why would you risk getting pregnant again?" Remarkably to Holmes, Andrea grew healthier during her pregnancy with Mary. She'd been off medication for a year when she gave birth on November 30, 2000.

Three and a half months later, Andrea's father, Andrew Kennedy Sr., whom she'd helped nurse through Alzheimer's disease for seven years, died at age 84. Since being sidelined by a heart attack and subsequent complications in 1986, he had been in continuous decline and depression. He spent the last six months of his life in a wheelchair. Rusty Yates felt the relationship between his father-in-law and mother-in-law was strained. But Andrea adored her father. She was the only family member who shared his enthusiasm for sailing. When her father had been well, she sailed every weekend with him in Galveston Bay. In 1979, the father-daughter team took first place in the Great Pumpkin Regatta. When he became too sick to sail, rather than sell or give the boat to someone else, Andrea said her father "sailed it to a watery grave."

In late February 2001, Mr. Kennedy had been admitted to a Houston veterans hospital, where doctors found he had failing kidneys and a subdural hematoma, which they drained. He rallied briefly, but then lost his ability to eat or drink. The hospital sent him home DNR: Do Not Resuscitate. Andrea tried to give him water, but the liquid only gurgled dangerously in his throat.

Andrea's brother Patrick, from California (who'd been estranged from his father), and sister Michele, from Alabama, had come to be with their dad. It was the first time all five Kennedy children had been together in over twenty years. With their mother, the kids gathered around their dad and said their good-byes.

Later that night, around 10:00, Andrea's mother called to tell Andrea her father had died. She went instantly to her mother's side. She arrived back home before first light, disturbed to have seen her father's dead body. She described to her husband how different her father looked from just a few hours earlier. "It was a horrific experience for her," Rusty remembered. Paramedics and police had come and because he'd died at home, an autopsy was performed.

As a nurse, Andrea knew her father could have lived a while longer with intravenous fluids and a feeding tube. But there was no way he could have been saved. Still, she blamed herself for his shortened life.

By the end of that week, her father had been cremated, the funeral service had been conducted, and Andrea Yates was once again showing signs of serious depression. This time Rusty recognized them. But what had taken months to evolve during her first psychosis now developed in only a matter of days.

During the last week of March, Andrea crashed. She exhibited the now frightening signs of standing and sitting like a zombie. What Rusty termed "the sewing machine leg" returned: Andrea pumped the heel of her foot up and down against the floor with the rapid action of an electric sewing machine needle. She picked at spots on her scalp until they bled. As with Luke during the last psychotic event, she held baby Mary in her arms nonstop, terrified to put her down. She stopped eating, drinking, and speaking, and was plagued by hallucinations she could not—or would not—describe. She slept only an hour or two at night. She didn't eat. She didn't speak.

Rusty called Starbranch, the psychiatrist who had successfully treated Andrea in 1999. She recommended immediate treatment at an inpatient mental hospital in northwest Houston. Spring Shadows Glen had been closed. Both the hospital and Starbranch's office were a forty-five-minute drive from the Yateses. With work and five children, including an infant, and his mother-in-law (and babysitter) still reeling over the death of her husband, it was a nearly impossible commute for Rusty Yates to juggle. According to Starbranch, he scheduled an office appointment for his wife on April 2.

During the next two days, on March 28 and 29, he called several local psychiatrists to see if they would prescribe his wife medications over the phone. Understandably, they wanted to see her first but didn't have immediate openings for new patients. On Friday, March 30, Rusty called nearby Devereux Texas Treatment Network in League City and was advised that it would be best to wait until the following day to admit Andrea because the facility was not staffed to admit her that night. On Saturday, March 31, Rusty's even demeanor began to fray. "I am not going through this again," he said, raising his voice in frustration, slamming his fist on the kitchen table as Andrea's mother and brother Brian looked on. He walked briskly out to the Suburban. Brian loaded his unwilling sister into the car. Together, the two men jackknifed her body into the seat as she stiffened her legs against them.

I was thinking, 'who will take care of the kids?' Mary wasn't taking the bottle very well, and I worried about her. Maybe I was afraid.[2]

Rusty drove his wife and her brother to Devereux, a collection of single level, nouveau colonial brick buildings housing locked wards and a registration and visitors' center.

At 11:00 that morning, Nurse Martin filled out the admission documents. Around noon, Rusty told Dr. Ellen Allbritton, the admitting physician, that his wife "could not survive another night at home."

Rusty said he gave Allbritton his wife's medical history, including information about her previous medications and suicide attempts. She had been treated successfully with Effexor and Wellbutrin, he told the doctor. Zoloft and Zyprexa didn't seem to work. Haldol did. Dr. Allbritton later testified that she was not told that Andrea Yates had previously been psychotic and had taken Haldol. Rusty described his wife's overattachment to 4-month-old Mary, carrying her around and never wanting to put her down. Andrea was sleeping only one or two hours a night, Rusty told Allbritton—lying in bed beside him, eyes wide open.

Andrea Yates refused to sign a consent form to be treated at Devereux. Nurse Martin consulted a list of hospital psychiatrists. After two calls, he found one who was available to take Yates's case: Mohammad Saeed. Martin noted on a March 31 mental status evaluation that Andrea Yates had been experiencing auditory hallucinations. Both Martin and his colleague Bobbie Findley described her as being "selectively" mute, giving a monotone yes or no answer—if she spoke at all—or a slight nod of her head. Each response included a long latency time between question and answer. "Sitting quietly," "a vacant look," "staring into space," "almost catatonic" was how Yates was repeatedly described in hospital notes.

As the day wore on, Andrea still refused to admit herself to the hospital. Not even her husband's coaxing could convince her to change her mind. At 3:00 that afternoon, at the hospital's suggestion, Sergeant Josette Budow made an application to Galveston County Probate Court for emergency detention of Andrea Yates without a warrant for preliminary examination.

---

2. *Letter of A. Yates to author, May 14, 2003.*

Allbritton, who had examined Andrea at 12:30 that day, said she was "selectively mute, nearly catatonic, [had] poor self care, [was] depressed, anhedonic, apathetic, [and had] poor sleep, poor appetite, poor concentration, [and] hopeless, helpless feelings." She joined in Sergeant Budow's application, writing that emergency detention for Andrea Yates was the least restrictive means by which necessary restraint could be effected. Yates "needs inpatient stabilization for safety of self and others. Will continue to have decline in future," she added. Significantly, Allbritton was the only physician other than Dr. Starbranch (in 1999) to suggest that this woman might be a threat to the safety of anyone besides herself.

Rusty walked his wife across the hospital grounds to her assigned room in the Unit 3 building. He gave her a kiss and a hug, told her he'd see her the next day, then he and Brian went home to relieve Andrea's mother, who'd been watching her five grandchildren.

Favorite brother—you know—Brian is charming, handsome and funny. Spiritually I'm closer to Pat.[3]

By the next day, April 1, Andrea was worse. Her total nutritional intake for the day was 16 ounces of liquid. Hospital progress reports established that she could, with "great effort," speak three- or four-word sentences. Her longest sentence was "I am not a good mother."

On April 2, 2001, after talking at length with Rusty Yates, Saeed wrote to Judge Gladys Burwell:

Honorable Judge Gladys Burwell
Galveston County Probate Court
Galveston, Texas 77550

Re: Andrea Yates

Honorable Judge Burwell,

Ms. Andrea Yates was admitted to Devereux Texas Treatment Center on March 31, 2001 with a diagnosis of Major Depression. She is

---

3. *Letter of A. Yates to author, May 14, 2003.*

catatonic and is refusing to talk, eat or drink fluids. She is also refusing to take her medications. She is currently under the care of Dr. Mohammed [*sic*] Saeed.

The doctor and treatment team members recommend that the patient be committed to Austin State Hospital.

The courts [*sic*] assistance and cooperation in this matter is very appreciated.

Sincerely,

Mohammed [*sic*] Saeed, MD
Attending Psychiatrist

Simultaneously, Saeed applied for an Order to Administer Psychoactive Medication, describing Andrea Yates's condition to the probate court as postpartum depression with possible psychotic features. Saeed wrote that Yates lacked the capacity to make a decision regarding the administration of psychoactive medication, including antidepressants, antipsychotics, sedatives, and mood stabilizers, because she "is severely depressed and possibly paranoid, has lost motivation, has had similar episode after birth of fourth child." Failure to administer psychoactive medication, Saeed claimed, would result in his patient's "further deterioration and possibly death."

Dr. Patricia Corke, an examining physician, joined Saeed in this application. Both doctors checked committal form boxes indicating that Andrea Yates was a danger to herself and that she was unable to make a rational treatment choice for herself. But one box was left unchecked: "Is likely to cause serious harm to others."

The basis for their opinion, the doctors told the court, was that Andrea Yates "would not talk," "refused to eat or drink," "refused meds," and was unlikely to improve without medication. Saeed's hospital admissions orders prescribed daily doses of Effexor (37.5 mg), Wellbutrin (100 mg), Restoril (30 mg for insomnia), Tylenol (650 mg), and Mylanta (30 cc). His treatment plan anticipated hospitalization until April 12, 2001, with a step-down to the day patient Partial Hospitalization Program and private treatment by Saeed.

At dinnertime that day, Rusty and all five children visited Andrea in the unit. She sat on a couch but interacted only minimally with her family.

Just after midnight, Rusty telephoned the duty nurse, concerned about his wife's low fluid intake and poor personal hygiene and wanting to know whether she was compliant with her medications. A nurse wrote in hospital progress notes that Yates "suggested dividing his wife's medications into smaller doses and offering them more frequent times since she seemed to accept fluids only when she took medication." The nurse assured Rusty Yates that she would pass the suggestion on to Andrea's treatment team.

In the afternoon, Rusty and the children visited once more, trying to get Andrea to eat and drink. The duty nurses told Rusty that his wife might be committed to Austin State Hospital (formerly known as the State Lunatic Asylum) if she didn't sign herself into the hospital. Rusty explained the situation to his wife. "I think the thought of going to a state mental institution scared Andrea," he said. In any case, Andrea relented and signed herself into Devereux, officially becoming patient 67357. Saeed withdrew his commitment application.

Saeed's notes indicate that he dropped by for rounds after Rusty Yates left. He wrote, "Patient still almost mute, but with husband's persuasion drank Ensure and appears hydrated. Continues to appear paranoid."

On April 4, 2001, Rusty and the kids and Andrea's mother visited again for several hours. "Encouraged by husband, patient accepted Ensure and a carton of chocolate milk," another nurse wrote. Dr. Saeed wrote that though his patient had attended her first group session that day, she still refused to eat or drink unless her husband was present. "It would take literally an hour to get her to drink one carton of Ensure mixed with chocolate milk," Rusty remembered. His secret weapon was that two of his brood, Mary and Luke, were still in Pampers. "You need to eat this," he'd tell Andrea, "because I've got to go home and get more diapers."

The hour-long group therapy sessions Andrea attended twice a day were provided by the Chemical Dependency Services Department of Devereux—the hospital had no groups that dealt with Andrea's illness. According to Devereux records, that first day of group therapy—when Andrea was paranoid, mute, refusing nutrition, and reluctant to take medication—was a "chalk talk" on alcohol. Yates, who never drank and was phobic about recreational drugs and prescribed medications, "gained insight on the effects of alcohol including death."

On Andrea's sixth day in the hospital, April 5, social worker Barbara Lane-Roberts tried getting some verbal responses from her about her feelings. What she saw was "a dullness to her eyes." "My mind is so full of things," Andrea told Lane-Roberts, but could not distinguish what "things" were on her mind. Ultimately, she mentioned that she had to go home to "be a mother" to her children. That same day, Dr. Saeed noted that Andrea continued to be severely depressed but was alert enough to give brief answers to the doctor's questions. But she became instantly mute when he asked her whether she felt suicidal. "Patient [is] still not eating or drinking unless husband is here. She drinks Ensure for him." That day she watched a video on relapse and recovery from drug addiction in group therapy.

On April 6, Nurse Marion Pollard noted for the first time the "pacing" behavior that spiraled out of control the sicker Yates became. For safety, she was monitored every fifteen minutes and continued to be described as severely depressed at each interval. From shift to shift and nurse to nurse, the reports remained the same: the patient was very depressed. From 11:00 AM to noon that day she attended group therapy and listened to a lecture on the signs and symptoms of "post acute withdrawal from drugs." From 3:30 to 4:30 PM, after another visit from her husband and children, she attended a second group therapy session. With fellow patients, she watched a video called *The Mind: Episode 4, Addictions.* She cried all the way through it. "Client gained an understanding of how chemicals affect the brain of an addict," Counselor Peggy Davidson noted in her daily report. Yates had lost three pounds since arriving at the hospital. She drank only Ensure and only when her husband fed it to her.

On April 8, Saeed's progress note reported that Yates took some solid food for the first time and denied having suicidal thoughts. Asked how she felt, she said, "About the same." The following morning she had "some O.J., bread and egg." The fifteen-minute suicide checks continued. A nurse summed up that day's ninety-six entries describing Andrea Yates in these words: "Sits and stares." The only other notation in the record with equal constancy described twice-daily visits of Rusty Yates with and without the children. Mrs. Kennedy, Andrea's brothers, and Debbie Holmes also say they visited, though Yates's records do not specifically identify visiting family or friends except her husband and children.

On April 10, Yates was back to refusing breakfast and pacing her room. According to Davidson's notes of April 11, her group session that day included watching a Discovery Health Channel video on "the signs, symptoms and treatment for 'chemical' depression." Later that day, she learned "ways to cope with chronic pain other than chemicals." Saeed indicated in her chart that Andrea Yates had made what might seem to some an amazing recovery. She was feeding herself for the first time, reporting she felt 90 percent better, denying suicidal ideas, agreeing to attend PHP, and requesting to be discharged. Her only question for the doctor was about the maleffects of the antipsychotic drug Risperdal, which he had prescribed. When Rusty Yates visited his wife and learned that Saeed planned to release her that day, he was shocked; so was Andrea's mother. Rusty wasn't a doctor, but to him his wife still looked like the sickest person in the unit. He asked Saeed to keep her in the hospital at least another day.

The woman who had been sick enough to be committed to a state hospital ten days earlier was discharged exactly according to the Managed Care schedule, April 12. Her discharge followed a group discussion on alcohol and drugs and her signature on an agreement to "remain clean and sober, not to harm or kill herself" and (somewhat contradictory to the antidrug education she had received) to take all the medications prescribed to her. She would keep her word.

Andrea began attending PHP at Devereux the following morning at 8:30. Lynnette Hunterman, Utilization Review LCDC, described Andrea quite differently than Saeed had when he had discharged her. She was "sad, depressed, withdrawn, and having suicidal feelings," according to Hunterman. Her goal at discharge from PHP was listed as "no longer risk to self." Again, there was no mention of her being harmful to others. On that first day of PHP, one specific goal was for Andrea to "be able to identify three reasons to live." The "Objective Met" box was checked over the signatures of both Dr. Saeed and Hunterman.

When Rusty Yates picked his wife up at the end of the day that Friday, April 13, she told him she didn't want to go back because the sessions were for substance abuse patients. Rusty called Bob Martin, the nurse who had admitted Andrea, to tell him she was leaving the outpatient program. Hospital records show she was discharged on April 18, 2001. "Patient not here for discharge," read the note written across the Devereux Texas Treatment Network Discharge Plan.

Then came the roller-coaster ride. Rusty Yates remembered Andrea's being "down but stable" for the first several days after she left the hospital. Then she began to decline. Dora Yates arrived from Hermitage, Tennessee, for a long-planned visit on the day Andrea was discharged. She was shocked to see her daughter-in-law's condition. She babysat when Rusty finally met Saeed in person during Andrea's first visit to Saeed's private practice office. The psychiatrist asked Rusty to join the session after ten minutes.

In the face of Andrea's obvious decline, Saeed increased her dose of Effexor. Rusty was perplexed that Saeed didn't prescribe Haldol. Risperdal was a much newer drug and was preferred by most psychiatrists for treatment of psychosis, but it hadn't worked for Andrea in the past and wasn't working now. Rusty asked Saeed to contact Eileen Starbranch, Andrea's previous psychiatrist, to discuss her success with Haldol.

On April 20, Rusty began giving his wife the new dose of Effexor according to Saeed's direction. She improved slightly but was still more depressed than when she had left the hospital. Over the next two weeks, as her depression deepened, Saeed prescribed higher doses of Effexor. The doses of Wellbutrin and Risperdal remained constant. When Debbie Holmes visited on Friday, April 27, she had no idea her friend was banking on prayer—not medication—for a cure for her mental illness.

By May 3, Andrea's eccentric behaviors returned. She paced the house, stood in front of the television screen and stared at it (once for as long as forty-five minutes), gazed into space (sometimes for as long as three hours), and was withdrawn and noncommunicative. Dora Yates noticed her daughter-in-law walking in circles as many as "thirty times—around and around." She convinced herself that Andrea was walking for her health, because it was too hot outside. She could put breakfast cereal into bowls in the morning, yet she spoke in monosyllables and did not remember to feed the children at lunch. It was confusing, Dora said.

Noah noticed his mom filling the bathtub with water. Mommy didn't take baths. She always showered in the master bathroom, which didn't have a tub. He knew she'd tried to hurt herself in the bathroom at Grandma Kennedy's house. She was sick again, and he was worried. When Dora asked Andrea why she was filling the tub, she answered, "In case I need it." That afternoon, when Debbie Holmes again came by the house to bring food, Dora said that Andrea turned her friend away at the door as if she were a stranger.

As with her 1999 hospitalization, it took Andrea Yates only a matter of weeks to wind up back in the hospital. At her scheduled appointment with Saeed on May 4, the doctor wrote, "The patient was near catatonic. Sat in the chair and did not move at all." Rusty suggested readmitting his wife to Devereux. "Well, she would qualify," Yates recalled Saeed saying. The doctor telephoned ahead to alert admissions.

On the way there, Rusty took Andrea to Burger King for a Whopper Junior and fries. When they arrived at the hospital, she didn't want to get out of the car. After appealing to her for twenty minutes without success, he physically removed her from the car and took her into the admissions building. In the waiting room, Andrea stood holding on to a wall, until a staff member asked her to take a seat. Unexpectedly, she sat down and filled out the admissions papers.

Once again Rusty walked his wife to a room in Unit 3, kissed her good night, and went home to help his mom with the kids.

Devereux was one of the few affordable psychiatric inpatient facilities remaining in the Houston area. Most patients and their families didn't know about the numerous complaints filed against the facility with the Texas Department of Health and Human Services between September 1, 1996, and August 31, 1999. In three of eleven records reviewed, psychosocial evaluations were performed by non-LMSWs and unqualified mental-health professionals. In one of eight records the psychiatric evaluation was missing. In another case, a director failed to monitor the staff. One patient had committed suicide by hanging himself with a bedsheet while on suicide watch. He had been dead at least five hours before his body was discovered.

Saeed had not attempted to contact Starbranch for Andrea's medical records. His choice of Risperdal certainly hadn't worked. He relented and began treating his patient with 2 milligrams of Haldol per day—"at the husband's request"—on May 4. He continued giving his patient Effexor, Wellbutrin, and Cogentin, and Restoril for sleeplessness. It was not until May 9, nearly six weeks after Andrea Yates had become his patient, that Saeed obtained her records from Starbranch's office. JoLynn Janda, the custodian of Starbranch's records, faxed Yates's records to Saeed's office. After Yates's outpatient discharge from Spring Shadows Glen Hospital on August 20, 1999, Starbranch had treated her with Haldol Decanoate, injected intramuscularly every three weeks. As she showed improvement, the injections were reduced to once every four weeks. In October 1999 Yates reported to Starbranch a conflict with the insurance company regarding coverage for the Haldol Decanoate. Starbranch's notes indicate that Andrea advised her of the disagreement and asked whether she was well enough to stop taking the injections.

Getting Andrea to eat was not such a struggle this time, though she continued to be depressed. Her stay at Devereux included two weekends, during which Rusty was able to attend family group therapy sessions with his wife on Saturdays and Sundays from 4:00 to 6:00 PM, as his mother remained in Houston and could watch the children. He found the sessions helpful, but Andrea didn't participate. At the beginning of each group session the participants introduced themselves. When it was her turn, she said, "Andrea Yates, Depression" and nothing more for the remaining two hours. During the May 5 and 6 sessions, she stared straight ahead into space, not following the conversation. The following weekend, May 12 and 13, she did occasionally turn her head as if she were listening. This emboldened Rusty to ask his wife, in front of the group, if there were anything she might like to contribute. She didn't answer. To Rusty, she seemed more depressed than anyone in the room. He was once again shocked when he came to visit his wife on the following day, May 14. Instead of being in her room resting, she was standing by the door with her bag packed. After eleven days at Devereux, she'd been discharged and referred once again into the only Partial Hospitalization Program Devereux had—for chemical dependency.

The next morning, he dropped his wife off at PHP around 9:30. By 10:00 she had signed her Behavioral Management Contract agreeing that it was her duty to abide by numerous guidelines, including the three rules of "being safe": not hurting herself, not hurting others, not hurting property. By noon that day Andrea was sitting uncommunicatively in a group therapy session where participants "talked about what causes a person to pick up drink or drugs." When Rusty collected his wife at the end of the day, she complained that there had been only one session that day and it was focused on substance abuse. Later that week, Rusty asked one of the PHP nurses about the lack of treatment sessions and why were there no sessions that addressed Andrea's depression. The nurse suggested he file a complaint.

After her discharge, the Yateses saw Saeed in his private office once in May and twice in June. Andrea remained stable at about 65 percent of her normal capacity. At the appointment on June 4, Saeed and Rusty Yates agreed that Andrea had plateaued; she'd been back on Haldol for one month. Saeed asked her to taper off Haldol. He would later testify "there was no definite indication . . . of psychosis" and that he had "considered the possibility that Haldol might be hindering the progress that . . . could have resulted from use of antidepressant medications, because some of the side effects of Haldol . . . produce a picture that could very well resemble depression, meaning their facial expressions are masked, their body movements are slowed down . . ." Saeed thought this was possibly the case with Andrea and "that we would be able to see more improvement in depression if we took that measure."

Rusty had been giving Andrea 2 milligrams of Haldol orally in the morning and another 2 milligrams in the evening, as prescribed. Saeed's new orders were to drop the morning Haldol dose for three days, then drop the evening dose entirely. The routine patient information sheet on Haldol advises: "After you have been doing well for a number of months, your physician may discuss the possibility of slowly tapering the medication. Usually the medication should be tapered very slowly, to determine the lowest effective dose." After going off Haldol, Andrea improved slightly for a few days, only to decline sharply thereafter.

On June 7, Bob Holmes ran into the Yates family at the grocery store. Like his wife, Debbie, he had known Andrea for seventeen years. He hadn't seen her in nearly four months. Andrea was pushing the grocery cart with baby Mary in it. Rusty pushed another with the boys grouped around him. "What shocked me was the look on Andrea's face," Holmes said. "It was a look of extreme paranoia—almost like the look of a caged animal." When Holmes said hello, "for a brief second the look left her face, but immediately it came back, and she mouthed a 'hello'—no sound came out. She looked away and did not look back at me for the entire time I talked to Rusty. I could hardly take my eyes off Andrea. I was used to seeing the kind, gentle eyes that sparkled whenever she laughed. Instead, I was seeing eyes that were communicating danger. It was like she was saying with her eyes, 'Don't mess with me, I will hurt you!' Andrea has never been a person who could hide her emotions. Whatever she was feeling, you could see on her face."

Holmes was astonished to see the children grouped around Rusty instead of their mother. Andrea was the center of her kids' world, providing for their every need, with Rusty sometimes suffering from the ignored-dad syndrome. But *this* Andrea didn't respond at all to her kids. "No wonder the children were grouped around Rusty. She wasn't giving them a thing," he said.

Holmes found it difficult to tell his wife what he had seen that night. When he did, she remembered she had seen the same look on Andrea's face when she had visited her friend in mid-June. It had frightened her. Andrea had been almost mute with Debbie, too. The last full sentence she had uttered to her was "Debbie, pray that Jesus will come into my heart." She showed a complete lack of interest in caring for herself or the children. Afterward Debbie confessed that she had sat in her car for ten minutes crying. Holmes told Debbie to prepare for something terrible to happen. He played out a couple of scenarios in his head. One was Andrea killing Rusty and then herself. He even fleetingly considered whether he'd have the courage to take on raising five more children. "Amazingly, *none* of them involved her harming the children," he said.[4]

At the Yateses' June 18 appointment with Saeed, the first thing Rusty said was "She's declined and I'm concerned." Saeed's notes for that office visit confirm Rusty Yates reported that "in the last 3–4 days" his wife had "declined." The doctor wrote that Andrea Yates denied hav-

---

4. Letter of R. Holmes to author, postmarked June 5, 2003.

ing psychotic symptoms and feeling suicidal. He didn't want to put her back on Haldol. According to Rusty, Saaed's reason was "It's a bad medicine," referring to its side effects. Saeed would later testify that he "did not find any evidence . . . that psychosis was playing any important role."

Saeed decided to continue on course. He added 15 milligrams of Remeron, in a form that dissolved under a patient's tongue, to the 45-milligram dose she was already taking. Rusty had read that 45 milligrams was typically the maximum dose of the drug; Saeed said it was okay to go higher. He told Andrea he was optimistic that increasing the dose of Remeron would help. She needed to help *him* out with a more positive attitude, he said. Chin up. Andrea told Rusty later that she thought Saeed was sick of seeing her face.

Rusty had read up on the drug Effexor, which his wife had been taking at an unusually high dose—450 milligrams per day. Saeed lowered the dose to 300 milligrams when her depressive symptoms failed to improve. The product brochure warns that "adverse events have followed the discontinuation of Effexor XR" and that "patients discontinuing Effexor XR after 6 weeks or more should have their dose tapered gradually over a 2-week period. In clinical trials, the dose was reduced by 75 mg at 1-week intervals. Individual patients may require different schedules for tapering." Saeed told Yates that going straight to 300 milligrams, without tapering the decrease, was fine.

Now Andrea Yates was on straight "rocket fuel," the term some psychiatrists gave to the combination of antidepressants Effexor and Remeron. She had been without antipsychotic medication for two weeks.

THAT DOCTORS HAD documented a possible "component of delusional guilt" as early as 1999 was an understatement of what was going on with Andrea Yates. More specifically, what was going on between Andrea and the Woronieckis. Rusty had told doctors he thought the patient "may be struggling with the concept of Salvation." This insight proved to be another warning that was ignored. Andrea was indeed grappling with the concept of Salvation. And, according to Michael and Rachel Woroniecki, her time was running out.

Long before the Andrea that her family had known disappeared into psychotic silence, she had pleaded with her mother and siblings to renounce Roman Catholicism. Shortly before her father died, she twice wrote to the Woronieckis asking them to send literature to her parents, three brothers, and sister. Next to the address she supplied for her parents, she jotted, "My parents—'Catholics.' Dad has 'Alzheimer's.' Mom's never really receptive to 'religious talk.' Mom is *so* stressed taking care of Dad. I pray she turns to Jesus for *mercy* and truth and not try to handle it 'on her own.' "[5] Among the last things Andrea focused on as she lost her grip on reality was this Woroniecki poem:

MODERN MOTHER WORLDLY

Modern Mother Worldly was very, very lazy,
All her children drove her crazy.
The Bible told her to spank and train them,
But society said she must never constrain them.
The fruit of rebellion she did now see,
On the day of judgment she will have no plea.
Modern Mother Worldly cast in hell!
Now what becomes of the children of such a "Jezebel"?

---

5. *Letter of A. Yates to R. Woroniecki, undated, circa 1998.*

CHAPTER 4

Thursday

On Thursday morning, June 21, 2001, Rusty Yates returned with his mother and brother to the house on Beachcomber. Overnight, an impromptu monument of flowers, teddy bears, yellow ribbons, and candles had accumulated on the front lawn.

Standing on the sidewalk, Rusty spoke to the assembled press about his wife's recurrent illness, his father-in-law's recent death, his children, T-ball, his wife's homemade Valentine cards for the kids with coupons redeemable for hugs and kisses. He talked about the couple's recent decision to limit the size of their family, their hopes for a manageable life, and his two-year struggle to understand mental illness. His in-laws were concentrating on legal representation for Andrea, he said, while he worked on funeral arrangements. He wouldn't be allowed to see his wife until the next day. "I've got to remember that she wasn't herself," he said. "She was thinking irrationally." He paused. "Andrea, if you see this, I love you." Little of what Rusty Yates said made its way into the public consciousness; some of Andrea's friends and family didn't believe what did.

Inside the house, the phone rang nonstop. Katie Couric, the NBC *Today* show host, was among the callers. "I was really struggling at the time," Rusty Yates said. "Katie Couric called and was just doing her normal stuff. She said that if there was anything she could do, to let her know."

"How about helping me find an attorney for Andrea?" he asked her.

Later that day, Rusty said he got a call from an NBC staffer with a list of three prominent Houston defense attorneys. He set up an appointment with one of the three, Mike Ramsey, for Friday morning. Attorney George Parnham was another name on the list.

AFTER HIS LUNCH, Assistant Harris County Medical Examiner Harminder S. Narula, MD, finished the last of the Yates children's autopsies, that of 3-year-old Paul Abraham Yates. With each of the children, the team of medical examiners made the familiar Y-shaped incision in the chest, rolled back the skin, opened the rib cage, extracted and weighed the organs, took tissue samples, returned what they could to its place, and sutured the chest closed. Noah, John, Paul, Luke, and Mary's bones had been X-rayed, their measurements taken, stubbed toes and scraped knees and bruised shins noted. For each child, the manner of death was determined to be homicide. The cause of death was "asphyxia due to drowning." All tox screens were negative—no drugs or alcohol or poisons present. Each child was described as "well developed" and "well nourished." Five-year-old John had the biggest heart: 104.6 grams.

CHAPTER 5

The Catchers
and the Keepers

At 7:30 on the morning of Friday, June 22, 2001, Andrea Yates, dressed in a bright orange jumpsuit with the words COUNTY JAIL stenciled across the back, walked into the 230th District Court of Texas. Her hands were folded across her waist. She stood motionless before Judge Belinda Hill.

Prosecutor Kaylynn Williford detailed the facts to Judge Hill. The accused had "intentionally and knowingly" caused the deaths of her five children "with a deadly weapon—namely, water."

"Do you understand the charges against you?" Judge Hill asked Yates.

"Yes, ma'am," she answered.

The court determined that Yates was indigent and appointed an attorney, Bob Scott. Scott asked the judge to impose an immediate gag order. Judge Hill took Scott's request under advisement. Yates was led out of the courtroom for a ten-minute meeting with her attorney.

On the sidewalk outside the Criminal Courts Building, prosecutors Joseph Owmby and Williford answered questions. Owmby was an assistant district attorney and lead prosecutor for Harris County in the Yates case. Judge Hill had been Owmby's mentor in the DA's office before becoming a judge. Williford, a graduate of Texas Tech University School of Law, was trying her first capital case as a Harris County ADA.

"Whether the judge issues a gag order or not, the effect is the same," Owmby said. "I'm not trying the case out here. I'm not going to talk about the case."

Andrea Yates had been charged with a single count of capital murder. John and Noah together—two or more people in the same criminal episode and a child under the age of 6—comprised a capital offense. What about the other children? "We haven't made all the charging decisions yet," said Owmby, who had prosecuted a dozen capital murder cases. "It is possible that we could prosecute just that case, or charge other cases, or charge different cases. Usually in a charge of capital murder, all acts like that come into the trial anyway."

What about the death penalty?

"Chuck Rosenthal is the district attorney in Harris County, and he'll make that decision," Owmby answered. "It's not an everyday occurrence anywhere. It's not an everyday occurrence in the world. I've been here fifteen years," Owmby said. "This is the most horrendous thing that I have ever seen."

ON THE MORNING of Friday, June 22, criminal defense attorney Wendell Odom was in his eighth-floor law office in Houston's Lyric Centre, reading a *Houston Chronicle* article that described his theory of a new legal order. Executives of Houston's beleaguered energy trading company, Enron, traditionally shared its millions with corporate attorneys who tended paper fortunes. But as last year's brilliant ideas became this year's felonies, the same deep-pocketed executives valued their newly (and often secretly) employed criminal defense attorneys more highly. Odom had just bagged his first client of the new order, Steven Gary Todoroff, an energy trader who pled guilty to laundering money.

Odom's partner, George Parnham, appeared in the doorway. Parnham's face wore a look of contained frenzy, but Odom didn't seem to notice. He couldn't wait to get back to the newspaper.

"Listen to this," Odom said, quoting aloud from the *Houston Chronicle.* "His attorney, Wendell Odom, said Todoroff made a terrible trading mistake, but it was a personal trade that was not supposed to involve EOTT." A nice bit of publicity, didn't Parnham think?

"I got a call on the Andrea Yates case," Parnham replied.

Parnham explained that he had received an urgent phone message from a lawyer named John O'Sullivan with whom he had worked on a murder case in Angleton, Texas, but hadn't heard from in a couple of years. He had delayed returning the call. "I just had that sixth sense," he said, "that he was calling me about this case." O'Sullivan had an office in Clear Lake City and had been the Kennedy family attorney for years. At 7:30 on the morning of June 21, O'Sullivan, Jutta Karin Kennedy, Andrea Yates's seventy-two-year-old mother, and Yates's three brothers, Andrew, Patrick, and Brian Kennedy, met in Parnham's office. They had hired him on the spot without consulting Rusty Yates.

Parnham called 230th District Criminal Court Judge Belinda Hill, the presiding judge, and notified her that he'd been retained to represent Andrea Yates. Then he prepared a Notice of Representation and went to see his client. Walking south from his office to the County Jail, he turned the corner onto San Jacinto Street and saw a gathering army of satellite news trucks. He passed unnoticed through the lines of reporters and cameramen for the first and last time.

He saw Andrea Yates's shadow first, falling against the jailhouse floor. His eyes followed the dark outline along the concrete floor, up her silhouette against the window, past the yellow jacket draped over her shoulders to her long, straight, matted black hair.

He was scared and he didn't know exactly why. What was he going to say? What was he going to do? How was he going to react to this woman who less than twenty-four hours ago had taken the lives of her five children? It reminded him of sitting in a hearing on the Clyde Durbin murders back in 1969, when he was a law student at the University of Texas. Parnham had a seat next to the victim's parents. When the back doors of the courtroom opened, revealing the pasty-faced kid who'd been sitting in prison since the killing, the parents gasped.

He wanted to "catch his breath," his expression for withdrawing from the kind of emotional intensity that could suck the breath out of him. He wanted to get beyond "what occurred" and on to the job of lawyering. But Andrea Yates was in a state of suspended animation.

What startled Wendell Odom on his first visit with Yates later that day were her eyes. They were like shark eyes, he thought; there were no pupils. He had never seen anything like Andrea Yates before in his life, and this wasn't "his first rodeo" (a Texas term coined by convicts who were "available" to compete more than once in the annual Huntsville Prison Rodeo). He'd had a lot of clients committed to mental institutions who weren't what you'd call mentally stable. But in his thirty years as a prosecutor and defense attorney, "there wasn't even a close second to Andrea Yates."

"Doctors are trained in medical terms, and they say it in a very scientific manner—'flat affect,' 'responding to internal stimuli.' Well, that just doesn't portray the picture. Her hair is totally matted. She's scratching constantly at the crown of her head, which she thought was marked with the sign of the devil—666." She'd rubbed her head raw trying to get it off. "She was mentally ill to the point that we were a sideshow," Odom recalled. "There were more important things going on in her head than the lawyers who were talking to her about whether she was charged for a capital offense or not."

AFTER CONDUCTING PROSECUTORS Joe Owmby and Kaylynn Williford on a 9:50 AM tour of his Beachcomber home, Rusty Yates was allowed to see his wife. He and Parnham went into an interview room. Later, Rusty felt he'd "grilled Mr. Parnham—asking like a hundred questions." He was "concerned." He knew it was critical to get a good attorney for his wife. Bottom line, Parnham told Rusty Yates what he wanted to hear: "I'm Andrea's attorney, that's it. I do what's in Andrea's best interest."

Rusty had difficulty communicating with Parnham. Parnham's conversation was sometimes circular—if not serpentine. "Sometimes you talk with Mr. Parnham," Yates said later, "and you don't know any more when you finish than you did when you started." But what he liked about Parnham was that he was "a very gentle, dignified man," someone to whom he knew his wife would respond. With his white hair and full beard, he "had a grandfatherly appearance." Andrea had always been comfortable with older people. The longer he knew Parnham, the more he knew he'd made the right choice. "He and his entire team care for Andrea," Yates said. "I would have never expected that from an attorney. To have that means as much to me as his being a good defense attorney. It's made this whole thing so much more bearable."

With Yates's stamp of approval, Parnham achieved his aim of a unified family front with the Yates and Kennedy families. But now, Rusty had to introduce Parnham to his wife.

"Stoic" is the word that kept coming up in police and jail personnel descriptions of Andrea Yates that day. Yes, she was absent joy or grief, but she'd also gained a persona that, under different circumstances, Rusty would have thought comical.

"You will be greatly rewarded" was what Andrea Yates said when she saw her husband, as if she'd just received breaking news from a crystal ball.

Rusty let that pass. "This is Mr. Parnham. He's going to be your lawyer."

"I don't need an attorney," Andrea said. "I'm not going to plead not guilty."

"Well, Mr. Parnham will help you with paperwork then," he explained, as he might have to an overtired child. Everyone in the family would help her through this, he promised.

Andrea shot her husband a skeptical glance. "Have a nice life," she answered.

> I was pretty sure I had lost Rusty forever and that's why I said, "Have a nice life."[1]

Rusty found only one word to describe his wife's behavior: "bizarre."

"I had a sense of how the law enforcement people, who were the catchers and the keepers—particularly the keepers—how they viewed Andrea's situation," Parnham recalled. "I believe that, to a person, they believed that no one in her right mind could do what she did. The second thing I realized is that all of the years I've been down to the county jail—thirty-five to be exact—that for whatever reason there was a certain deference they were providing. I was important."

Two hours later, Rusty Yates, the Kennedys, and George Parnham took the elevator down to the ground floor to face a phalanx of reporters, microphones, and cameras that extended from the lobby all the way down the exterior steps a hundred feet away. Beyond them was an infinity of satellite transmission trucks. "I looked out that window

---

1. *Letter of A. Yates to author, August 4, 2003.*

from the ground floor," Parnham said, "and I realized this family didn't know what was in store for them."

"She is doing as well as can be expected," Parnham told the press corps, "considering the circumstances—which I know you understand are extreme." He had "accumulated evidence in the last twenty-four hours that strongly suggested that the mental status of my client will be the issue, which means entering a not guilty plea by reason of insanity." Rusty Yates's meeting with his wife had been one of a "very personal" nature. "You can imagine that it was as intense, as private, and as heart rending as any meeting between two individuals that I have ever witnessed." The family would not be making any more statements until after the funeral, he said. Fearful he would inherit the gag order his predecessor had requested, Parnham himself went on a forty-eight-hour television blitz, not stopping even to sleep.

Later, Parnham said he went back to the jail with his associate Molly Odom, sister of Wendell Odom, to check on Andrea Yates. "That's when she said what she said," he recalled. " 'Please don't leave me alone.' "

RANDY YATES TOOK the sheets off the bed where the children had lain, stuffed them in a plastic garbage bag, and put them out on the street for the next trash collection. Then he got down on his hands and knees and scrubbed the bathroom floor and tub. When he was finished, he took a shower there. He didn't like the task, but he did it for his brother. Five children he loved were dead—that he'd never get over. But the bathroom was just a bathroom. Dammit.

CHAPTER 6

Five Small Coffins

O ur hearts are full of questions, and answers are few," minister Byron Fike told the more than three hundred mourners assembled at the Clear Lake Church of Christ on Wednesday, June 27, 2001. The church, an active community center of friendly Texans, is located only four blocks from the Yates house. Fike had volunteered the church and his services for the children's funeral, though he didn't know the Yateses.

Growing up Methodist in Tennessee, Rusty Yates had thought of Church of Christ members as a snooty bunch who didn't allow musical instruments and whose male congregants attended largely for the business connections. In time, more people than he would wonder how different the Yateses' lives might have been had they joined the congregation. Andrea Yates would have had fellowship, mothers' days out, coffee klatches, and a society of parents who might have provided checks and balances as her illness spun out of control in the isolation of raising children.

When Rusty, dressed in a dark suit and white shirt, first heard the a cappella choir singing "Near to the Heart of God" from the rear of the sanctuary, he thought it must be what angels' voices sounded like. The white caskets of his children, draped in flowers, stood in a half circle at the head of the contemporary-style church. He sat with his and his wife's families in the front pews. Andrea Yates had not been granted permission to attend her children's funeral.

"When tragedy strikes we turn to God and ask, 'Why, God, why did you let this happen?' And God is oftentimes silent," Fike said. Without realizing it, that day he sounded several biblical themes favored by Michael Woroniecki. From Psalm 19: "The heavens declare the glory of God, the skies proclaim the work of his hands. Day after day they display knowledge." And from Job: "Job in the Old Testament suffered in horrible ways. He lost all of his possessions. And then he lost all of his children. And then he lost his health," Fike said. "And his friends question and accuse; Job struggles. But right in the middle of the book, in the midst of all this terrible mental and emotional and physical turmoil that he's in, he says these words: 'I know that my Redeemer lives, and that in the end He will stand on the earth. After my skin has been destroyed, yet in my flesh I will see God, I myself will see him with my own eyes, I and not another. How my heart yearns within me!'

"But today, today is not very good," Fike said. "And today you acknowledge your pain. Today you acknowledge your unspeakable grief at what you've lost. . . . But we hold on to hope. The last chapter has not yet been written."

In fact, the promise that they were going to see Noah, John, Paul, Luke, and Mary again was what was getting Rusty and his wife (under completely different circumstances) through the day. "We can live through it, if we can have an eternal perspective," Rusty Yates said afterward.

"Rusty is now going to talk to you about his children," Fike said, introducing him. "He is wanting to communicate so badly to you how much each child means to him as an individual. . . . And when Rusty finishes that, we will conclude this service with a message of hope and encouragement." Fike sat down. Rusty Yates stood among his children's coffins. At the front of the sanctuary, a large screen, typically used for projecting the words of hymns and verses, featured a slide of Noah.

"This has gotta be the hardest thing I've ever had to do," he began. "I wanted to tell you really, you know, a little bit about each of my children. And I know some of you knew them pretty well, others didn't. And I can't tell you everything, you know, there is to know about them, but I can give you a little glimpse into who they were." He referred only fleetingly to his wife.

During the days leading up to the service, Yates had told his out-of-town relatives stories about his kids over the dinner table, and that was how he wanted to describe them today. "So if I say anything, you know, a funny story, don't feel too awkward about laughing," he said.

Noah was the firstborn, who liked to play alone. At 7 years old, he could replace the broken speaker from one musical toy with the working speaker from another, using only a miniscrewdriver and a glue gun.

One night, the family rented the movie *Air Bud*. Noah loved it. The next night, at his 9:30 bedtime, he asked if he could watch the video again. His father told him no, it was too late. But Noah was persistent.

"Well, Daddy, how about you ask me a president question, and if I get it right, then I get to watch the movie?" Yates recalled. Each of the children had his own rubberized placemat at the kitchen table. Noah's was of the presidents of the United States.

Fine, Rusty thought to himself, he'd pick the most difficult question on the placemat, Noah would get it wrong, and that would be the end of it. "I said, 'When was James Garfield born?' And just before I could hardly get the sentence out of my mouth, Noah said, '1831.'" He had memorized the entire placemat. "I just shook my head and said, 'Okay, here,' you know, 'watch the movie.' And I sent his brothers to bed. He liked that."

Noah was crazy for rainbows and butterflies. His bug jar was ubiquitous. He captured caterpillars from the milkweed plants his mother grew and watched them turn into the dark gold-speckled cocoons of Monarch butterflies. When they hatched, he loved to set them free. "That's kind of the way I feel about Noah. It's time to set him free," Yates said, tearing up and touching Noah's casket. "I love you," he whispered.

> I wish I had dreams like my mom and a woman who came up to Rusty
> and said she dreamed that as the children passed away they would go
> up to the edge of Heaven and wait for each other. The younger ones
> were waiting for Noah so he could lead them into Heaven.[1]

"John, he was quite different than Noah," Yates said as the on-screen photo changed to one of John with his big, contagious grin. "My mom always told me that . . . after she had me she didn't know there could be any other kind of guy, you know. And then here comes

---

1. *Letter of A. Yates to author, postmarked January 6, 2003.*

my little brother who was totally different. And that's the way it was with all my children, you know, they're all different. And I kinda thought, well, maybe after two that will stop. Maybe there are not that many different kinds of children. But I think if we kept having children, there'd still be more kinds."

Noah once had a Discovery Toy space rattle. "When he was 4 months old, he would take that toy and he'd get his finger and gently move the sun," his dad remembered. "And John, at the same age, he'd get that toy and just shake it and throw it across the room." There was laughter amid tears.

The two kids liked roughhousing. Yates played a game where he'd hold each of the boys upside down and swing him back and forth like the pendulum on a cuckoo clock. "Noah liked it," Yates said, "but just one time. And John, he was little and I'd do that to him, and I'd set him down, and he'd just jump right back up and say, 'Do again, do again!'"

John's uncle Randy had next-door neighbors in Florida with a diesel truck that fascinated John, who loved *all* trucks. "He used that word, like 'heavy duty,' you know. And when Randy would call he'd go, 'heavy—.'" Yates's voice cracked. "I can't say it. . . . He'd say, 'Heavy duty, Uncle Randy.'"

Yates patted his son's small casket. "I love you, John."

I want so much to reach out and hold them and give them a squeezie hug. I'd give John an extra special hug and make him laugh.[2]

The slide changed to a picture of Paul. According to his dad, Paul was the "best liked," nicest to his brothers and sister, and "best behaved" of all the Yates kids. "Perfect Paul." "My mom used to complain that when I was a little baby . . . I wouldn't put my head on her shoulder, you know," Yates said. "I wasn't very snuggly. Then, you know, Noah and John and Luke and Mary were all *exactly* the same way. . . . But Paul was exactly the opposite. Paul was very cuddly and he gave the best hugs."

"I asked Noah one time, I said, 'Noah, which one of you guys is the best behaved?' And he just, without even hesitating, he said, 'Paul and then me and then John or Luke—I'm not sure.'"

---

2. *Letter of A. Yates to author, March 8, 2003.*

One of Paul's books had a story with a bull moose in it. "He just loved the bull moose," Yates said. "Instead of calling him Paul, a lot of times I'd call him Bull Moose. And he got this shirt that we, we picked this shirt up at a garage sale. And it's got this cute little bull moose on the back with his little arms out. And he wore this shirt like every, I mean every other day. It was like he'd wear it, it would be dirty, we'd wash it, and the next day he'd have it on again. . . . The way the little moose has his little arms out, it kinda reminds me of Paul."

"I love you, Bull Moose," Yates said quietly.

> On one visit Rusty asked me in what order the kids died (I have trouble saying that—also the word ki— and murd—). Usually I say I "took their lives away" or the time "they lost their life." Contrary to what was reported in the paper and book *Breaking Point,* it was Paul, John, Luke, Mary and Noah. Surely enough, this was the order that the lady said happened in her dream.[3]

Of all the children, Luke "had the hardest time grasping boundaries," Yates recalled, as a slide of Luke appeared behind him. "I remember I was sitting in the hallway when he couldn't even walk, and he tried to get by me. He wanted by and that was all there was to it . . . he was going to get by whether he'd push me or poke me in the eye, whatever he needed to do."

Yates coached the homeschoolers' T-ball team. When Andrea was sick in the hospital, he had to take all five children to the game. If Noah and John missed a game, there weren't enough kids on the team to play. Yates crossed his fingers that a sympathetic mom would keep an eye on the younger kids. Mrs. Pratt volunteered. As she held baby Mary, he instructed Paul and Luke to sit still on the bleachers next to Mrs. Pratt. Paul sat through the entire game, as instructed. "Luke," Yates smiled, "when I told him, he had his hand on the bleachers and that's the last he saw of the bleachers. He was all over the park."

Luke thought of himself as ten feet tall, his dad remembered. Once, sitting on the ground in the moonshine, Yates said he turned to catch a glimpse of his youngest son stretching his arms out to the sky. "He was trying to grab the moon."

---

3. *Letter of A. Yates to author, postmarked January 6, 2003.*

"I know it's kind of awkward, I'm just telling you this like I would any day, but he had—he had really beautiful eyes. . . . He'd done something, I don't know what it was. And I . . . was giving him a little lecture. That's the only time it ever happened to me in my life where I was talking to somebody, and I have kind of a hard time looking people in the eye anyway . . . but while I was doing it, his eyes were just so absorbing, you know, that I just got lost in his eyes and . . . I couldn't even speak . . . you know, and I just stared at his eyes for a while and I said, 'Okay, Luke, you know, go on.' "

> Mom dreamed that her parents, aunt, husband and Dad's sister were sitting in Heaven watching the children play. I think those are God's ways of comforting those who are grieving.[4]

Much of what the world would know of the Yateses' family-planning efforts came from what Rusty Yates said next, in eulogizing his only daughter, Mary, whose face now lit the screen. When they had children, many couples wanted just one of each, a boy and a girl, Yates said. But he and Andrea "decided to have whatever kids we had." The Yates side of the family tree was distinguished by being exclusively male. When Andrea asked her husband whether he wanted boys or girls he said, "Well, I want to get a basketball team, and then we'll talk about girls." The mourners chuckled at the familiar line.

By the time of Andrea's fifth pregnancy, Rusty felt destined to repeat the Yates family all-boy pattern. "Andrea was carrying the same and she had the same heart rate and everything, and when Mary came out, I was like 'Wow!' . . . I couldn't believe we had a girl." He was so used to sons and Mary looked so much like Paul as a baby that once, he arrived home from work, saw Mary, and thought, "What's one of my boys doing in a dress?"

His daughter was already ticklish and gave her daddy kisses. Yates loved the image of Mary in the grocery cart being borne along by her four older brothers holding on to the sides.

Yates was close to finishing what he intended to say, but he would rather have stayed suspended indefinitely in memories than move on. Under the circumstances, he had said little about his wife and nothing

---

4. *Ibid.*

at all about the Kennedy family. Wiping away tears, he thanked those who had helped him through the week, "people that I haven't really done much with in several years, and one reason is that these guys [his children] have become my friends, you know." He placed their worn baby "blankies" in their caskets and closed the lids.

"I read this the other day and started crying," Yates said, referring to the text of Job 1:21, which was displayed on the projection screen. "I'm going to read it and that's the last thing I'm going to say up here. This is exactly what—you know, Job—he lost his children, he lost his health. 'Naked I came into this world, naked I'll leave. The Lord giveth and taketh away.' That's what he's done. He gave me all these children and now he's taken them."

The choir closed with "It Is Well with My Soul," written in the 1800s by Horatio Spafford. Spafford lost his son and subsequently his wealth in a Chicago fire. A few years later, he lost his four daughters in a shipwreck; only his wife survived. She sent him a two-word telegram from England: "Saved alone."

> When peace, like a river, attendeth my way,
> When sorrows like sea billows roll;
> Whatever my lot, Thou has taught me to say,
> It is well, it is well, with my soul.
>
> *Refrain*
> *It is well with my soul,*
> *It is well with my soul,*
> *It is well, it is well, with my soul.*
>
> Though Satan should buffet, though trials should come,
> Let this blest assurance control,
> That Christ has regarded my helpless estate,
> And hath shed His own blood for my soul.
>
> *Refrain.*
>
> My sin, O, the bliss of this glorious thought!
> My sin, not in part but the whole,
> Is nailed to the cross, and I bear it no more,
> Praise the Lord, Praise the Lord, O my soul!

Refrain.

And Lord, haste the day when my faith shall be sight,
The clouds be rolled back as a scroll;
The trump shall resound, and the Lord shall descend,
Even so, it is well with my soul.

Refrain.

NEWS HELICOPTERS SPUN hot air down onto satellite trucks scrambling for position as the funeral cortege pulled into the drive of Forest Park East Cemetery. Greg Bolton was a communications director for Service Corporation International, a funeral and cemetery company headquartered in Houston. SCI owned Forest Park East. Bolton had seen funerals across the United States, in small cities like Oxnard, California, and big ones like New York. He'd seen them in capitals across Europe. Once, he'd been caught short by a 7-year-old girl in a velvet dress, patent leather shoes, white ruffled socks, and hair ribbons, lying on a gurney in a refrigerated prep room waiting to be placed in her casket. But watching five black hearses drive onto the cemetery grounds jolted Bolton harder than rolling Texas thunder.

He watched as attendants unloaded each vehicle. What would remain glued to Bolton's brain was the descending lengths of the coffins. "You could tell which child was in each casket just by its size," he said. Two years later, the memory would still bring him to the edge of tears.

THAT DAY, THE flags flew at half-staff at Johnson Space Center. Just as they did when U.S. astronauts died.

Rusty Yates was served with a gag order barring him from discussing his wife's case with the media under penalty of a $500 fine and/or up to six months in the Harris County Jail.

CHAPTER 7

Jailed

I am Satan," Andrea Yates answered when jail psychiatrist Melissa Ferguson asked if there were anything she wanted to share with her Harris County Mental Health and Mental Retardation Administration (MHMRA) treatment team on June 22. Yates looked pointedly at Ferguson. "You know what I mean."

Ferguson was certain that Yates had included her in what she clinically described as Yates's "illusion." Ferguson, a graduate of the University of Texas Medical School at Houston, had done her psychiatric residency at the University of Southern California. She kept asking questions.

"She didn't discuss, she made statements," Ferguson said. "To fulfill the prophecy, Satan must be destroyed," Yates said. "It is better to tie a millstone around your neck and drown in a river than to stumble." The children had to be killed because they could not be saved any other way, Yates told her. "Andrea Yates believed there were cameras in her home, put there by media, to watch her performance as a mother," Ferguson recalled. "Her statements about being a bad mother changed from years to months to weeks [old] without being anchored in time. She said cameras had been monitoring her for years."

Yates assured Ferguson she did not need medication: "The voices were as clear as you are hearing me right now." Ferguson started Yates on the antipsychotic drug Risperdal (changing to Haldol the following day) and prescribed more Ativan and Trazodone. The MHMRA team rapidly attempted to gather Yates's past medical records for guidance. She was also given a pregnancy test, routine for women prescribed psy-

chotropic medication known to affect fetuses. News of the test leaked
to Houston's KTRK television and Reuters news service, causing the
unfortunate rumor that Yates was once again pregnant. She was not.

Prisoner Yates hadn't been furnished yet with a "suicide blanket,"
the heavy dressing gown (similar in weight to lead X-ray aprons) worn
by prisoners who might harm themselves. On Sunday, June 24, at 3:30
in the afternoon, she stood naked at her cell door, chanting, "Eat, drink,
and be merry because we all shall die." The words were a paraphrase
from a parable about greed found in the Gospel of Luke, chapter 12.
"Eat, drink, be merry," a rich man exclaimed after a bountiful harvest.
"You fool," God replies, "this night your life will be demanded of you
and the things you have prepared, to whom will they belong? . . . Thus
it will be for the one who stores up treasure for himself but is not rich
in what matters to God."

To the nurses and technical assistants who monitored her behavior
every fifteen minutes, Yates said little more than yes, no, okay. She
steadfastly denied hallucinating or having thoughts of committing suicide, but no one believed her. At 5:15 PM she accepted a visit from her
mother. At 5:45 she spent fifteen minutes with her attorney, George
Parnham. She wore a hospital gown to the visitation cubicles for both
visits. Afterward, the gown and orange plastic jail shoes were stored in a
plastic bag and hung from the door handle of her cell.

On June 25 she appeared more depressed and revealed that she'd
heard "noises from hell."

"Mrs. Yates, do you know how sick you are?" Ferguson asked.

"I am not mentally ill," Yates said and began to weep.

A day later, Yates confessed to having auditory hallucinations: she
heard the voice of Satan over the intercom system in her cell. Several
days before she came to jail, as her children were watching cartoons, a
message was broadcast personally to her that she was a bad mother and
her children were eating too much sugar. Some time before that, when
she'd gone with her husband to see the film *O Brother, Where Art
Thou?*, a Satanic character in the film had told her directly that she had
eluded him long enough. Rusty Yates later remembered being perplexed by his wife's crying when the couple exited the film, a Coen
Brothers comedy based on the *Odyssey*. When he asked what was
wrong, Andrea had mumbled something about "life's choices" and

dried her tears. Ironically, the central character, played by actor George Clooney, broke up a demonic Klan rally, lost a golden treasure in a gargantuan flood, and was returned to his wife and family from prison only by the intercession of a state governor.

"Satan is in me and Satan will be destroyed," she told Ferguson.

How was she going to destroy Satan? Ferguson asked.

"I can't destroy Satan," Yates answered. "Governor Bush would have to destroy Satan." At the time, the former governor of Texas had been president of the United States for almost two years. She asked Ferguson for a razor to shave away some hair on the crown of her head to see whether the "mark of the beast" was still there.

> I had three sores on the top of my head that I constantly picked at until they were bloody (ask Rusty—he hated me doing that). I believed I had the mark of the beast on my head, and if they shaved my head, they would see it was there.[1]

Yates said she had stopped breast-feeding Mary because the Trazodone overdose (which emergency room doctors had pumped from her stomach two years earlier) was somehow still trapped in her breasts. But according to her mother and brother Brian, as she grew sick following the births of Luke and Mary, her body had stopped producing milk. The babies couldn't get enough to eat at the breast.

During the two months after her father's death she had fallen down on the job of teaching her children. Her homeschooling lesson plan stopped the day her father died, March 12. She was concerned that the children were "tainted and might be retarded." Her children were "not righteous," she said, because she was evil. "They had to die to be saved." Ferguson suspected her patient was having visual hallucinations in jail as well as hearing voices. Yates later confirmed that the visual hallucinations were of men on horseback, teddy bears, and ducks, all pouring out of the cinder-block cell walls.

By June 27, Yates admitted hearing a man's voice outside her head, continually saying bad things about her. She again mentioned the

---

1. *Letter of A. Yates to author, August 4, 2003.*

prophecy and Governor George W. Bush. She revealed having been bulimic in high school and afterward. She'd previously told no one but her friend Molly Maguire-Stephano that she used laxatives—purging—to lose weight. Her brother Pat hadn't seen his sister purge, but he "had suspicions" about her bulimic behavior. According to her brother Brian, after the trial one of Andrea's friends revealed that she had spoken of wanting to kill herself when she was seventeen. She'd binged and purged "a few times" in the six months after Mary's birth. She insisted she wasn't depressed: "I never cried."

As far as Ferguson could see, Andrea Yates had "zero understanding of psychosis."

P.S. How did you get to review my medical records? I thought they were confidential.[2]

ON JULY 2, the day before Andrea Yates's thirty-seventh birthday, MHMRA psychiatrist Debra Osterman returned from vacation and took over daily treatment of Yates from Ferguson, her supervisor. Osterman graduated from Rice University in 1976 and from the University of Houston Medical School in 1988. Yates had lapsed back into catatonia and didn't speak as freely as she had with Ferguson.

"The Ativan [prescribed June 21 for sleep] helped her be able to speak more freely in that initial interview [with Ferguson], and she had closed back down by the time I met her," Osterman explained later. Yates's recollection of any prophecy was sketchy. Recalling one from the Bible's twelfth chapter of Revelation might—or might not—have helped: "Then another sign appeared in heaven: and behold, a great red dragon having seven heads and ten horns, and on his heads were seven diadems [crowns]. And his tail swept away a third of the stars of heaven and threw them to the earth. And the dragon stood before the woman who was about to give birth, so that when she gave birth he might devour her child . . . and her child was caught up to God and to His throne. Then the woman fled into the wilderness where she had a

---

2. *Letter of A. Yates to author, November 1, 2002.*

place prepared by God, so that there she would be nourished for one thousand two hundred and sixty days."

Though Yates denied wanting to kill herself, in Osterman's opinion, she was at "extraordinarily high risk for attempting suicide." She continued having auditory hallucinations and "seeing the signs" in the cinder-block walls. "She really did not think that she was mentally ill at that time," Osterman said. Yates's condition remained unchanged on her birthday, Friday, July 3.

By the time Osterman met with Yates on July 6, Yates believed she would be punished "for being a bad mom, not for killing her children," according to Osterman. "On that particular day, she couldn't recall why they [the children] had to die." Osterman increased Yates's dosage of Haldol that day, attempting to get the auditory and visual hallucinations under better control.

July 9 was a striking day, Osterman said. Yates "denied suicidal ideation. But when I asked her if life is worth living; there was a long silence with a slight twitch of her jaw muscle, but she would not answer that question." Sometimes a lack of response was more telling than an answer, to Osterman's way of thinking. The next day brought continued "Satanic signs," but Yates could not explain how teddy bears or horses were Satanic. "Sometimes a psychotic person will not make any sense to people who aren't psychotic," Osterman said. "It's risky to put logic to psychotic thinking." Osterman described psychosis as the difference between waking and dreaming experiences. For psychotic people, the dream "*is* their reality." Sometimes you don't remember it after you wake up, or if you do, it often makes no sense.

Don't say it's a dream, say it's more like a nightmare.[3]

By July 11, Yates did not remember telling Ferguson that she expected the State of Texas to execute her. That day more medical history arrived from Dr. Starbranch. Yates began showing glimmers of improvement, but it took more than a month to bring her out of psychosis—an unusually long time. The first time Debbie Holmes vis-

---

3. A. *Yates message to author, conveyed through R. Yates, December 8, 2002.*

ited Andrea in jail after the murders she said, "Debbie, it came back. The Bible was right, it came back. It was seven times worse. No, it was a hundred times worse. I could not control it."

Yates's Haldol dosage stabilized at 15 milligrams a day; 2 milligrams a day is a typical maintenance dose for chronic psychiatric illnesses that are responsive to the medication. Now, whenever she saw "men and children and horses" coming out of the cinder-block walls, she told Osterman, "I just try not to look." July 23 was the last day she reported visual misperceptions or auditory hallucinations.

PSYCHIATRIST LUCY PURYEAR sat in an interview room at the Harris County Jail gazing across the table at Andrea Yates and wondering how she had let herself be talked into this. As an international expert specializing in the treatment of women with reproductive psychological disorders and a long-term associate of Baylor College of Medicine in Houston's Medical Center, she was an obvious candidate to evaluate Yates.

It was thirteen days after the murders when Puryear met with Yates for fifteen minutes and confirmed for herself that Yates was psychotic, suffering from a delusion regarding her children and herself. Puryear had four children of her own, one less than a year old, and had just opened her own psychiatric practice. After deliberating with her husband about the repercussions of a demanding trial on their family life, she agreed to evaluate Yates for the defense team. She scheduled a video interview on July 27, 2001. Forensic psychiatrist Phillip Resnick had made a fourteen-minute videotape of Yates two weeks earlier, on July 14. For five weeks, Yates had been taking 10–15 milligrams a day of the antipsychotic drug Haldol, as well as Effexor and Wellbutrin for depression, and Cogentin to counteract the side effects of Haldol.

On the day of the interview, Yates was still disheveled, Puryear noted. She hadn't been showering or wiping herself after bowel movements, according to jail notes. Rusty Yates had described his wife as someone who was modest about her body and dress, but during their hour-long conversation and subsequent taped interview, Yates seemed not to notice the sleeve of her orange jail shirt slipping off her shoulder, exposing her white bra strap. Her glasses, which she was not allowed to use in her cell because of suicide precautions, were held together at her right temple by a Band-Aid. Ordinarily, she wore contact lenses. Someone had plaited a strand of Yates's hair, which fell across her collar bone, easily mistaken for a video or audio wire.

After reintroducing herself on tape and making certain Yates was oriented to the time (3:30 PM) and place (Harris County Jail), Puryear asked her whether she'd ever had anxious thoughts about Noah when he was an infant. She was surprised by Yates's response.

"I was washing my hands in the sink and . . ." Tap, tap, tap, tap. Yates's foot knocked against the leg of the interview table. "There was a knife there, and a voice telling me to . . ."

"Telling you to what?" Puryear pressed, quickly.

"To hurt Noah."

"To hurt Noah?"

"Yeah."

"With the knife?"

"Yeah." She spoke in the tone of a child sick to her stomach. "I didn't pick anything up . . ." Yates recalled the knife in detail. It was a long, thin slicing knife with a wooden handle.[4]

"How were you able to stop?"

"Just try to blank it out of my head."

"Okay. Did that thought or voice come back when Noah was little—or was that the only time you had that?"

"It was going away as Noah was growing up."

"It was going away as Noah was growing up," Puryear repeated. "So you had that thought more than one time, but eventually it went away?"

"Yes."

"Okay. And was that a frightening thought?"

"Yes."

"Did you tell anybody about it?"

Ten seconds of silence passed. "No," Yates finally answered.

"No? Why didn't you tell anybody?"

"Because I thought if I stopped . . ." Rata-tat-tat-rata-tat-tat, went the sewing machine foot. "Stopped thinking about it . . ."

---

4. *Letter of A. Yates to author, June 13, 2003.*

"If you stopped thinking about it?"

"It would go away."

"And if you talked about it? What might happen?"

"It may happen," Yates answered haltingly.

"It may happen that you might hurt Noah?"

"Hmmm."

"Okay. So it was a frightening time for you."

"Hmm."

Yates's answer didn't surprise Puryear. It is common knowledge that women who suffer from psychosis after childbirth frequently have the paranoid delusion that talking about a specific fear will make it come true. Though the seminal textbook *Infanticide*, edited by Margaret G. Spinelli, MD, wouldn't be published until months after the Yates trial, the "waxing and waning" pattern of the disease was well established. Moments of frightening psychoses often alternate with moments of lucidity, allowing a psychiatric emergency to go unnoticed or untreated until it is too late. Hippocrates called it "a kind of madness" around 400 BC.[5] Puryear scribbled a note to herself. Yates had actually been at the beginning stage of her illness as far back as the birth of her first son, but the intrusive thoughts had not been constant or overwhelming.

"Did anything happen while you were pregnant with John or after he was born?" she asked.

"Unh-unh."

"Things went okay?"

"Hmm."

"You didn't have thoughts like that?"

"I don't remember, we were pretty busy then."

"Your mood was okay?"

"Yeah."

"Were you depressed or sad or—"

Yates's eyes darted. Tap-tap. Tap-tap. Tap. Tap. "I don't think so."

"So that was an okay time for you." If she'd had thoughts about harming her second child, Puryear noted, they were being blocked. "What were you busy with?"

---

5. *Margaret G. Spinelli, MD, ed.*, Infanticide: Psychosocial and Legal Perspectives on Mothers Who Kill (*Arlington, VA: American Psychiatric Press, 2003*).

"Selling the house and moving into the trailer," Yates recalled incorrectly as she squirmed in her chair. The Yateses had rented out, not sold, their house when they purchased the Jayco travel trailer.

"You moved into a trailer?"

"Yeah."

"Why did you sell the house and move into a trailer?"

"We just wanted to simplify things. Not have a bunch of junk around and have to maintain it." Tap. "So we got a . . ." Tap-tap-tap. "Travel trailer . . ." Tap. Tap. Tap. "And moved in there."

"How was that for you? Living in a trailer?"

"It was okay. We were there a couple of months . . . a couple of years . . ."

"A couple of years. And that's when you had two children?"

"Yes."

"Okay. How many bedrooms were there in the trailer?"

"Two."

"So you and Rusty had one and the kids—"

"Were in the other."

"Okay. And then after you had John, you had—"

"Paul."

"How old was John when you got pregnant with Paul?"

"He was . . . 17 months." John had been a year old when Yates became pregnant with Paul.

"Okay. Were you excited to have all these pregnancies, or was it stressful or were they planned?"

"They were planned."

"Okay. Were you trying to get pregnant or just letting it happen?"

"Just letting it happen."

"So you weren't trying to stop it?"

"Unh-unh."

"Okay. And you had Paul, and how was that pregnancy?"

Tap. Tap-tap-tap. "That went fine."

"That went fine?"

"Uh-huh."

"Any depression, or unusual thoughts or scary feelings?"

"Can't remember." She still sounded thick-tongued with nausea.

"When you had Noah and John and Paul, where did you all live?"

"We were still in the trailer."

"Was that here in Houston?"

"Yes."

"How old was Paul when you got pregnant with Luke?"

Ten seconds passed. Yates made one false start at answering the question, then stammered, "About . . . uh . . . 20 months or so . . . 17 months . . ." Again, Andrea's math was wrong.

"Something like that? So he was still little?"

"Yeah."

"Did you breast-feed all of your children?"

"Uh-huh."

"How long did you breast-feed?"

"Usually I breast-fed for a year, but I had to stop Luke at 4 months because of the medicine," Yates said, referring to her 1999 suicide attempt with the drug Trazodone. Her husband later explained, more clearly, that his wife's menstrual cycle was like clockwork. With each of her pregnancies she had conceived two months after discontinuing breast-feeding. She'd had one miscarriage between John and Paul and had become pregnant again in less than two months. After the suicide attempt and subsequent medication for psychosis, the couple had used birth control until Andrea was off dangerous medication.

"Did you breast-feed while you were pregnant?"

"Not very long." Not at all, if Rusty Yates's recollection of detail is correct. As it usually was.

"Once you found out you were pregnant, you would wean?"

"Uh-huh."

"So you were pregnant or breast-feeding for a long period of time."

"Uh-huh."

"You got pregnant with Luke, and were you still living in the trailer?"

"We moved into the bus."

"On the same property?"

"Uh-huh. A converted bus."

"Why did you move from the trailer to the bus?"

"Well . . ." Time passed. "It had a little more room." Tap. Tap-tap-tap. "And it had some appliances like a washing machine, instead of me going to the Laundromat, and extra refrigerator and some features—"

"Okay. So it was bigger and more comfortable?"

"Uh-huh."

"How many rooms did it have?"

"It had the front area, the restroom, and the back area."

"Okay. And where did you all sleep?"

Tap. "Rusty and I slept . . . they [the previous owners] had the bed that folded out."

"Uh-huh."

"And the boys went to sleep on the, we called it 'the hole,' because it was part of the luggage compartment. They had put some carpet around there and some little beds," Yates said, describing the forward baggage hold of the bus that had been made accessible through a trap door in the bus's interior floor.

"How did you get to that part of the bus?"

"You had to just jump in."

"From inside?"

"Yeah, there was a door that opened."

"So you had put some beds and some carpet down there?"

"The people that sold it to us did . . . their children slept there, too, previously."

"Would you leave the door open when the children were down there?"

"Yeah. We, uh, wanted to be careful no one fell in it. So we put in a vent for some air," Yates said, moistening her lips.

"To get some air down there?"

"Yeah."

"Okay. So when you were pregnant with Luke, that's where you were?"

"Yeah."

"And when Luke was born, that's when you started having some frightening thoughts and feelings again."

"Uh-huh."

"Do you remember what they were?"

Yates couldn't get an answer out. To Puryear's trained eye, it was here—at her question about Luke—that Yates began to lose coherence and veer back into psychosis. Long pauses and extra movements punctuated her extended answers.

Ten seconds. "Uhm . . ." Eight seconds. "Uhm . . ." Tap. Tap. Tap-

tap. Fourteen seconds. "Uh . . ." Tap. "It was the fact of hurting one, uh . . ." Tap-tap. Then suddenly racing toward the words, "Can't remember." Tap-tap-tap-tap-tap. "Whooooo . . . who . . . specifically who . . ."

"But you were having thoughts about hurting one of the children?"

"Yeah," she moaned.

"Not all of them?"

Seven seconds. Yates's jaw muscle pulsated involuntarily inside her right cheek. "No, we didn't . . . it was just . . . worried about raising them up right." Tap-tap-tap.

"So you were just worried about one of the children?"

"All of them."

"You were worried about all of them, but the thought was just that you were going to hurt one of them?"

Yates nodded.

"Did you think there was something causing you to have those thoughts or someone putting that thought in your head, or—"

Tap.

"Or making you think that way?"

"It seemed that way."

"Who would have been doing that?"

Yates's jaw muscle throbbed. "I guess . . . I thought it was Sss . . . it was Satan doing it."

"Satan was putting that thought in your head. What did you think? Was that a frightening thought?" Puryear asked.

"Yes," Yates answered.

"So that was very scary to have that thought. Did you want to hurt the children?"

"No." Yates answered immediately.

"You tried very hard not to?"

"Yeah."

"Was that thought all the time?"

"I started feeling it in the bus . . . got kinda crowded . . . a lot of stress . . . and, uh, I called one morning it was particularly bad . . ." Tap-tap-tap-tap-tap. "And I called Rusty to come home, and I think that's when I had that nervous breakdown. I was crying . . . and worried," she said.

"Okay. And you went to the hospital."

"No, not yet. I went to stay with my mom."

"Okay."

"And, uh . . ." She stopped, looking ashamed. "The next morning I took the overdose."

"You took an overdose of Trazodone? Your dad's medicine?"

"Uh-huh."

"Why did you want to kill yourself?"

"'Cause I didn't want to hurt the kids," Yates replied, as if it was obvious.

"You wanted to save your kids? You thought if you killed your-self, you'd be saving the children?" Puryear asked, adding some spin of her own.

Yates nodded.

"Besides Satan putting that thought in your head, were you getting any messages from anybody else or anyplace else?"

"Unh-unh."

"No?"

"Until later."

"So you took the overdose and went to the hospital. That was Methodist [Hospital]?"

"Ben Taub [Hospital]."

"And then they transferred you to Methodist?"

"Hmm."

"Did you get better?"

"No."

"They put you on medicine and it didn't seem to help? And you went home? Were you still having those thoughts about hurting the children?"

Fifteen seconds ticked. Yates's jaw muscles spasmed again. "At what point? When I came home from Methodist?"

"Right."

No answer. She appeared to be busy with an internal conversation. "I think I was still worried about that," she said finally.

"Did you tell anybody then, about those kinds of thoughts?"

"Still worried about that."

"Did you tell anybody about that?"

"Rusty. He was a good husband and wanted to help, you know. I told him I was overwhelmed." Again she avoided describing any thoughts of harming the children. "He tried to make things better. He bought a house. Because the bus had gotten to be . . . pretty . . ."

"Crowded," the two women said, overlapping.

"So I moved in the house."

"But you didn't tell anybody you were having these thoughts about hurting the children?"

Ten seconds passed. "Can't remember."

"You got home from Methodist, and then did you try and hurt yourself again?"

Yates nodded.

"What did you do?"

"I took a . . ." Tap. Bang, bang, bang. "Took a kitchen knife and went into the bathroom. Rusty was in the house. He saw me. He opened the bathroom door and . . . took the knife out of my hand."

"Were you planning on stabbing yourself or what were you planning on doing?"

"Probably . . ." She gestured to her neck with her fingers. Bang. Bang-bang-bang. "Probably cut my throat."

"Why did you want to kill yourself?"

"'Cause I didn't want to hurt the kids."

"So you were still having those thoughts, and thought you were going to act on them, and so you wanted to hurt yourself instead?"

"Uh-huh."

"Then you went to Memorial Spring Shadows [Glen Hospital], and did you get better there?"

"A little," Yates said, her tongue seeming to get thicker. "They tried a few medicines on me." One of them was Haldol. It affected motor skills, such as speech.

"So when you got out of the hospital, you were doing better than when you went in?"

"I thought so."

"Were you still having the thoughts about harming the children when you came home from Spring Shadows?"

"No."

"They had gone away?"

"Uh-huh."

"You did okay then for a while?"

"Uh-huh."

"How long after you got out of the hospital did you get pregnant with Mary?"

"Maybe March." Yates's memory was correct.

"How old was Luke?"

Sixteen seconds. "Maybe . . ." Tick-tock. "March . . . maybe two and a half months." Yates had gotten pregnant with Mary seven months after her release from Memorial Spring Shadows Glen Hospital, not two and a half months.

"And how old would Luke have been?"

"How old was Luke?"

"Uh-huh."

"Sorry. When I gave birth . . . ? "

"When you got pregnant with Mary, how old was Luke?"

"Luke was probably 20 months." She was off by seven months. Luke was only 13 months old when she became pregnant again in March 2000.

"So you got pregnant with Mary and you were feeling okay at that time? . . . And you weren't having thoughts of hurting the children?"

Yates nodded no.

"After Mary was born, how long before you started having those thoughts again?"

"She was probably 3 months old, and my dad had passed away."

"Right. You had said maybe when she was a month old, you started feeling depressed or started feeling not well?"

"I didn't think it was that early."

"Things really got bad when your father passed away?"

"Hmm."

"What kinds of thoughts were you having?"

"Thoughts. I was depressed after the first month . . . withdrawing from . . . from them." Yates's voice trailed off and then returned. "Started homeschooling them . . . Noah was in kindergarten . . . and John in preschool, I think."

"How was that going?"

"It was okay. We tried the second year . . . and it got more difficult . . ."

"What got more difficult?"

"Tasks. I had more to do. And . . . my thoughts weren't clear." Tap. Tap-tap-tap. "You know."

"And you were having thoughts about hurting the children again?"

For fifteen seconds, Yates didn't answer. "I think so."

"And those thoughts got stronger and stronger?"

She nodded.

"Did you tell anybody you were having those thoughts?"

Bang. Bang-bang. Thirty seconds more. Yates appeared to be terrified by the unspoken answer to Puryear's question. She was involved in some other conversation inside her head, Puryear observed. "Rusty was watching me closely, you know, to make sure . . . it was all right," she said.

"So you didn't tell him what you were thinking?"

"Not that specific thing," she answered, her voice trembling slightly.

"Do you remember there was a time when you filled the bathtub with water?"

A sound came through Yates's lips that meant yes.

"What were you thinking then?"

"Um . . . Um . . . I was a . . . having images . . . the images I was having . . ." Bang. Bang-bang-bang. "The images like, lose the house somehow, you know, having all those payments, you know, with utilities and stuff," she answered haltingly. "And, um, I was thinking we hadn't paid our bills, and we'd lose the house, so when we went for a walk we passed this water facility, and I thought they were shutting our water off. And I put water in the tub to wash dishes or whatever."

"Okay. Were you having thoughts about drowning the children at that time?"

"Not then, no," she answered shakily.

"When did the idea about drowning the children come?"

Thirty seconds passed. "Probably," she said struggling to hold back tears, "the day before, or—"

"The day before? Okay. And why was—what about drowning them? Why drown each of the children? Was there a particular reason that you thought of that?"

Puryear waited patiently as another thirty seconds passed, but Yates couldn't compose a sentence.

"Was the drowning for a special purpose or special reason?" she tried again.

"No."

"Other times you tried to kill yourself to stop it. Did something happen this time, that made it seem to make more sense that that's what you should do? Do you remember what you were thinking at the time?"

Yates sat in silence. "The reason I chose drowning?" she asked, finally.

"The reason you decided it was time to hurt the children?"

Half a minute passed, then her foot came to life. Tap-tap. "I can't remember."

Puryear concluded that Yates was unable to answer that question at all. Either her thoughts were blocked, or the "fog" of psychosis had rolled in. Puryear later described her state as the equivalent of the state of persons seen on street corners babbling. Haldol treated those symptoms.

"Do you remember feeling like you were a bad mother?"

Yates nodded.

"How were you a bad mother?"

Yates strained to hold back tears. "Because they weren't developing emotionally," she said, wiping a tear from under her glasses. She bit her lip, then nodded yes in answer to a question that no one present had posed. Seconds passed in silence.

"Were you worried about them?"

"Yeah."

"What were you worried about?"

"That they weren't, uh . . ." Tap. Tap-tap. "They weren't progressing," she said, hanging hard onto the last syllable to keep her voice in control. "Um, the right way in school, and teaching them manners and social manners and something kids . . ." Tears flowed now. "It's, um . . ." Outside the interview room, random laughter ricocheted through the jail corridors. Yates bit her lip to stop talking and disappeared within herself.

"Are you okay?"

She nodded. More laughter from the corridor. She pounded her foot against the metal table leg.

"Let me ask you a different question. You said you felt like you were a bad mother and you were worried about the children not progressing. Were you worried about their religious beliefs or up-bringing?"

"All those things."

"Were you worried they weren't growing up as God wanted them to?"

"Yeah."

"And that time when you were having the thoughts about hurting the children, did it feel again like Satan was putting messages or thoughts in your head?"

"Seemed like it."

"Did you feel like Satan was inside of you, is that what you told me?"

"I told you that?" Yates asked, looking scared to death.

"Do you remember saying that?"

There was no immediate answer. Tap-tap. "In reference to what?" Tap. Tap. Tap.

"Your having thoughts about hurting the children. You had thought that Satan was trying to put those thoughts into your head," Puryear reminded her.

"Uh-huh."

"At one point you said that you thought it was possible that Satan was inside of you. Do you remember that now?"

"Well, I thought he was just sending messages."

"What did you think would happen to the children when they were killed?"

"Their innocence . . . they'd go to heaven . . ."

"Were you worried about them not going to heaven?"

"Yeah." Now she sobbed.

"You were worried about them going to hell?" The cackle of a woman's laughter from the hallway pierced the interview room.

"I just thought, that they were so young," she cried. Tap. Tap-tap.

"Did you worry if they grew up, that they might not go to heaven?"

Yates couldn't or wouldn't answer. Then, at length, she said, "Yeah."

"What did you think would happen to you after you killed the children?"

"I'd be arrested," she answered without any pause.

"And then what would happen?"

"Go to jail," she replied, her voice trembling like a child's.

"Is that what you wanted?"

More than twenty seconds passed. "I broke the law and have to be punished for it."

"Uh-huh. Did you want to be punished? Did you feel like you needed to be punished for something?"

"For being a bad mother," she said, her tone rising insistently at the end of the sentence.

"Did you think that it was a way to get rid of Satan?" Puryear lobbed a big, fat slow ball right over the plate. If ever Andrea Yates had a chance to hit one out of the ballpark—prove herself a nut job—this was her opportunity. Instead, she tapped her foot fourteen times against the metal table leg and said nothing.

"What? . . . Wha—what?"

"Huh?"

"Wha—what?"

"It's okay," Puryear reassured her. "When you're quiet for a long period of time, what are you thinking about?"

"Trying to remember." Consistently, when Yates didn't answer after long periods, her response had to do with not remembering her thoughts.

"Are your thoughts confused or mixed up at all?" Puryear continued.

"Sometimes."

"Are you hearing voices now?"

"Just the noises."

"Just the noises outside. Do you ever still feel like somebody or something is putting messages or ideas in your head?"

"Right now?"

Puryear nodded.

"I think so."

"Who might be putting messages in your head?"

"Maybe Satan."

"Satan's still trying to do that?"

"He, uh . . . there was a radio and they were playing some music in my cell and I heard a voice."

"And what did it say?"

"I can't remember."

"Do you think it might have been Satan's voice?"

Yates nodded.

"Let me ask you just two more questions and then I'm going to stop for today, okay? If you can remember, what were you thinking this time about not killing yourself? The other two times, you had tried to kill yourself. Do you remember why you didn't think about that this time?"

Yates sat for twenty seconds before answering. "It did cross my mind."

"Do you remember why you decided not to?"

She shook her head no.

"Do you remember, you told me about a man you met in the hospital? He said something to you? Can you tell me what he said?"

"He said, 'They're coming for you, you're going to burn in hell.' "

"They're coming for you, you're going to burn in hell?" Puryear repeated.

"Uh-huh."

"What do you think he meant?"

More silence. Tap, tap, tap, tap. "They're coming for me to . . ." The noises coming from the jail hallway were spine-chilling enough to disturb the sane. "That's all I took it for, what he said . . . ," she eventually replied.

"Did you have feelings and thoughts that somebody was going to hurt you or come get you?"

"Come get me."

"Come get you? Who might that be?"

"Maybe the police?"

Puryear had been going for "Satan," but Yates had just changed tracks and times. Or maybe she was simply trying hard to please an authority figure with a right answer.

"So you weren't worried that someone was watching you or trying to get you?"

"No-o. It wasn't yet."

"Okay, was that after the children died or before?"

"What?"

"He said that to you *after* the children died or before?"

"Oh. Before. A few weeks before."

Puryear ended the interview. Andrea Yates went back to the voices in the hallway—real and unreal.

THE KIND OF free stuff one can find in one's mailbox simply by waking up in a good zip code in Houston, Texas, includes the ninety-four-page paperback book *National Sunday Law* by someone called A. Jan Marcussen. The book contains chapter titles like "The Mark of the Beast," "The Beast Described," and the "Beast Identified." Sort of a reverse Cliff's Notes to the last book of the Bible, Revelation. (Reverse because the book is many times longer than Revelation itself.)

Andrea Yates had been pondering the last book of the Bible. Specifically, Revelation 13:18: "Let him who has understanding calculate the number of the beast, for the number is that of a man and his number is six hundred and sixty six." Despite the fact that one early biblical manuscript translated the number as "616," "666" is the number that has come to represent the devil in certain circles.

National Sunday Law, for example, instructs that 666 is the sign—or code—for a specific man who is the devil. The logic for this interpretation is Byzantine, at best. One of the Pope's ceremonial mitres or headdresses perhaps carries the Latin inscription "Vicarius Filii Dei," which translates as "Vicar of the Son of God." If one capitalizes the Latin characters and gives a Roman numeral value to each letter and adds them together, this is the result:

V = 5

I = 1

C = 100

A = 0

R = 0

I = 1

U = 5 (assuming one agrees that U is interchangeable with V as a Roman numeral)

S = 0

F = 0
I = 1
L = 50
I = 1
I = 1

D = 500
E = 0
I = 1
Total = 666

Clearly, Revelation means to tell its readers that the Pope is the devil. Far simpler to skip the Roman numerals and go with 616, the telephone area code of Michael Woroniecki's hometown in Michigan. It makes as much sense.

CHAPTER 8

The Death of a Butterfly

Preacher Michael Woroniecki couldn't get Andrea Yates and her children out of his mind. He knew exactly what had happened. But he hadn't come forward. No one had asked him.

"For whatever it may be worth, I want to reiterate that Andrea's sole motive for her diabolical actions was *revenge*," he said. "It was deep and it was intense. She had told me on several occasions of her intense hatred for Rusty. She pleaded with me for an answer on how to live with him. She despised him. Matters concerning God had absolutely nothing to do with any of it. All the usage of Christian rhetoric, by her and the media, was nothing more than a smoke screen to cover her true motive.

"There is only one major variable. To what degree was Andrea drug-induced at the exact time of her actions? If she was severely *intoxicated* with those drugs (as I am convinced she was by Rusty whose motives in dispensing these drugs was *sinister*, contrary to what he outwardly conveyed). He wanted to silence her while at the same time using her as his slave to take care of the kids. In this case, there is no doubt that Satan took full advantage of her by filling her mind with diabolical delusions with twisted 'Christian' conclusions."[1]

"These are five people that don't live, that are not going to be able

---

1. *Letter of Michael Woroniecki to author, postmarked October 24, 2002, Florence, OR.*

to have an access to Jesus Christ, that I won't ever be able to share with. And the Scriptures do not take that lightly."[2]

THE LAST TIME any of the Woronieckis saw the Yates children alive was in Miami, Florida, in June 1998. "Noah was 4," Rachel Woroniecki recalled. That made John 3 years old and Paul 9 months. "They had caught a caterpillar. They kept it in a jar and put a little twig [inside]. And they actually watched the caterpillar spin the cocoon and become a butterfly. Andrea shared it with our children. . . . She was so vividly excited because she could; you know, Second Corinthians 5:17 talks about when you come to Jesus, you become a new creation. And this butterfly symbolized that new creation that I believe she had a desire to become at that time."

"It was a time of great hope for her," Woroniecki said.

And, one wanted to think, a time of great hope for the Woronieckis, who did not often find people as willing as Andrea Yates to give up worldly possessions and follow—literally—the life described in the Bible. "But also, it [the butterfly incident] also told me she is really desperate because she's latching onto this with such strength. . . . This seemingly insignificant thing said something about her life because she wanted to escape that life. She wanted to leave that life. It was not right. She was not—she was miserable. And she conveyed that to us.

"I'm remembering exactly a time when she said, 'Michael, what do you do, if your husband doesn't want to follow the Lord, you know, have a relationship, basically?'" Woroniecki said. "If Rusty could have just said 'I love you. Man, I'm sorry for blowing it with you, honey.' . . . If Rusty could have just said, 'Michael, I need help. I don't know what to do. I don't know how to love her like I should. I'm such a selfish and proud man. What do I do?'

"Instead he chose arrogance. 'We don't have a problem. Everything's okay. Everything's in control.' No. Things are out of control. And they're only getting worse. And you better wake up. Because this is not

---

2. *M. Woroniecki*, Dateline NBC, *March 2002*.

going in a good direction—especially when you rob a person's hope, you know?"

"She left [Florida] full of hope," Rachel interjected, recalling the Florida visit.

"That's right. And to see that disappear, I think that crushed her."

That was one way of looking at it. The other was that even Michael and Rachel saw "something breaking down in our relationship [over the bus]," Woroniecki said. "What we expected to happen did not happen, you know? That they would get serious."

If Rusty Yates couldn't trust a guy to sell him a vehicle, how could he ever trust him with his—and his family's—spiritual life? In addition to the leaks in the roof, there were safety code violations and improper electrical wiring that he thought could start a fire or be dangerous to the kids. He'd need to gut the bus to correct those problems. He was flat-out disillusioned. He stopped writing to Mike. Andrea seemed to remain neutral, continuing to write, "hinting around" about the bus problem, according to Woroniecki. She urged Rusty to renew his contact with his former religious mentor. But Rusty knew. Like a kid burned by touching a hot stove for the first time, he did not want to go back for seconds.

Woroniecki admitted the bus wasn't in tip-top shape, but it depended on whose standards you used to evaluate it. "By the high-end standard of America, it was low-end," he said. "But if you evaluated it in Mexico, you're rich—you've got a refrigerator and air-conditioning.

"Finally he [Rusty Yates] wrote," Woroniecki said. "He *was* bummed out about the bus. It irked me, because I knew he did not know how to drive that bus. And he didn't want to learn . . . and I *know* if you do not know how to drive that bus."

Andrea continued the friendship on her own, through letters and frequent phone calls. The last call was as recent as a month before the children died, according to Rachel Woroniecki.

IT IS EASIER to say what Michael Woroniecki is not than to say what he is. The term "itinerant preacher" legitimately describes Woroniecki, who obtained a master's degree in divinity in 1980 from Fuller Theological Seminary in Pasadena, California, but is not an ordained minister. He does not like to be called a preacher or a minister or to be associated with any organized religion, cult, following, or church.

My first letter to Woroniecki in January 2001, requesting to talk to him about his ideas on mental illness and its relation to evil, received this reply: "In response to your note I have absolutely no idea what you are asking, Suzanne." My second letter, better grounded in Woroniecki-speak, went like this: "Your witness of the living Jesus came to my attention through Andrea Yates. I would like to meet you and interview any of you who have the courage to speak with me. . . . As you know, your friend Andrea has murdered her children."

TO SAY THAT Woroniecki and his wife and children (ages 13 to 22) lived in a bus was true, but misleading. New conversions of the Woronieckis' used 40-foot luxury bus, manufactured by Prevost, sell for as much as $1 million. Rock stars and celebrities, such as plane-shy sportscaster John Madden, tour the country in similar buses. The Woronieckis were members of a network of recreational camps that anticipated their comings and goings, took reservations, gave member discounts, and featured conveniences such as campsite offices, telephone service, fax machines, Laundromats (although the bus was equipped with its own washer/dryer), full bathroom facilities, and the occasional swimming pool. His mailing address in Eugene, Oregon, was a service for dozens of well-heeled retirees who enjoy a toll-free number for picking up messages and the low vehicle registration fees Oregon residency offers. Many Americans, having spent their lives job-bound, aspire to retire to this lifestyle. Woodall's *Campground Directory* for North America is the size of the Manhattan phone book. For Woroniecki, a man who grew up the youngest son of a factory worker with a wife and six children in Grand Rapids, Michigan, it may well have been the realization of a dream.

With four licensed drivers in the family, the Woronieckis could drive as many as 1,200 miles in a day. At one time the family worked in a Florida marina for several months, bringing in eight paychecks. Money also came in the form of donations and Rachel's good credit rating. Cash advance credit card lines enabled them to purchase a used 1993 Volkswagen Eurovan from West Houston Volkswagen for $5,600 in cash in April 2001.

Born on February 4, 1954, Michael Peter Woroniecki was the youngest of six; five boys and a girl. Aside from his male-pattern baldness, the blond-haired, blue-eyed, mustachioed Woroniecki still looked the part of a former college fullback. Growing up, his family belonged to the Basilica of St. Adalbert, a Catholic church on the Polish West Side of Grand Rapids. Michael's father, Charles Woroniecki, was a member of the Usher's Club of St. Adalbert; his mother, Rose, was a religious woman with a big heart. She participated in St. Adalbert's Catholic charismatic prayer meetings beginning in the early 1970s. Following his retirement as a door handle "buffer" at the Doehler Jarvis tool and die company in 1965, Charles Sr. and his wife owned a maternity store called The Stork Shop.

After their parents' deaths, the oldest three Woroniecki brothers—Charles, John, and James—lost touch with Michael. Another brother, Gerald, once a graphic artist for a Chicago newspaper, lived in the family's small brick home at 919 Lake Michigan Drive in Grand Rapids until 2000, when he retired to a St. Cloud, Florida, trailer park.

At West Catholic High School, Jim Schaak coached the 130-pound freshman to the Grand Rapids City Wrestling Championship. But one thing troubled him about Woroniecki: "He always wore a wrist wrap in wrestling matches, so if he lost, he'd have a reason." Another of Woroniecki's teachers, Bob Misner, talked him into going out for football in his sophomore year. "He was shy. I saw sports was the way to motivate him academically," Misner said. At 18, Michael was, by his own description, "a Pollack from the West Side—a beer-drinking, fighting, football-playing tough guy." Football was his only passion and his "claim to fame." He was desperate to get out of Grand Rapids, "hoping there was more to life" than what he saw around him.

In 1972, Michael made a deal with God. If God would help him to a one-way college football scholarship out of his hometown, he'd go with his mom to charismatic prayer meetings (standing discreetly in the back, of course). That year, #22 made All-City Fullback. Central Michigan University offered him a full-ride scholarship.

Woroniecki hit college with gusto: football, weightlifting, drinking, drugging, partying, staying out all night. He neglected studying and grades and developed a reputation as both a hell-raiser and the fastest, strongest guy on the team. He was, according to one of his college coaches, popular with his teammates but "the *last* guy I'd ever expect to become a minister." Crowds rhythmically chanted his nickname, "War-War-War." He loved it. He played in ten of thirteen games in his sophomore season and was the team's sixth leading rusher. But there was a physical toll for the 5-foot-11-inch, 190-pounder. He separated one shoulder and then the other, broke his hand and his nose, and tore up his knee, losing his opportunity to become a starter in his junior year. His succession of injuries was so impressive that he says the local newspaper referred to him as the biblical "Job" of the team. When his girlfriend dumped him, he hit as deep a bottom as he thought existed.

In June 1974, Woroniecki and his family attended a monthlong conference of charismatic Catholics at the University of Notre Dame in South Bend, Indiana. Lost and without hope, he found himself reading about Jesus of Nazareth and wondering whether Jesus could have any relevance to him. He clearly remembered participating in an event in the football stadium and thinking about accepting Christ as his personal savior. At some point, he says, he knelt down and prayed: "Lord, I don't know what this expression 'born again' means, but if you have something for me, show me." He thought of himself as a simple man and his statement was as simple as he knew how to make it. He felt "filled with the spirit." When he looked up, the first image he remembered seeing was a well-known mural of Jesus on the side of Notre Dame's library building, visible from inside the stadium. Though it hadn't been the artist's intention, Jesus' arms were raised like a referee signaling a touchdown. Many referred to the mural as "Touchdown Jesus." *I just met Jesus*, he thought. *And he has a sense of humor.*

Outside the stadium Woroniecki ran into his sister, Mariane, and told her what had happened. "She looked at me with bewilderment and, in a sense, jealousy," he recalled, "because she knew there was something different about me and there was no way she could imitate it." He spent the month of July hitchhiking in the East and described his religious awakening to anyone who listened.

He returned to CMU in time for "hell week"—grueling August two-a-day football workouts—which he and his buddies chased with beer at a local bar. "I was the 'Crazy War,'" he said, "the leader of the pack. I did the most insane, bizarre things. Everybody looked to me for stimulation of insanity." In a way, he didn't disappoint them. In the bar after practice, Woroniecki told his teammates about his discovery of Jesus. His best friend on the team asked him whether he was on drugs.

His teammates' rejections took him by surprise. "That kind of rejection would send you plummeting into despair," he said. "Your best friends, your identity—you're *gone*." He thought of quarterback Roger Staubach, a Christian athlete whose career was then at its peak with the Dallas Cowboys. Why couldn't he be a success like Staubach? And how was he going to replace the physical rush of athletic fame? Ultimately, he decided "it wasn't about compromising so as to be accepted; it was about being who I was and being *rejected*. Jesus says, 'I have chosen you out of the world. That is why the world hates you' (Jn. 15:19)."

Woroniecki plastered a large black cross on the back of his football helmet. That year, 1974, he and his team made CMU history, winning the National Championship in the Middle Atlantic Conference for the first and only time. He didn't give a damn about the championship ring until years later, when his daughter Elizabeth found it while going through a box of mementos at her grandparents' home. Engraved on the ring was the year 1974, the year of his salvation.

FOLLOWING GRADUATION, MICHAEL attended Melodyland School of Theology in Anaheim, California. It was 1976, when the Children of God, an offshoot of the Jesus People, in their "prophet buses" flourished in Orange County. One book called them "doom-saying exclusivists."[3] The words fit Woroniecki as well. He described his year's study there as a phenomenal experience. He met men who seemed to him to be anti-Catholic, a challenge that made him defensive but inspired him to work toward constructive change in the religion of his birth. That goal, coupled with his mother's death, led him to interview for the Catholic priesthood.

He was invited to interviews at a Dominican seminary near Chicago, but was rejected in his final round. He remembered that when he returned home to Grand Rapids, he and his father cried together over the disappointment.

---

3. R. Enroth, E. Ericson, and C. Peters, *The Jesus People: Old-Time Religion in the Age of Aquarius* (*Grand Rapids, MI: Eerdmans,* [1972]).

Not dissuaded, he tried the Franciscans. After a semester of studies at Aquinas College in Grand Rapids preparing for the novitiate, he was rejected by the Franciscans, too. "They didn't want me, and it blew my mind. Why? I mean, I love the Lord. I can stand up there in the Catholic Church and bring these people, tell them . . . I scared them." The more he was rejected, the more disillusioned he became. And the more Christlike he felt. He spent "time praying and fasting for God's will."

He applied and was accepted to the protestant Fuller Theological Seminary, where he studied Latin, Greek, and Hebrew, among other things. But like Groucho Marx, Woroniecki was apparently reluctant to join any club that would have him for a member. Fuller's "scholars" were hypocrites of the highest order, he thought. One day he stood on a hill as his Fuller colleagues came out of chapel. He preached to them from St. Paul, "It is written: 'I will destroy the wisdom of the wise, and the cleverness of the clever I will set aside.' "

In the summer of 1979, Woroniecki interned at the Crusade for Christ in Trenton, Michigan, near Detroit. Throughout his quest, he'd continued his relationship with Leslie Jean Ochalek of Detroit, a former CMU cheerleader two years his junior, who also worked at the Crusade for Christ. Leslie, too, had been raised Catholic, but she hadn't been disappointed when the priesthood didn't work out for her boyfriend. She waited five years for Michael to gain the wisdom and experience in the Lord he felt was necessary to become a husband and father. On August 7, 1979, the couple married. Leslie changed her name to Rachel Woroniecki and cut off contact with her birth family.

That fall, the newlyweds returned to Pasadena so that Michael could complete his divinity degree at Fuller. He saw hypocrisy everywhere he looked. He returned to preaching on campus and was ostracized as he once had been at CMU. He grew to abhor Catholicism, Judaism, Islam, Protestant religions, Church of the Latter-Day Saints, Scientology, Buddhism, *any* kind of organized or disorganized religion. When he got his degree, he tried to get a ministry in Africa. He tried to go to India. He tried for jobs in campus ministry. No. No. And no. "Too zealous" was the complaint common to every rejection. If he'd had the time, he was certain he could scare the hierarchies of all 22,000 religious sects and denominations throughout the world.

The couple returned to Grand Rapids, the town Woroniecki had bargained with God to get out of eight years earlier, and settled into a two-story frame house with gingerbread trim at 824 Prince Street, S.E. Michael began a ministry of his own, called Cornerstone Christian Fellowship. Two years after their marriage, the first of their six children, Sarah Joy, was born. By then, Woroniecki had begun racking up arrests for disturbing the peace with zealous preaching on the streets of Grand Rapids, usually carrying banners that said things like "Stay Home and Read the Bible" and "You are Born a Worthless Sinner Headed for Hell."

He had attracted a hopeful assortment of Christians in their early twenties (many had attended the same Catholic charismatic prayer meetings Woroniecki had). According to one regular, they met at the Prince Street house for fellowship on Sundays and listened as the 26-year-old man they simply called "Mike" stood behind a podium and "talked about proclaiming the gospel."

Then things took a distressing turn. "Jobs began to be lost," one woman recalled. "Guys began to emulate Mike's character and didn't respect or honor the wishes of their employers. Mike accepted the money from the individual families who supported him, and at the same time seemed to scoff at their employment. I remember sitting in his living room and thinking: Everyone can't quit their jobs, Mike. If they did, who would support *your* family?" Lives were damaged, minds and marriages tested. More than twenty years later, some were still not repaired.

Besides proclaiming the gospel on Sunday, Woroniecki spent considerable time confronting people on the street corners of downtown Grand Rapids. He often used a bullhorn. Many considered his demonstrations intrusive. He was arrested several times for disturbing the peace and eventually faced a jury trial. He represented himself, winning a dismissal on the grounds that the law was vague regarding what decibel level distinguished "loud speaking" from "disturbing the peace."

BY THE TIME the teacher who had talked Mike into playing high school football encountered Mike on the downtown Grand Rapids mall, Woroniecki had begun shouting at passersby and towing a life-size crucifix over his shoulder. Bob Misner wondered whether he had helped to create a monster. "It wasn't confidence" he saw in his former student, "it was arrogance."

Eventually, Mike's aggressive preaching resulted in a criminal misdemeanor charge with the prospect of a second jury trial and possible jail time. In September 1981, he agreed to pay a fine of $150 and move to Atlanta as part of a plea agreement after thirteen people signed a complaint against him for disturbing their religious meeting. According to Woroniecki, "I went to him [the city attorney] and told him I would leave if he would drop the remaining ten charges against me. He agreed and kept my blow horn until I was gone for three months, then gave it to my dad."[4]

Devoted fellowship members staked Mike to ownership of a recreational vehicle and gave him some cash. He took off for Florida—via Atlanta—with his wife and child and a band of followers: three women (including his sister Mariane) and several men, including a husband who left behind his pregnant wife. Later, Woroniecki and his family were arrested in Morocco, the Vatican, and Tampa, Florida, to name a few places.

Mike could not understand why he was being persecuted—unless he'd been called to be a prophet like Jeremiah. A Presbyterian minister named Dave Van Dam had once suggested this possibility offhandedly to Mike at a Fellowship of Christian Athletes retreat.

Years later, when Misner heard Woroniecki's name in the national news in connection with the drowned Yates children, the words Mike shouted that day on the mall echoed in his mind. They haunted him still: "You cannot be saved until you are cleansed in the water."

IF MICHAEL WORONIECKI were to write a book about Andrea Yates, he "would title it something like *The Death of a Butterfly*."[5] "This little book, *Hope for the Flowers,* fell into my hands and meant so much to me when I came to Jesus," Woroniecki said of the book he'd recom-

---

4. *Letter of M. Woroniecki to author, postmarked Las Vegas, NV, May 8, 2003.*
5. *Letter of M. Woroniecki to author, October 24, 2002.*

mended to Rusty Yates so many years before, when they first met at Auburn. "It was the beginning . . . of my end," he said, referencing the last line of the 150-page book of words and drawings by Trina Paulus. "It hurt, but such pain began to open my eyes. I never even blinked over the thought of being a worm [Job 25:6]. No doubt. My question was whether I could, in reality, become a new creation, and such as that of a *butterfly*?"[6]

> Have you read *Hope for the Flowers*? It is such an inspirational story. It was one of Noah's favorites, and you know why—butterflies! He would get weepy at the part where Yellow and Stripe separate.[7]

For anyone who struggles to understand the role Woroniecki played in the Yateses' lives, *Hope for the Flowers* is a touchstone. The book was published in 1972 by the Paulist-Newman Press, a publishing company named for St. Paul and for the Catholic student centers around the country ministered by Paulist Priests.

> An early "born again" believes we may tend to divide things into "right" and "wrong"—or "good" and "bad." According to Paul—I'm looking for the scripture—something like "all things are lawful: but not all things edify."[8]

Rusty Yates had bought the book for Andrea when they began dating. Andrea, in turn, read the book to her children.

> I believe that Michael recognized that the book was a good symbolic story of the transformation of the "ugly bug" caterpillar "sinful" man into the "beautiful" butterfly/"saved" man: That by leaving the caterpillar pillar (John used to call it "catapillah-pillah!") or "rat race" and becoming a butterfly (Christian) there was "hope for the flowers" (the "harvest of righteousness" [Hebrews 12:11]).[9]

---

6. *Letter of M. Woroniecki to author, April 2002.*
7. *Letter of A. Yates to author, December 5, 2002.*
8. *Letter of A. Yates to author, postmarked January 6, 2003.*
9. *Ibid.*

Hope for the Flowers was beloved by Woroniecki's children, who sent the book as a birthday gift to me as I was covering the Yates murder trial in 2002. Correspondence from the Woronieckis was frequently decorated with butterfly stickers and drawings—and once, a one-of-a-kind self-portrait of Michael Woroniecki himself as a butterfly. Woroniecki signed another letter "Stripe," with the postscript, "When things get really difficult find a tree—then spin a cocoon."[10] Andrea Yates, too, liked to hand-decorate her correspondence with butterflies.

> Besides its awesome beauty and the miracle of its transformation, can you see why I love butterflies so much? [drawing of a butterfly][11]

For all of Woroniecki's rhetoric, his theology of salvation doesn't differ substantially from Roman Catholicism. Man, in the person of Adam, alienated God and was cut off. Redemption required a blood sacrifice. In the Old Testament, when a man sinned, he sacrificed a goat, a lamb, a bull—whichever satisfied the ritualistic requirement for atonement for the specific sin committed. Abraham's willingness to sacrifice his only son, Isaac, foreshadowed what was to come in the New Testament—the perfect sacrifice, Jesus Christ—son of God and son of man. Only the blood shed by Christ on the Cross was ransom enough to be acceptable to the Creator and human enough to represent man in the bargain. That sacrifice alone, according to both the Catholic church and Woroniecki, bought back all men for all time.

As Woroniecki explained it in a teaching tape called *True Salvation,* "Ezekiel says that every soul that sinneth shall die, that Satan has rights to every man, that you and I are born into this nature of Adam—the first man—and this sin is in our very *blood.* It is in our very bodies, it is in every cell, every hair—every molecule has been corrupted in rebellion to God." Essentially, he said, God told Satan, " 'Here, here's the blood you require.' Satan laughed and was ecstatic that he had killed man's only hope. Obviously, three days later Jesus Christ showed him what the blood, the Resurrection and the power was all about. . . . The one power that Satan has left is that every soul that sins will die. So he

---

10. *Letter of M. Woroniecki to author, August 29, 2002.*
11. *Letter of A. Yates to author, postmarked January 6, 2003.*

gets everybody ultimately, unless a man is bought back, and that's the whole idea of ransom. . . . Jesus bore our sins in his body on the Cross, on the tree, so that we might die to sin. He bore all that junk, all in his body, for all time."

Here is where the Woroniecki doctrinal muddle sets in. Whether to the casual observer or to those who had tried to follow Woroniecki for years, the streets of heaven seem empty. In spite of the ransom given for all men for all time, the numeric set of the "saved" seems to number only eight people: Woroniecki and his wife and children. If you count his mother—who was on the "maybe" list—nine. For those who were drawn to Michael Woroniecki for the sincerity of his beliefs and his walking the walk he talked, there seemed little, if any, hope to equal his personal success. For those who, like Andrea Yates, were both sincere and driven to please, following Woroniecki could lead to ruin.

On April 6, 2002, Bruce Nichols reported in the *Dallas Morning News* that "Mr. Woroniecki says he is devastated by the tragedy but rejects blame. He says he simply delivered God's message and that the Yateses—particularly Rusty Yates—misinterpreted it."

CHAPTER 9

The Full Extent

On August 9, 2001, the Harris County District Attorney's Office filed Notice of the State's Intent to Seek Death as a Penalty in the Andrea Yates case:

CAUSE NO. 880205 & 883590

THE STATE OF TEXAS	°	IN THE 230TH
VS.	°	DISTRICT COURT OF
ANDREA PIA YATES	°	HARRIS COUNTY, TEXAS

Comes now the State of Texas, by and through the undersigned Assistant District Attorney, and pursuant to Articles 34.04, 35.13, 35.15, 35.17, and 37.071 Texas Code Crim. Pro., and in accordance with Section 19.03 Texas Penal Code, in open Court hereby notices this Honorable Court and Defendant that the State will seek death as a penalty in the above styled and numbered cause.

Respectfully Submitted,

Joseph S. Owmby
Assistant District Attorney
Harris County, Texas

IF HARRIS COUNTY were a state, in 2001 it would be fourth in the number of people on death row, behind Oklahoma, Texas, and Virginia.

"But you have to temper that with this," District Attorney Chuck Rosenthal said: "Harris County is also the third largest jurisdiction in the United States in terms of population." Justice for the Yates children was what spurred him on, he said. "They allegedly were killed by the person in the world they loved most."

The Yates family did not appreciate Rosenthal's sympathy. By offering the citizens of Texas what he described as "the broadest range of punishment available" for Andrea Yates, Rosenthal narrowed the jury's choices to death or life in prison and gained the advantage of a "death-qualified" jury. By Texas law, only citizens willing to impose the death penalty can be seated on a jury in a death penalty case. "Seeking the death penalty was never used as a ploy to get a better jury," Williford said. "It was always used as an avenue to seek justice for those children . . . some crimes are so bad that they justify the death penalty." Williford had stalled three weeks before looking at the children's crime-scene and autopsy photos—interviewing witnesses, doing investigative work, reading *The New Predator: Women Who Kill*.[1] She would never understand how Andrea Yates had done this, nor forget Noah's clenched fists, bruised body, and the terror she imagined he felt fighting for his life in the bathwater alongside his already dead sister.

Parnham and Odom were baffled. They had believed that there was no way the state would ask the death penalty for a defendant with a well-documented mental illness. By seeking the death penalty, DA Rosenthal had an unlimited budget to prosecute the case. "As far as I know, there's not a per se limitation on the money that can be spent in a capital case," said Scott Durphee, General Counsel for the Harris County District Attorney's office. "It's a matter of prosecutorial discretion. . . . Ultimately, we don't have any constraints, within reason."

A conservative estimate of the taxpayers' tab on the Yates trial was three quarters of a million dollars. Operating a Harris County district courtroom for the four-week-long trial and hearings cost $11,000 a day, including the salaries of a district court judge, bailiff, clerk, court reporter, and district attorneys. The expenses and salaries of ADAs, investigators, and staff for the eight-month-long preparation for trial

---

1. *Deborah Schurman-Kauflin,* The New Predator: Women Who Kill: Profiles of Female Serial Killers *(New York: Algora Publishing, 2000).*

doubled—or perhaps tripled—that sum. Experts, audiovisual presentations, and excerpts of trial transcripts tacked on more than $200,000, according to invoices available under the Texas Public Information Act.

Andrea Yates had her husband's $80,000-a-year salary. According to Rusty Yates, he and Mrs. Kennedy had more or less split the fees paid to Parnham and Odom. Rusty paid $80,000, including about $35,000 donated by colleagues at NASA and from the Clear Lake community. Andrea's mother, a retired JCPenney employee, paid $50,000, including $10,000 from a relative.

On September 9, 2001, three days before the Yates sanity hearing was scheduled to begin, Karen de Olivares of Dallas wrote to the Honorable Mr. Charles A. Rosenthal Jr., District Attorney of Harris County.

Dear Sir:

I've been troubled since I read the article in the Monday, September 3, 2001 *Dallas Morning News.* The article, "With Yates case, new Harris DA gets a chance to define his style," by Bruce Nichols reported that you 'see a biblical basis for capital punishment.' I'm afraid I don't understand. Whether I agree or not, I could understand that you feel an obligation to uphold the law. What puzzles me is that you would seem to find support for the death penalty in Christianity.

I grew up in the Methodist Church believing that Christian values were ones that would help us to become better people; that Christianity taught forgiveness and how to persevere with love. These are some of the lessons I learned in Sunday School. I learned that Saul had a profound conversion on the road to Damascus; a conversion which fundamentally changed the way he thought and acted. I learned that New Testament was about teaching people kinder ways to behave.

I do not believe that learning to feel compassion and exercise understanding means that people should not be held accountable for actions which cause great harm to others, however, I also believe that we can hold people accountable and not allow them to perpetrate further harm without becoming like them.

Sincerely,

Karen de Olivares

Rosenthal responded to Olivares on Harris County District Attorney letterhead on September 20, 2001, two days before the competency verdict.

Dear Ms. Olivares:

Mr. Nichols, the author of the *Dallas Morning News* article was speculating about the Yates case defining my style. I never said that.

In terms of Biblical assurance I begin with the premise that the Bible teaches that Jesus is God. The first chapter of the book of John talks about the fact that Jesus has existed for eternity. So, when God made his covenant with Noah in Genesis 9:6 Jesus was there and a part of the Devine [*sic*] half of that agreement. The one thing that God cannot do is to contradict Himself. That is why Exodus 20:12 prohibits murder. You may further look to the words of Jesus in the Sermon on the Mount recorded in Matthew 5:17 and 5:20.

Now, if you turn to Paul's letter to the Romans beginning at chapter 13 you see God's inspired word to Christians about the role of government. The same Paul whose conversion was alluded to in your letter.

I do have an obligation to uphold the law. I have an obligation to the five victims whose lives were snuffed out by Andrea Yates. I have an obligation to try to keep others from taking the lives of children when they become burdensome or when some need in the murderer's life is not being met. Furthermore, it offends my religious beliefs to force my beliefs on others. This letter is calculated to only answer your questions. You certainly have the right to differ with my judgment in this case and differ with the Texas legislators about the propriety of the Death penalty.

Sincerely,

Charles A. Rosenthal, Jr.

Michael Woroniecki weighed in during February 2002. Andrea Yates, he said, "violated the 'Ancient boundary' of the code of righteousness written in the conscience." His sources were chapters 22 and 23 of Proverbs and the second chapter of Paul's letters to the Romans.

In regards to the death penalty, there is only one source of murder: Satan (John 8:44). Whether it be between a woman and her children or the government and the woman. Whether it be between nations or individual neighbors, murder is NEVER an option found in God's Word. God says "woe to those who call good evil" (Isaiah 5:20). In the Old Testament justice was rendered "an eye for an eye" and the death penalty implemented (Exodus 21:24 ff/Matthew 5:38–39). The teachings of Jesus are not directed towards the worldly governments but individual seekers of truth. Often times officials use various Scripture verses to justify such issues. Romans 13:1 ff does not speak of murder or any other crimes, but rather of basic order and the conduct expected of a servant of God.

God bless you Suzanne,

Michael[2]

What Romans 13 states is: "There is no authority except from God and those which exist are established by God. Therefore whoever resists authority has opposed the ordinance of God; and they who have opposed will receive condemnation upon themselves. . . . 'You shall not commit adultery, you shall not murder, you shall not steal, you shall not covet,' and if there is any other commandment, it is summed up in this saying, 'You shall love your neighbor as yourself.' Love does no wrong to a neighbor; therefore love is the fulfillment of *the* law."

---

2. Letter of M. Woroniecki to author, postmarked February 2002.

CHAPTER 10

Four Days to Sanity

Though there are now as many Starbucks, Gaps, and Pottery Barns in Texas as elsewhere in the country, the state is still very much part of the Bible Belt, as well as a fertile religious melting pot. It is not unusual to find almost as many new mosques as new churches and synagogues. Some young Islamic women work out in 24-Hour Fitness gyms wearing chadors. Football players, businessmen, and community leaders alike—not to mention the president of the United States, Texan George W. Bush—attend Bible study classes. Men fill stadiums to support one another in becoming "Promise Keepers" to their wives and children. A daily Bible verse appears on the editorial page of the *Houston Chronicle*. The Pledge of Allegiance can be said at public gatherings without incident. Heaven and hell are concrete places, not states of mind. And the name Satan often refers to an actual person, not a figurative evil.

Houston jurors got down to the interim business of deciding whether Andrea Yates was competent to stand trial for her life on September 18, 2001. The hearing had been delayed one week from its scheduled start on September 12; understandably, jurors had been too distracted by the World Trade Center and Pentagon attacks to concentrate. Apart from the sensational crime, the social dynamics of the trial were considerable. A white woman was being prosecuted for multiple murders by an African American male assistant district attorney, backed up by a white female assistant district attorney before an African American woman judge. In the pretrial hearing, eight of twelve jurors were minority women. Only one white male, an academic, sat on the panel. Yates's attorneys, both white males, bet on women of color being more sympathetic to Yates than men, an assumption they would later have reason to question.

The scene would have been unthinkable forty years earlier, when few women were attorneys and "whites only" signs were still posted at Texas drinking fountains, swimming pools, and Laundromats.

ANDREA PIA YATES was barely visible from the entrance to Judge Belinda Hill's packed Houston courtroom. But eventually her bright orange jumpsuit grabbed the eye as surely as her unthinkable crime had captured the national consciousness. She sat at the defense table, staring through large glasses at the nearest wall, her hands motionless in her lap. On this September day her long dark hair was washed and neatly combed, not unkempt as it was in her jailhouse photos. Before arriving, Wendell Odom had taken a look at his client's appearance, prepared to make the usual juror-friendly adjustments. Looking Yates over, what he thought was "Perfect." He wouldn't change a thing.

At the bench, attorneys conferred with Judge Hill. They talked and walked around Andrea Yates as if she were a fatality in an overworked emergency room.

After three months of antipsychotic medication and treatment in the jail's psychiatric unit, the state believed Yates was competent to stand trial for the murders of her children. State District Judge Belinda Hill, who was rated the most outstanding of twenty-one criminal district judges, according to the results of the Houston Bar Association's Judicial Evaluation Poll for 2001 (her 2002 rating dropped by 7 percentage points following the Yates trial), hammered the courtroom to order. The immediate business of this competency hearing, Attorney Joseph Owmby explained to the jury of eleven women and one man, was whether "Yates is rational today—not was she rational at the time of the crime." There would be time to decide that later.

In those months the name Andrea Yates had become a lightning rod for public opinion. Say she did go crazy: maybe she drowned one child—but five? That took conviction; it wasn't like someone who instantly regretted pulling a trigger. A 7-year-old like Noah was strong—how could she drown him? Did she drug him first? Didn't the husband notice his wife was psychotic? Where was her family? Her doctors? Child Protective Services? Where, some wanted to know, was God?

At the time, few understood the superhuman strength that could be generated by "rocket fuel." And few not intimately involved with the case knew of the two-year-long struggle with mental and physical illness and the multiple hospitalizations she and her family had endured. Her 2,000-plus pages of records from doctors, nurses, therapists, and social workers registered as no more than tabloid headline fodder for the feeding-frenzied press. No one knew what was *really* wrong with Andrea Yates, and by the end of the competency hearing—indeed, by the end of the trial—the case would still be a mystery.

FOR THE THIRD day in a row, Andrea Yates sat impossibly still and stared at the courtroom wall. Gerald Harris, a University of Houston psychologist and defense witness, recommended that Yates be treated further and reevaluated in ninety days. The legal concern, he said, was that "you're not going to defend yourself if you believe your death is getting rid of Satan."

"Delusional or not, she believes she committed a crime?" Owmby asked Harris.

"That's not the purpose of her wanting the death penalty," Harris shot back.

Parnham objected but was immediately overruled. Ownby's words hung in the air. This brief exchange might ultimately have been all that was needed to convict Andrea Yates of capital murder. The standard for insanity in Texas is whether defendants know their acts are *wrong* at the time of the crime.

THE MCNAUGHTON RULE—the "not knowing right from wrong test"—originated in 1843 with the case of Englishman Daniel McNaughton, who shot and killed the British prime minister's secretary and was acquitted "by reason of insanity." Though he spent the rest of his life in a mental institution, the case created a public outcry. Queen Victoria ordered the court to develop a stricter sanity test.

In the 1970s, some states, including Texas, broadened the rigid

McNaughton test and subscribed to a new rule for insanity developed by a panel of experts called the American Law Institute. The Model Penal Code (MPC) considers a defendant not responsible for criminal conduct when, as a result of mental disease or defect, he or she lacks "substantial capacity either to appreciate the criminality of his conduct or to conform his conduct to the requirements of the law."[1]

Following the successful insanity defense of John Hinckley after his attempted assassination of President Ronald Reagan in April 1981, the civic backlash was so strong that Congress passed the 1984 federal Comprehensive Crime Control Act, requiring the defendant in a federal case to prove that "at the time of the commission of the acts constituting the offense, the defendant, as a result of a severe mental disease or defect, was unable to appreciate the nature and quality of the wrongfulness of his acts."[2] More than half of all states, Texas among them, returned to the original British standard. In fact, the wording of the current statute is stricter than the one written in 1843. Insanity pleas are raised in less than 1 percent of all felony cases; acquittals for reasons of insanity occur in no more than 25 percent of those cases, according to veteran criminal defense lawyer Kathryn M. Kase who practices in both New York and Texas. The April 2002 edition of *Psychiatric Times* reported that 75 percent of those acquittals (or fewer than 0.18 percent of all felonies) are reached by agreement between opposing attorneys. In other words, the prosecution agrees that society is better served by giving the accused a long-term civil commitment to a secure treatment facility rather than a prison.

George Parnham thought the unusual confluence of religion, psychiatry, and the law in the Yates case could easily result in a "false positive" for the legal sanity test. Andrea Yates knew that killing was wrong, she knew she killed her children to save them, she knew she sacrificed herself to kill Satan. Parnham pointed out the single rub. "Show me one person in this courtroom who ever said, 'I am Satan and I deserve to be punished, and George W. Bush will see that it's done.' Show me one person," Parnham said. "There is only one. She's sitting there."

---

1. *MPC insanity standard is based on the District of Columbia Circuit Court's decision in federal appellate case* United States v. Brawner, *471 F.2d 969 (1972).*

2. *18 U.S.C. 17; see also Insanity Defense Reform Act of 1984, 18 U.S.C. 4241.*

• • •

IN THE JURY room, the initial vote was 8 to 4 for incompetence. But over the course of the eight-and-a-half-hour deliberation—unusually long for a Texas competency hearing—a stunning reversal took place. The jury panel unanimously voted Andrea Yates competent to stand trial. As the jurors—some visibly disturbed—left the courtroom, Yates patted her lawyer on the back. "What verdict were we hoping for?" she was overheard asking.

Within days of the sanity hearing, both Rusty Yates and Harris County District Attorney Chuck Rosenthal violated the spirit of Judge Hill's gag order by participating in a taped interview with Ed Bradley of CBS-TV's *60 Minutes* which aired on December 9, 2001. The judge was not pleased. Though Rusty feared he might be jailed for contempt, he couldn't be punished without the same treatment for Harris County's district attorney. George McCall Secrest Jr. was appointed special prosecutor to investigate. In April 2002, he concluded that Judge Hill's order had violated the trial participants' First Amendment rights. "The prohibition with respect to communication with the media was not specific enough," he wrote.

Although journalists were not strictly subject to Hill's order, they were bound not to listen to anyone who was. Officially, there was no penalty; unofficially, Hill saw to it that independent journalists who published interviews with sources who may have been covered by her unconstitutional gag order were not issued media credentials for the trial itself. Author Suzy Spencer, whose credentials were not reissued following publication of her book *Breaking Point,* challenged Judge Hill in Federal Court and lost.[3] Still, the suit was a public relations debacle. Spencer, and others like her (this author included), eventually covered the trial as members of the general public, paying the penalty of having to arrive at court an hour and a half early each morning, wade through security, and stand in line for one of the fifty laminated passes available to the general public each day.

---

3. *Suzy Spencer,* Breaking Point *(New York: St. Martin's Press, 2002).*

CHAPTER 11

Other Voices

Beachcomber Lane was not quiet. Curiosity-seekers drove by to see the house where Noah, John, Paul, Luke, and Mary were drowned. Rusty Yates was living in his six-room house alone. He had given away the four-bunk-bed system he built in the boys' room and many of their toys—except their favorites, which he had put away as mementos. "I kept some of them, you know, for later," he said.

> One of my precious memories is all four boys, Rusty, and I. Each [of us] had sandpaper to sand the wood quadruple bunk bed Rusty made . . . even little big boy Luke, . . . Rusty's been hurt so much these past 2 years. He has been so loyal and forgiving, I just feel so unworthy sometimes.[1]

For months Rusty slept on a new queen-size mattress set in the tiny room that would have been Mary's. He'd hauled the bed on which his dead children had been placed out to the curb for trash pickup. It was the mattress on which he'd played the game "Great Big Immovable Dada" with the boys. Rusty would lie limp on his back in the middle of the bed and challenge Noah, John, Paul, and Luke to pull him off. Together, he said, they were powerful enough to do it, but they worked

---

1. *Letters of A. Yates to author, June 15, 2003, and June 13, 2003.*

against one another, each pulling an arm or leg in a different direction. He suggested they work as a team. Over time, they did—and shoved him off. Andrea, too, romped with the boys, raising and lowering them on the "elevators" of her feet. The family, including Andrea, had been an after-work fixture on the block, playing basketball in their driveway with a medium-height hoop for the taller boys, a Fisher-Price hoop for the smaller ones.

THROUGHOUT THE PRETRIAL hearing (and later, the trial itself), Yates spent his days sitting on an oak bench outside the courtroom, usually from start to finish of each day's proceedings. Because he had been called as a witness, he was barred from the courtroom. Like most of the public, he knew nothing of what went on inside except what he heard in the hallways or read in newspapers or saw on television. On and off, over time, family members sat outside the courtroom with him long enough for each of them to finish reading *Women's Moods* by Deborah Sichel and Jeanne Watson Driscoll.[2] First Rusty read it. Then his mother. Then his aunts. And finally, his brother, Randy.

Yates was learning to live as a single adult again. The first time I interviewed him, I suggested we meet for dinner instead of at his house. "Anywhere you want to go," I said. "The sky's the limit."

He seemed uncertain of where to go to eat. Most of his dining had been at home with Andrea and the kids, "but I used to like to go to a place called Houston's," he said. He called back ten minutes later to say he had changed his mind. He had forgotten he was famous. What would it look like, him dining alone with a woman? I prevailed on him to try Morton's of Chicago, an upscale steakhouse conveniently located on the second floor.

Arriving at the restaurant, Yates parked his blue Chevy Suburban, the kind of SUV any parent of five might drive, in the lot adjacent to the Container Store. He had been there before, he explained, when he and Andrea had bought plastic containers to organize the

---

2. *Deborah Sichel, MD, and Jeanne Watson Driscoll, MS, RN, CS,* Women's Moods: What Every Woman Must Know About Hormones, the Brain, and Emotional Health *(New York: Quill, 2000).*

kids' toys. In fact, most of Houston's shopping strips reminded him of his former life. He had dined at Mr. Gatti's and Jason's Deli on kids-eat-free nights. Noah invariably wanted to show off the reading skills his mother taught him at Barnes & Noble's kids' place. He ordered iced tea and whistled in genuine disbelief at the price of a Morton's filet mignon ($33.95), but still ordered one, medium. Yates had been called self-centered, controlling, and abusive on late-night TV and talk shows, but once we were tucked away in a corner, no one looked his way. The party of six nearby didn't seem to notice him or his unsteady laugh.

When I asked him about the bitterness toward him, he said he didn't understand it. "How can people hate my family without even knowing them?" he asked, "How could I have done it better? Tell me, because I really want to know."

Yates was then seeing his wife only through a glass partition during twice-weekly fifteen-minute meetings in Harris County Jail and was allowed to talk to her once a week for twenty minutes by phone (at a cost of $3 per minute).

"She cries a lot," he said. "She doesn't understand how I can forgive her." The truth was, he could forgive her, but could he forget? "I told her that her brain was sick. I asked her, What if I had a heart attack while I was driving with the kids and had a wreck? What if I was the only one who survived? Would she blame me? She said no."

But he knew that many people did blame him: he hadn't intervened forcefully enough in his wife's treatment, hadn't insisted on outside day care, and, worst of all, had fathered a fifth child when Andrea was at risk for postpartum illness. But what others thought of him was their business. Short of being able to prescribe medicine to her himself, he didn't know how he could have done better.

Whether his wife was sane or insane, guilty or innocent, a sentence of a kind had already been dispensed for many people, including Rusty Yates. "If Andrea gets well and works through her guilt and can go on, we've got a chance," he said. "But I know I can't hold her hand for fifty years while she cries. I just don't have the strength to do it."

· · ·

CYNTHIA SCHROER SAT feeling the weight of her master's thesis in her hands.[3] Nearly eight years earlier, on June 6, 1994, Schroer had submitted the 296-page paper to Vermont College of Norwich University. Noah Yates had been 3 months and 10 days old. His mother had just begun thinking about killing him. Schroer flipped the pages to case study number thirty-one and poured over the familiar words there.

"The morning I went to the hospital, I had been up most of the night. This was the morning after looking for the light. I had dozed off lying on the sofa. As I stirred, I looked out the window. The sun was just breaking the horizon—golden. Simultaneously, my husband walked through the front door on my left (the sun on the right). I was filled with rage and growled like a 'bear' at my husband—my face contorted and I reached out with a claw-like hand and attacked his arm. He yelled in fright and pulled back. I held on. When he broke loose, he backed off into the kitchen and protected the girls. I took a hand mirror and continued growling and making awful faces as I watched myself. I put in a CD of Handel's 'Ode to St. Cecelia [sic]' and tried to calm myself. I thought 'Music to calm the beasts.'

"I told my husband to call 911 and get an ambulance to take me to the hospital. I had to tell him where we lived and what to say. Then I went and hid in the coat closet—feeling ashamed.

". . . Upon the arrival to the rescue unit, I felt the woman who spoke to me was an angel. I felt as soon as she radio-ed [sic] in a code 44 that this meant I was moving on to the next spiritual plane. 44 stood for completion. I became very peaceful—like all my troubles were over. I also thought 'How exquisite! How unexpectable!—to go out in a rescue unit.' Once inside the unit, I became terrorized by the thought that I was to be beaten and raped by all these 'helpers'—this was atonement for my sins.

"My daughter and I [had earlier] played a memory [card] game of hers under the Christmas tree. I made associations with each of the

---

3. Cynthia A. Schroer, "Treatment Responses to Postpartum Psychiatric Disorders: Using Subjective Experience as a Bridge Between Traditional and Alternative Treatment Perspectives," June 6, 1994, Vermont College of Norwich University, master's thesis.

pictures she selected—some for herself and others for me. All pictures had a message.

". . . They seemed to weave together an undercover operation that I was then responsible for the making known through the writing of a novel, which I did begin at that time. It would be a collaborative work with my cousin, who lives in New York and does write. I could use her contacts to get published—the writing turned on the theme of darkness and light being two sides of the same coin, and that both were needed to understand the other—and had equal value, rather than light being above the dark.

MY CARDS WHICH MY DAUGHTER GAVE ME:

dark boy, half Arabian, dark-skinned = 7-year-old neighbor
brightly colored bird = Muslim woman I know
mountains = where the body of this young boy would be found, or
    whatever was left of him
firehat = emergency
helicopter = a search was going on
pencil = I was to write
apple = I was to teach
purse = make money
boat = "other man's" boat
turtle = proceed slowly
chicken = the Muslim woman
astronaut = "other worldly," someone from the outside
umbrella = protection
car = to use as a getaway
drum = beat the drum, make it known.

MY DAUGHTER'S CARDS:

cat = wants a cat
star = she's the star of revealing this murder conspiracy
little girl = my daughter
flower = my daughter's genitals
paintbrush = that my daughter is an artist

"Along with this game, she [my daughter] would run to the tree and tinkle various glass bells. These bells had pictures on them. This action also had a secret message: I was to 'ring the bells'—draw attention to— 'declare' the 'truth.' One bell I associated with my sister and another with my brother, her twin. At this point, I believed my sister had been sexually abused and so had my brother, but I had less of a feel for my brother. During this game, my daughter said to call 911. She was at her play phone and wanted to pretend calling a 6-year-old neighbor. I was confused. Was I to call her friend? I was taking direction from my daughter, trying to interpret her 'secret language.' . . .

"I had called a friend to come over. I felt she was a long-lost twin sister. I also had thoughts of her being an angel in disguise. I also felt her therapist friend whose initials are J. C. was really Jesus Christ and that I was to be privileged to have Jesus Christ in our house. I had told my friend this. While she was over helping put lunch together, my daughter was watching the videos, *Dumbo* and *Bambi*. I felt they held hidden messages for me. There seemed to be a childhood memory of watching *Dumbo* and being called 'Dumbo' by my eldest brother with a strong feeling of ostracization. In *Bambi*, I identified with the bird that panicked, flew and was shot in the heart—that this was a warning not to panic and fly off, else I might be shot in the heart. I was extremely paranoid to walk in front of the large kitchen window for fear of being shot. I told my husband to be careful of the window."[4]

After pausing to reflect a moment, Schroer went to her computer and began composing an email.

I HAD FORTY-SIX first cousins; sometimes we didn't see each other for years. Cynthia Schroer is one of them. She had not read my reporting on the Yates case but had heard I'd written for *O, the Oprah Magazine*. On March 14, 2002, the day before Andrea Yates was found guilty, I read the email Cynthia sent me. Thirteen years earlier, following the birth of her second child, she'd become psychotic. Like Andrea Yates, she was treated with Haldol and Cogentin, recovered, and went on to have another child. Unlike Andrea Yates, she had not killed her children. She was one of the thirty-one anonymous case studies in her

---

4. *Ibid.*, pp. 202–207.

master's thesis. Until her email, I knew nothing of her illness or treatment. She has spent the last ten years integrating her experiences with Postpartum Adjustment Disorders and serving as a community organizer and educator for mothers and their families. She offered to come forward, to identify herself as a former sufferer of PPP and PPD, and to describe her psychotic experience.

"WHEN A WOMAN is in the delusion state of a postpartum psychosis she may believe that she or her infant must die," read a sentence from *Women's Moods.* "Perhaps God has chosen her to be Mary or some other figure who will remove Satan from the world. If the mother embroils her baby in the delusion and identifies him or her as the "devil," the infant is at great risk."[5] The book was published only a year before Andrea Yates drowned her children. Sichel had had one PPP patient whose psychosis was about Satan and the Virgin Mary. She was Mary, her baby was Jesus and somehow the child had to be sacrificed. The patient was an Orthodox Jew. Why would this be her delusion? Sichel wondered.

"Mrs. Yates, on the day of the drownings, believed that her children were going to hell, that Satan was going to get her, telling her to kill her children," Dr. Sichel said from Boston after carefully reviewing Andrea Yates's medical records. ". . . Her only option to save her children was killing them—they were still innocent enough that by drowning them she might get them into heaven—'god might take them up' . . . it's human nature to try to make sense of things, even Mrs. Yates herself was trying to make rational sense out of what she had done. You can't."

---

5. *Ibid., p. 75.*

CHAPTER 12

The Killer Rooms

On January 7, 2002, "at 11:55 AM, the Court welcomed sixty good men and women at which time the entire [jury] panel was admonished," Court Reporter Jennifer Slessinger typed into her steno machine.

Joe Owmby and Kaylynn Williford were seated at the prosecution table on the left side of the courtroom. Judge Hill presided from above. To the right, at the defense table, were Wendell Odom Jr., Andrea Yates, George Parnham, and Molly Odom. Andrea's hair was combed. She looked neat in a white, long-sleeved, turtleneck shirt and gray-green jumper. The judge's coordinator, Janet Warner, stood observing from the rear of the courtroom.

Judge Hill reminded the more than two hundred visitors to her Harris County courtroom of the house rules, as she did every day thereafter. She was especially firm about cell phones: she had a one-strike policy against them. Even the sound of a phone powering off was grounds for confiscation with no return. There was already a boxful in the hallway leading to her chambers. She ordered the first three rows of the courtroom cleared. The panel of prospective jurors began filing in.

"Single-file line," yelled Harold Bittner, the white-haired bailiff. A cell phone sounded a beep.

"It sounds like someone didn't hear me," said Judge Hill. Bittner confiscated the man's phone.

Jurors 1 through 60 moved briskly to their places. "Jurors 1, 2, 3, all the way over, please," Bittner ordered. "Jurors 42, 43, and 44? Over," he motioned.

"Number 50?" he asked, stopping one man.

"Number 60," the juror corrected, seemingly at his own peril.

"Good morning, ladies and gentlemen," Judge Hill said. No one could hear her. She made a minor adjustment to her bench mike and repeated the greeting with no better result. So it would remain throughout the trial. Hill preferred it that way.

Andrea Yates looked more responsive as she let her gaze fall toward the right-hand bench, where her husband was seated. Watching her swivel slightly in her chair was like seeing someone add a sudden spring to his walk. After concluding some matters of law with the judge, Parnham escorted Andrea out of court and into a back room. The court was dismissed for lunch.

When court reconvened at 1:05 PM, the panel was reseated in open court. "At this time the court explained voir dire procedures, basic allegations of the case, and general principles of the law," Slessinger typed. Specifically, Judge Hill asked whether any prospective jurors had formed an opinion or conclusion as to the guilt or innocence of Mrs. Yates. Eleven hands shot up.

"Juror 5? Ms. Jangda, you've already formed an opinion?" Hill inquired.

"Yes."

"Ms. Jangda, juror 5, has formed a conclusion of guilt or innocence," Judge Hill repeated for the record. "Mr. DeGollado?" Hill continued. Juror 6 had also raised his hand.

"Yes, Your Honor, I've formed an opinion *and* I'm against the death penalty."

"Juror 2, Mr. Kolar, you've formed an opinion?"

"Yes."

"Will that opinion influence your verdict in this case?"

"Yes."

Juror 26, Mr. Hammond, in the second row, had formed an opinion. So had 38, Mr. Chapa; 41, Mr. Neff; 42, Mr. Dittrich; 50, Mr. Pate; 53, Ms. Cook; and 55, Ms. Signorelli.

The definition of capital murder in Texas, Hill explained, is killing a person under 6 years of age, more than one person during the same episode, or a police officer. "Mrs. Yates is charged with two separate indictments of capital murder," she continued. "An indictment is no evidence of guilt. It is like a traffic ticket in that it initiates a criminal process. . . . Is there anyone here who believes that simply because she was indicted Mrs. Yates is guilty already?"

No hands went up.

"Proof beyond a 'reasonable doubt' is the standard of proof the prosecution must achieve," Hill continued. "The definition was given by the courts [in the mid-1990s]—and then taken away. Simply, *you* decide what 'reasonable doubt' means. The law tells us what 'reasonable doubt' is *not*. It is not beyond all doubt, beyond a shadow of a doubt, not inconsistency of evidence—like whether someone was wearing a green shirt or a red shirt. If it's not in the indictment, the State doesn't have to prove it. The burden of proof is the same in *all* criminal cases. Juror 9, Mr. Valadez? Do you understand?"

"Yes."

"Juror 17, Ms. Teoh?"

"Yes."

"As to Question 3," Hill proceeded, "can you hold the State to the burden of proof placed on the State? Mr. Greer?"

"We can handle that," Greer answered.

"Are you speaking for the whole row?" Judge Hill said, allowing a rare glimpse of her sharp sense of humor. She moved quickly on to Question 4—whether the jurors were able to presume Mrs. Yates to be innocent, in particular if she didn't testify. Could the jurors treat police and doctors the same as other witnesses?

"The Insanity Defense is an 'affirmative' defense," she said, "and is based on the preponderance of evidence—a lower standard of proof than reasonable doubt. The legal definition in the state of Texas is: the insanity defense is an affirmative defense to crime if, at the time of the conduct charged, the defendant, as a result of a severe mental disease or defect, did not know that her conduct was wrong.

"Has anyone already formed an opinion as to state of mind of Mrs. Yates?" Judge Hill asked.

Four hands shot up: two men, two women. Those jurors were noted.

"Texas trials have two parts," Judge Hill pressed on. "Part one determines guilt or innocence. Part two is the punishment phase. There are only two possibilities for punishment in a capital murder case in the State of Texas—life or death."

There were, however, two "special issues" to be considered after a guilty verdict in the punishment phase of the trial. First, was there a probability that the defendant would commit criminal acts of violence that would constitute a continuing threat to society? If the jurors answered the question yes, all twelve of them had to agree. If they answered no, only ten jurors had to agree. Hill emphasized that "probability" was the important word. It was not sufficient to believe that the defendant would "possibly" be a continuing threat to society.

It was proper to consider many factors in making this decision: the circumstances of the offense, the state of mind of the accused, the nature of the acts, forethought and deliberation, the existence of a prior criminal record, the severity of that record, the defendant's age and personal circumstances at the time of the crime, whether the defendant was acting under duress, the psychiatric evidence and character evidence.

The second special issue the jurors would have to decide in the event of a guilty verdict was whether—having taken into consideration all of the evidence, including circumstances of the offense, the defendant's character and background, and "personal moral culpability"—there were sufficient mitigating circumstances to warrant that a sentence of life imprisonment be imposed rather than the death sentence. On this issue the twelve jurors had to be unanimous, whether the answer was yes or no.

Judge Hill looked up. "Is there anyone who cannot impose the death penalty?" she asked. Seven of the sixty prospective jurors raised their hands. Hill took note. By Texas law, this was to be a "death-qualified" jury. Only jurors able to impose the death penalty could serve.

Jurors would be paid $6 a day, starting immediately. Hill estimated that jury selection would continue for four to five weeks, until a jury of twelve and two alternates was selected. When the selection process was complete there would be a week off before testimony began. Hill estimated the actual trial would take three to four weeks, commencing February 18 or 25, 2002, and concluding around March 18 or 25. She planned to sequester the jury during the deliberations, but had not determined whether they would be sequestered during the trial. Last, Hill asked whether any jurors had additional reasons for being excused.

"Juror 3, yes?"

"I'm self-employed," he said.

"Jurors are not excused for financial reasons," Hill answered. That was the law. Next. A prospective juror was nine months pregnant. Another was both pregnant and had cardiological problems. One was starting college the following Monday. Another had to be at Cape Canaveral January 15 through 18. And the wife of one prospective juror had just been scheduled for surgery. Ten of the sixty jurors were excused "for cause." Three additional jurors, pregnant women, were excused by agreement of both the prosecution and defense. In all, 240 jurors, four groups of sixty, were prescreened before moving to a smaller courtroom for individual voir dire.

ANDREA YATES SAT tucked against the wall between the counsel table and the empty jury box in the second of two eighth-floor "killer rooms." The white-walled 20-by-30-foot minicourtroom was so nicknamed because its primary use was for voir dire (pronounced "vore dyer" in the South), one-on-one questioning of individual jurors, in capital murder cases. The building itself, located at 301 San Jacinto, had been vacated once in favor of an impressive new criminal courts building. But when the new facility was flooded during Tropical Storm Allison in June 2001, employees had to return to work in the dilapidated old building. Wide-slatted venetian blinds hung on the killer room's five windows and were shut tight against the daylight. An uncovered air vent in the flocked ceiling knocked relentlessly.

Andrea Yates wore the same white turtleneck shirt and gray-green jumper she had worn on day one of jury selection. After two weeks of voir dire, she looked as if she now comprehended something of what was being said. Her right hand twitched backward and forward in a disjointed fashion over her chair's armrest. A moment later, though, she successfully passed paperwork between attorneys George Parnham and Molly Odom.

"Is there anything I haven't asked that you think I should ask?" Owmby inquired of the former special education teacher seated in the witness chair.

"No," the potential juror replied.

"What role do you think a treating physician's not doing something for a patient plays in a verdict?" Owmby asked.

The juror herself had suffered from postpartum depression. "There's definitely sympathy," she answered. "How far that sympathy would go, I don't know."

Williford leaned over in her chair and whispered to Owmby, "Strike the juror." Owmby agreed.

Judge Hill rested her head on her left pointer and middle fingers, then clasped her hands over her brow. From this position she might have been able to rest her eyes for an instant. A female guard seated at the exit flipped vacantly through her copy of *Self* magazine. Andrea Yates rubbed a spot between her eyes and jerked herself out of Parnham's way as he moved forward to question the next juror.

"What do you think about the possibility of you being on this case?" Owmby asked Juror 75.

"Me?"

"Right . . . what do you think about your potential service as a juror?"

"I would be proud to serve on this case," he said. "I'm an American and it's my duty . . . to do this for my community and for Harris County." He'd never served on a jury before. He'd had a best friend who suffered from "postpartum blues" and knew her family and friends were important in helping her get better. But he still thought a mentally ill person could know his or her conduct was wrong, like in the 1995 murder of the singer Selena.

"But do you feel there might be a situation where a person . . . didn't know what they were doing?" Owmby continued.

"Yes."

"When you say, 'Didn't know what they were doing' it sounds to me like that means the same to you as 'didn't know right from wrong at the time'?" Owmby asked, referring to Section 8.01 of the Texas Penal Code.

"Yes," Juror 75 answered.

Williford pointed to a note on a legal pad and mouthed the words "capital punishment" to her cocounsel.

"Do you think it's fair to consider the death penalty in a capital murder case?"

"Yes, I do."

"[I]f you convicted somebody . . . , do you think they should receive the death penalty or would you be open to consider more than one penalty?" Owmby asked.

"I would be open to consider more than one penalty."

"In a murder case could you consider a punishment of 5 years probation up to 99 years or life in the appropriate case?"

"Yes."

Owmby had ten minutes left to question Juror 75. He spent them determining the weight the prospective juror might place on mental illness. A betting man in favor of giving Yates the death penalty would not sit Juror 75 on this jury, but so far he'd said nothing that disqualified him. What the hell, Owmby took a parting shot.

". . . [Y]ou think you can be a fair juror to both the state and the defense?"

"Yes, I do."

"I'm through now," Owmby said. "Thank you."

Now it was Odom's turn.

The questioning proceeded swiftly, right up to Section 2.04 of the Penal Code, dealing with the definition of "affirmative" defenses, such as not guilty by reason of insanity. As Judge Hill had instructed the jury pool en masse, an affirmative defense required a lower standard of proof than "beyond a reasonable doubt." It required only that "the greater weight of the *believable* evidence" be in the defendant's favor.

Odom asked whether Juror 75 understood the difference.

He said he did.

"What is it about you that—is there a reason why you think you should be accepted in this jury, and secondly, why shouldn't you be accepted on this jury?" Odom asked.

"I can't answer that question. I don't know," Juror 75 said. Then he added that the pretrial publicity he'd heard would probably make things harder for the defense. Being harder on the defense was not what Section 2.04 required.

"I'm sorry," Judge Hill interrupted. "Require more than what?" Something was brewing.

A reporter sat on the church-pew-style bench with her legs contorted like a pretzel. Her foot jiggled with nervous energy as Odom and

Owmby exchanged legal dialogue over the juror's understanding of a "preponderance of the evidence." Aside from her tics and tremors, Yates sat still. Her eyes were closed. Her head nodded as if to a silent tune.

"We have a challenge for cause," Odom said finally.

After exercising his opportunity to ask Juror 75 a few more questions Owmby pronounced the juror "qualified."

Judge Hill wasn't so sure. "Do you understand," she asked Juror 75, that "Mr. Odom talked to you about a preponderance. The law says that the defendant . . . bears the burden of proving that to the jury by a *preponderance* of the evidence?" Preponderance meant the greater weight of the credible evidence. "That's sufficient. That's *it*. . . . Okay?"

"Okay."

"Mr. Odom's question to you centered around whether or not you would raise the burden and require the defense to convince you of an insanity defense at a burden higher than a preponderance. Are you following me?"

"Yes."

"Did you follow that when he asked you that?"

"No, I didn't."

Judge Hill exhaled. Juror 75, it seemed, was eager to please the prosecution, the defense, and the judge. "Mr. Odom, it's the court's observation that [Juror 75] did not understand the last series of questions, so I'll give you a couple of minutes."

What was clear to the five lawyers, five reporters, four court employees, three family members, and one judge was that Juror 75 wanted to be on the Yates jury very badly. *Every* juror seemed to want to be on this jury. The gallery stifled amused smiles as Wendell Odom dutifully tried to pry an acceptable answer from Juror 75. Even Judge Hill loosened her iron grip and allowed the laughter. Only Andrea Yates's face was unsmiling—the odd woman out who didn't get the joke.

Ultimately, Juror 75 was "rehabilitated." Judge Hill denied Odom's challenge, and Owmby accepted the juror.

Odom cast a nod toward Parnham. He nodded back. "We will use our peremptory, Your Honor," he said, hoping that in her judicial wisdom, Hill would hand him back a strike later in the process.

Juror 75 was excused.

The day was over. Four press pool reporters filed out of the tiny courtroom and prepared to give their report to the assembled media outside. The lawyers packed up their briefcases and exited; potential jurors sitting on benches in the corridor went home. Odom lagged behind, casting a glance back over his shoulder before leaving the room. Later, he would hate remembering this day. All he needed to do was seat one juror who thought like himself. One. A single person who would be convinced that Andrea Yates was insane and vote his or her conscience, no matter the wording of the Texas insanity statute. Jennifer Slessinger, two female court officers, Judge Hill, and a tardy reporter remained behind. And Andrea Yates, who might as well have been a piece of furniture.

Then she moved.

Her shoulder dropped—maybe an inch. The weight of her right hand seemed to pull the rest of her arm with exquisite slowness to the white Styrofoam cup at the base of the chair leg. She grasped the cup. Slowly she rose and moved two paces to the counsel table strewn with half-consumed cups of coffee. She gathered them up like fragments of her life, carried the cups to Jennifer Slessinger, still busy at her steno machine, and held them out.

"Ants," she whispered. Was a psychotic incident occurring? God knew what haunting vision turned a courtroom into hot-and-cold flowing ants. Marching ants. Leftover ants. Her tics, her motionlessness, her closed eyes all made sense.

Slessinger looked up. What did a court reporter do with a defendant who might be gracefully losing it?

"Were they crawling on you?" she asked.

Yates nodded.

"Judge Hill," Slessinger said, "there's still ants."

"I called maintenance," the bailiff said. "They were *supposed* to vacuum and exterminate."

Hill remained immersed in her paperwork.

"I have some ant spray at home," the bailiff volunteered.

Judge Hill looked up. "Bring it," she said.

CHAPTER 13

Trial by Error

On February 16, 2002, one letter to the editor of the *Houston Chronicle* asked for "a modicum of civility" for the former Enron chief, Kenneth Lay. "There has been enough conduct reminiscent of McCarthyism and the days of the House Un-American Activities Committee [in the 1950s] and too little constructive inquiry," the letter concluded, referring to a recent Senate investigation of the energy trading company and its key executives. In another letter, Lay was applauded as "a risk-taker with integrity." Shortly, Enron Field would become the Ballpark at Union Station and ultimately Minute Maid Park, as Enron's naming rights were resold to compensate betrayed Enron employees.

Andrea Yates was news that day, too. One reader wrote, "I think the Yates case in the long run will benefit many mentally ill people to get the help they need before they harm themselves or others." Another suggested, "Yates deserves all the compassion she showed her children."

As the Yates trial began in earnest on February 18, 2002, President George W. Bush's initiative against the "Axis of Evil" was in full swing. The Salt Lake City 2002 Winter Olympics were winding down, with the United States closing in on twenty medals. Princess Margaret, the younger sister of Britain's Queen Elizabeth II, died at age 71. Jack Henry Abbott died as well, an apparent suicide in his prison cell. Abbott was a convicted killer and bestselling author who had been paroled in 1981 with the aid of Pulitzer Prize–winning novelist Norman Mailer. Abbott killed a restaurant waiter just six weeks after his release and was returned to prison.

The "Bathtub Killings Trial," the *New York Times* dubbed the proceedings. There were so many news tents on Preston Street, the scene looked like a spring bazaar. Video cameras, boom mikes, and media personnel jammed the entrance to the courthouse, obscuring the famous "Goo-Goo Eyes Ordinance" of 1905 etched in the sidewalk: "Any male person in the City of Houston who shall stare at or make what is commonly called 'goo-goo eyes' at, or in any other manner look at or make remarks to or concerning or cough or whistle at or do any other act to attract the attention of any woman or female person in an attempt to flirt would be guilty of a misdemeanor." The now-extinct ordinance had been mostly a convenience for indiscriminately prosecuting black males.

IN SIZE AND design, the courtroom was not unlike the church from which the children had been buried. Spectators sat on pewlike benches. Members of the media had reserved seating, with local journalists assigned the best seats. The friends and families of the victims and the accused were, in this unusual case, the same people. All of them devoutly wished the State of Texas would go away; consequently, they were left to duke it out for seating among the general public.

A wooden rail separated the spectators, including journalists, from the attorneys, court reporter, court officers, and Andrea Yates, who again wore the same gray-green jumper over a white knit shirt she'd worn often during jury selection. In black robes, Judge Hill sat at the elevated judge's bench; U.S. and Texas flags stood on ceremonial flag poles to her left and right.

Cause numbers 880205 and 883590 were read aloud, charging Andrea Yates with drowning Mary Deborah Yates, Noah Jacob Yates, and John Samuel Yates with a "deadly weapon," namely water. She was not being prosecuted for drowning Paul and Luke. Because there is no statute of limitations on murder, if something went horribly wrong with the prosecution's case, the state could simply prosecute again on behalf of the two other children.

"Mrs. Yates, how do you plead?" Judge Hill asked.

"Not guilty," Andrea Yates answered.

A long list of witnesses, including Rusty Yates, his mother, and his mother-in-law, was sworn in en masse and sent out of the courtroom to wait until they were called to testify. Joseph Owmby began his opening remarks by slowly ticking off the names: "Luke . . . John . . . Paul . . . Mary . . . Noah," in no particular order. He described Andrea Yates's 911 call, the drownings of the children, and the activities of the police at the murder scene. "You will hear that her motive was altruistic. . . . [S]he thought it was right and good to do this to these children. . . . You will also hear evidence that she knew it was an illegal thing. That it was a sin, that it was wrong. . . . [Y]ou will hear about treatments that are effective. And what shoulda, woulda, coulda been done and whose fault this is. We don't have to prove whose fault this is. We don't have to defend the mental health system of the United States of America. . . . The medical examiners will testify to the bruises that were on these children from holding their heads under water. Andrea Yates is presumed to be sane. The evidence will show that beyond a reasonable doubt she is guilty of the murders of Noah, John, and Mary Yates." Owmby was simple and direct, if occasionally flat wrong.

George Parnham rose from his chair at the counsel table and approached the jury box. "The moment for which you were selected has arrived," he began. "How does a mother who has given birth, who has nurtured, who has protected, and who has loved the(se) five children . . . interrrupt their lives? How are nature's acts of birth, protection, and love inverted to cause what happened on June 20?" he asked. Andrea Yates's actions were, Parnham said, the "definition of insanity." Parnham carefully substituted synonyms for verbs and nouns he might ordinarily use. He wondered how a mother could "interrupt," rather than "end," her children's lives. What might have been killing or drowning mutated to "what happened" to the children. With these few words, Parnham initiated the circuity that plagued many of his arguments throughout the trial.

"You will hear evidence relative to mental diseases. . . . You will hear testimony concerning a disease known as postpartum psychosis," he continued. "The loss of reality testing, including delusions. Postpartum depression with psychotic features is the cruelest and most severe mental illness. It takes the very nature and essence of motherhood to nurture, protect, love, and changes the reality."

Parnham hit the highlights of Yates's struggle with mental illness, its severity, and her inability to get proper treatment. "All antipsychotic medications [are] eliminated from her body by June 7th or 8th, and on June 20," Parnham said, "the inevitable happens."

Experts will testify that "not only did she not know on June 20th what she was doing was wrong, she believed it was right," he concluded. "As she sits here today, she is taking a daily dose of 15 milligrams of Haldol to prevent her from slipping into psychosis."

The battle was joined. Yates sat and stared.

The first witness for the prosecution had charge of the 911 call log. She established that Dorene Stubblefield was the telecommunicator whose voice was heard opposite that of Andrea Yates on the two-and-a-half-minute 911 call of June 20, 2001. Stubblefield was the second witness. Over several days, Officers Knapp, King, Stumpo, Svahn, Bacon, Mehl, West, Jordon, and Smith and Medical Examiners Sanchez and Moore carefully laid the prosecution's groundwork for admission of crime-scene evidence into testimony.

On the morning of day two, Owmby attempted to introduce into evidence the clothing worn by each of the Yates children when they were killed.

"Your Honor," Parnham objected, "there is no probative value whatsoever to display the clothes of those children, her children, to this jury. . . . The sole issue, the ultimate issue in this case, is the mental state of this woman . . . we are *willing* to stipulate that Andrea Pia Yates drowned those kids."

"The clothing of these children shows the jury, better than any other exhibit we have, the size of these children," Owmby insisted.

Judge Hill sent the jurors out of the courtroom and asked the two lawyers about the proposed stipulation.

"We will stipulate that Andrea Pia Yates, on the 20th of June 2001 . . . drowned her children . . . we will also stipulate as to their names, dates of birth, and ages," Parnham said. "The prejudicial value of these exhibits [the children's clothing] outweighs any probative value."

"I did not hear Mr. Parnham offer a stipulation [that] it was Andrea Yates's conscious objective or desire to kill each of these children," Owmby fired back.

Owmby had heard Parnham correctly. The words "conscious objective or desire" contradicted his legal argument for insanity.

"They are not willing to stipulate. . . ." Judge Hill interrupted, "Do you have photographs that would do the same?"

"There are no photos of the children with rulers in the photo," Owmby said. "On screen they'll appear seven feet tall. In an 8-by-11 photograph they'll appear too small." The actual clothing, he argued, was the only reasonable alternative.

"We have two medical examiners that are going to take the witness stand," Parnham said. "Judge, I challenge the good faith on the part of the prosecution. . . . I think it is a subterfuge to get this [child's] jumper . . . in front of this jury."

Owmby, as he would do frequently, blew like a baseball manager protesting an intentional bean ball. He gesticulated and walked the width of the courtroom in an exaggerated roll (uncharacteristic of his gait *outside* the courtroom). "Your Honor, I have no reply. If Mr. Parnham is saying I'm lying—"

"Gentlemen." One word from Judge Hill restored quiet.

The jury returned. They didn't give a damn about the legal backbiting that might have taken place in their absence. They were more interested in the drama of the visitor whose cell phone rang and who was concurrently being expelled from the courtroom in shame by the indefatigable Harold Bittner.

Dora Yates, 63, the children's widowed paternal grandmother, was the first nonprofessional witness to testify. Eight months earlier to the day, she had said good night to her five grandchildren on a Tuesday, and when she returned to babysit Wednesday morning, they were all dead. If only she hadn't been worn out. If only she had slept an hour less, her grandchildren might still be alive. If only she had come *half* an hour earlier, she could have saved Noah and probably Mary—maybe even Luke. Who wanted to do that calculus?

Owmby had first met Dora Yates two days after the killings, when he and Kaylynn Williford and several police officers toured the crime scene. Dora's two sons had been there along with her sisters, Fairy and Kathy. Seven months later, Williford contacted Dora, but she declined to speak with the prosecution. This was true, Dora agreed under oath. Wasn't it also true that sitting at a backyard picnic table just hours after the murders, she'd had a tape-recorded conversation with investigator Boyd Smith of the Houston Police Department? Yes, it was.

"What is your relationship to the defendant?" Owmby asked.

Dora sat in the witness box not fifteen feet from Andrea Yates. One could imagine the space between the two women as solid matter. Dora opened her mouth to speak words; sobs came out instead.

In that instant, it crossed Owmby's mind that he had made a serious miscalculation in calling Dora as a prosecution witness. *Quick, pass the antidote.*

"Would you like some water—or something?" Owmby asked.

Dora accepted a tissue from Judge Hill and began again, filling each word with heart. "I would say that . . . Andrea is my very precious daughter-in-law," she finally managed.

Dora Yates's ordeal brought her sisters—and many spectators—to tears. A NASA grief counselor comforted Fairy and Kathy with pats on the back.

Owmby proceeded. He asked Dora to identify her grandchildren from their photos, a technicality he realized might have been timed better. She lived in Hermitage, Tennessee, and had visited her older son and his family during Christmas 2000. She came back again four months later, on April 19, with the intention of returning home on April 25. After she arrived at the airport and saw how sick her daughter-in-law looked, she extended her stay indefinitely and contemplated moving to Houston. Rusty and Andrea had never told Dora about the two suicide attempts in 1999.

"She trembled," Dora explained, "her arms especially. She would sit and stare—for an hour, two hours. She would scratch her head until it was just bald in spots. She bit her lip. She wouldn't eat."

You didn't tell Sergeant Smith that, Owmby noted. "You told Sergeant Smith 'she needed help with the five children, as anyone probably would, but Andrea was also ill.' "

". . . I was probably in shock at that time," Dora said.

Owmby wasn't wasting any more time. ". . . because you know Andrea could . . . tell the difference between right and wrong?"

"I could not tell what she was thinking."

"What made you think she could *not* tell the difference between right and wrong?"

"I could not tell what she was thinking," Dora repeated.

"You couldn't?"

"Not in the state she was in, no. . . . Because she could not respond when you asked her a question—she was not like herself."

Now Owmby knew exactly where he was going. "It took her too long to answer and she was not like herself, and from *that* you concluded she didn't know right from wrong?"

"I don't think she knew how to cope. We never discussed right and wrong."

". . . Even after you decided that you no longer needed to come to the house at 9 AM?" Owmby demanded. "Did you still have the opinion that she didn't know right from wrong when you left her alone with the children from 9 AM to 10 AM?"

"I didn't think about right and wrong," Dora answered.

Owmby allowed his implications to linger a moment before the jury. "On June 19th, you saw her staring at a TV set how long?"

"It was a long time," Dora answered. "The children were watching cartoons, but I wondered why she was standing there. I thought she might be watching to see if the cartoons were all right for the kids to watch. She did not interact with the kids or laugh at the cartoons. . . . I came back on June 20 at a few minutes after ten . . . and the tragedy had happened. . . ."

"Your observations didn't cause you to want to call a doctor?" Owmby pressed.

Parnham objected.

"Let's just leave it that you didn't call the doctor," Owmby said. He asked whether she'd taken the opportunity to talk to forensics expert Park Dietz. She hadn't.

"Do you know who Dr. Dietz is?" Parnham asked on cross.

"I know him some, yes," Dora said.

"He's an expert witness hired by the prosecution to convict this woman and put her to death."

"Objection!" Owmby fumed.

"Sustained," Judge Hill said. Parnham had made his point. "Mrs. Yates, you may step down."

Aside from the division of Men and Women, everyone except officers of the court and defendants stand in the same lines to use the restrooms. It is always odd, this routine of waiting with mothers, sisters, aunts, and friends of an alleged murderer, people so close to the center

of an event so extraordinary. The urge to ask just one question sometimes outweighs allowing that person her privacy and dignity.

"How do you begin to forgive her?" a reporter asked Dora Yates, a
former flight attendant and retired high school English teacher.

"It's not a matter of forgiveness," she said. "Andrea is very, very
sick." Dora could as easily have hated her daughter-in-law, called her a
murderer, and gone home to Tennessee to try to forget.

Much of Wednesday, February 20, was devoted to wrangling over
which of the thirty-seven crime-scene photographs and sections of
video the jurors would be allowed to view. On Thursday morning, they
saw twenty-six of the photos, including the gruesome tableau of the
dead children on their mother's bed, and a seventeen-minute video
projected onto a seven-foot-tall screen. The audiovisual aids stirred Andrea Yates to sobs difficult to produce on such a high dose of Haldol.

The public prosecution of Rusty Yates continued as well. "If the
State of Texas allows Russell Yates to go unpunished for his part in the
drowning deaths of his children, it will be a shame," Jody King of
Cleveland wrote in a letter to the editor of the *Houston Chronicle* published that day. "Knowing that his wife was mentally ill for two years
prior to the drowning deaths, Yates should not have allowed Andrea to
become pregnant nor be left at home alone with them without supervision from a third responsible party." On Friday, February 22, Owmby
and Williford questioned assistant medical examiner Harminder
Narula, MD, resting their case in chief before lunch.

Parnham and Odom called as their first witness psychiatrist Melissa
Ferguson, the medical director of psychiatric services at the Harris
County Jail, who had seen Yates at least twenty-five times. Ferguson
began describing the wild ride of Yates's treatment in jail. Court recessed at 5:07 PM for the weekend.

When Ferguson resumed her testimony on Monday, February 25,
she described for the first time how Andrea Yates had been urged by
audio hallucinations to kill her five children with a knife, the weapon of
choice for biblical sacrifices. Yates resisted. Using a knife was "too
bloody." She also ruled out drugs. "I deserve to be punished. I am
guilty," she told Ferguson.

February 26 would have been Noah's eighth birthday. George
Ringholz, MD, a neurologist who also held a doctorate in psychology,

testified that Andrea Yates was schizophrenic and did not know her actions were wrong as a result of this disorder. She fit the definition of legal insanity—even in Texas, he said. When Ringholz had administered the Thematic Apperception Test, which asks a patient to tell stories about various scenes depicted on cards, Yates described sadness, depression, discord. The last card was blank. For this one, Yates described seeing a butterfly hatched by her son Noah.

Later in the day, Dr. Eileen Starbranch testified that during Yates's nearly three weeks of hospitalization at Memorial Spring Shadows Glen Hospital in 1999, Rusty Yates visited his wife daily. "He was very attentive, begging her to eat . . . drink," Starbranch said. "We gave him special permission to visit outside of regular visiting hours, because I felt his presence was going to be positive . . . because she was so shut down."

Asked whether she had ever told the Yateses it was okay to have more children because a recurrence could be treated with Haldol, Starbranch answered, "No. I never plan for psychosis."

Along the way, Owmby suggested to her that a lot of psychiatric medications had been discovered by accident. That, in fact, lithium (used in treatment of bipolar disorder) had been discovered in West Texas water.

"Lithium was actually identified as a therapeutic agent in Australia in 1949 or 1950," Starbranch corrected. Wherever Owmby had been going, he didn't get there. "I'm not guessing when I prescribe medication," Starbranch chastised Owmby. "If I'm guessing, I should prescribe nothing."

Rusty Yates had called Starbranch's office on March 28, 2001. His wife was sick again. "I remember specifically stating that I wanted Rusty to bring Andrea in that day, that I wanted to see her," Starbranch said. Rusty had a presentation at NASA and couldn't come that day, but scheduled an appointment for April 2. Two days before the scheduled appointment, with pressure from all sides to get immediate care, Andrea Yates reluctantly admitted herself to Devereux.

"To this day, have you ever been contacted by Dr. Mohammad Saeed?" Parnham asked on cross-examination.

"No," Starbranch replied. She had never spoken to Saeed on the phone, wouldn't know him if he were sitting in the courtroom, never received a message or correspondence from him. What was more, she was unaware of ever talking to anyone from Devereux.

She concluded that Andrea Yates "would probably rank up with . . . the five sickest patients I have ever seen with regard to . . . how difficult it was to get her out of her psychosis."

THAT TUESDAY, FEBRUARY 26, I flew to New Orleans to meet Michael Woroniecki and his family in person, for the first time, at the Audubon Zoo. Finding Woroniecki and convincing him to talk had been a months-long endeavor that included correspondence; travel to his hometown of Grand Rapids, Kalamazoo, Central Michigan University, assorted Texas recreational vehicle camps; and tracing a trail of parking tickets handed out to the Woronieckis at college campuses across the country.

Along with my coproducer, Joe Delmonico, and a *Dateline* crew, I watched the Woronieckis play touch football, eat po' boy sandwiches, preach on Bourbon Street, and record a more than two-hour-long interview on camera with reporter Keith Morrison. The content of that interview remained secret until it aired exclusively on *Dateline NBC* on March 20, 2002—five days after the trial ended. Woroniecki, however, gave me a statement responding to reports that he contributed to Andrea Yates's mental deterioration and describing his relationship to the Yateses. He asked that I release the statement to a Texas newspaper. An abridged text of the statement was first published at DallasNews.com, the website of the *Dallas Morning News* on February 28, 2002. Later, before making their final arguments, prosecutors Owmby and Williford approached me, asking for the full text of the Woroniecki statement. Because the document had been released as a statement to the press, I did not provide it.

I was back in the Houston courtroom Wednesday morning.

THE DAYS HE testified, Wednesday and Thursday, February 27 and 28, were the only times Rusty Yates had been seen in a suit and tie since the children's funeral. His perpetually wide-open blue eyes were on trial along with his wife. "Never trust a man who doesn't blink," June

Worrell, a crusty Texas antiques dealer, advised. She added that he should be strung up and hanged from the tree in her backyard. Hers was a popular sentiment. Since November 2001 two senior prosecutors in the District Attorney's office had been investigating whether Rusty Yates shared criminal responsibility with his wife on charges of child neglect or endangerment. In June 2002 the Harris County DA's office announced there was insufficient evidence to pursue any charges against him.

"You knew that Dr. Starbranch had put her on Haldol and you knew that Haldol worked. . . . You knew that Dr. Saeed didn't, and she declined. Why in the world would you take your wife back to Devereux?" Parnham demanded.

"At that time, I just saw all psychiatrists [as] the same," Rusty Yates admitted. "They all have their diplomas on the wall. It was my mistake." It was one of the few admissions of error he made. "On May 4, when we met with Saeed, I pretty much insisted he put her back on Haldol and put her back in the hospital."

Rusty Yates's voice was hoarse and shaky on Thursday morning. It wasn't a good thing, getting through the night before a second day of testimony. "I remember talking to her about a dream she had . . . I guess on the night of the 16th—maybe two days before we went to see Dr. Saeed. She was screaming . . . she said something about in her dream she was trapped in her bed. [I woke her up.] She said thanks and went back to sleep."

"She would not undress in front of you?" Owmby asked.

"That's a pretty personal question, but generally that is true. She's shy." Rusty didn't mention it, but even her mother called Andrea a prude.

One thing Parnham and Odom were concerned about was the matter of Rusty Yates's fidelity. Yates had been a very married man, but he was also 38, and had been physically separated from the love of his life for eight months at the time of the trial. Rumors circulated in the courthouse. The public speculated. The Kennedy family speculated. And so did Owmby and Williford. "I would love to have asked him about that [adultery]," Owmby said. "But we never had any evidence." For the prosecution, evidence of adultery during the marriage would have given Owmby a motive for Andrea Yates's crime. Even a post-crime affair would have been useful.

For Parnham and Odom, playing the adultery card was not an option, even if there had been evidence. Insanity defenses that blamed the spouse or family of the mentally ill succeeded more often than those that blamed the medical profession. Discrediting Rusty might have been statistically advantageous, but would have created speculation that Andrea killed her children out of revenge against her husband.

According to Rusty Yates, he had never been unfaithful during his marriage.

And in the time since his wife's imprisonment?

"Let's just say I'm desperately . . . *desperately* . . . lonely."

In an interesting juxtaposition, Debbie Holmes testified almost immediately following Rusty Yates.

"Are you very fond of Rusty Yates?" Parnham asked her.

"It's [*sic*] her husband," she replied.

"If I had to be in a foxhole with only one other person, I'd want that person to be Debbie Holmes," Odom said privately.

By March 1, the Yates case was shaping up as a duel between two of the nation's most famous forensic psychiatrists: Dr. Park Dietz for the prosecution and Dr. Phillip Resnick for the defense. As a professor of psychiatry and the director of the division of Forensic Psychiatry at Case Western Reserve University School of Medicine in Cleveland, Resnick had been studying parents who kill their children for more than thirty years. Filicide, it is called, from the Greek word meaning son or daughter. Resnick had proposed a new term for the crime: "neonaticide." He taught courses on the subject to agents at FBI headquarters in Quantico, Virginia. He was also an expert in the faking of mental illness. He was a past president of the Academy of Psychiatry and the Law (1984 and 1985). He'd consulted for the U.S. Attorney on the Unabomber case, as well as for the government in its case against Tim McVeigh and Terry Nichols in the Oklahoma City bombing. He'd testified to the insanity of John DuPont, "the wealthiest individual ever charged with murder in the United States," disagreeing with Park Dietz's opinion in that case. He'd helped prosecute serial murderer Jeffrey Dahmer, siding with Dietz, his sometime colleague, in judging Dahmer sane. He'd been consulted by the defense in the Susan Smith case, but concluded that he could not "be helpful to the defense with regard to an insanity defense in that case of child killing." He was more than qualified to evaluate Andrea Yates for her defense attorneys—at $300 per hour, a markdown from his usual rate of $400.

At half past noon that Friday, March 1, 2002, Judge Hill broke for lunch. The gallery, officers of the court, and defendant reassembled in the courtroom at 1:30 PM. "All rise," Harold Bittner said, as Judge Hill resumed her place at the bench and hammered the courtroom to order. Parnham looked up from the counsel table to continue Resnick's testimony. But something was missing: the jury. In a rare lapse of command, Bittner had forgotten to seat the jury. It was a misstep so out of character for Bittner that Judge Hill allowed everyone, including herself, a chuckle.

Resnick testified that three and a half weeks after Andrea Yates's arrest, he visited her in jail.[1] She'd been on increasing doses of Haldol for most of that time. Certain aspects of the psychosis Dr. Ferguson charted had changed. On the day following her crime, Yates said Satan was within her, that she needed to be executed to fulfill the prophecy regarding Satan's death. By the time Resnick interviewed her in July, she still claimed that Satan was within her, but she had no memory of the prophecy or her references to Governor George Bush or the fires of hell. In fact, he said, she asked Resnick about the prophecy. By November, when Resnick interviewed Yates a second time, there were even more alterations in her memory. Between June 21 and July 2, she had believed she could rid the world of the one and only Satan and save her children from burning in the fires of hell for eternity if she were executed by Bush. By November, she remembered only that if her children were not raised righteously, they would get in trouble with the law and be a burden on society.

It was Resnick's opinion that Andrea Yates suffered from delusions and auditory hallucinations in 1999. He diagnosed her with a combination of schizophrenia and the mood disorder, clinical depression. Virtually every mental health professional familiar with Yates, including Resnick and Dietz, agreed that she suffered from a severe mental disease on June 20 when she killed her children.

---

1. *Dr. Phillip Resnick, July 14, 2001, 3:39 PM. Videotaped evidence, time and date stamped.*

Resnick had spent three hours and fifty minutes with Yates on July 14, 2001, and another three hours and ten minutes on November 3, 2001. He made a concise fourteen-minute videotape of Andrea Yates that reflected the substance of their first interview. The recording was particularly important, he thought, because over time a patient often forgets his or her thinking or puts a more rational spin on it as psychosis resolves.

"Your Honor," Parnham said, partway through Resnick's testimony, "at this time we would like to play the videotape of the interview that Dr. Resnick had with her on July 14, 2001, as Defense Exhibit 23." The prosecution, defense, and Yates watched small monitors at their tables. The jurors watched the large screen at the defense side of the courtroom, returning with Resnick to visit Andrea Yates only twenty-four days after drowning her children. Resnick's was the first video record made of Yates after the drownings, the earliest that existed, predating Puryear's.

"Mrs. Yates, thanks for your willingness to make this videotape," Resnick began, sitting kitty-corner from Yates at a brown Formica table in an interview room at the Harris County Jail.

No response.

"You and I have been talking for a couple of hours now, and I wanted to go over certain highlights of what happened to record this on videotape."

Again, no response.

Andrea Yates's bangs were so long, they fell beneath her lower eyelashes onto the cheekbones of her skeletal face. Her eye sockets were black, her posture concave. Her back was to the corner of intersecting cinder-block walls. Her appearance might have repelled even morbid curiosity seekers. When she did speak, her grammar was uncharacteristically poor.

"First of all, you're here in the Harris County Jail and you're charged with the killing of your five children," Resnick continued, undeterred by Yates's nonresponsiveness. His questioning was more succinct than that of other physicians who interviewed her. "That occurred on June 20th of this year. So this is now a little more than three weeks after the events, and what I wanted to focus on in this interview were the events leading up to the killings and what your thinking was."

Nothing.

"Would you tell me when you first had the thought of taking your children's lives?"

Yates puckered her full lips and tried to speak. "Probably . . . couple months ago," she said in the deeper registers of her voice.

"A couple months before you actually did kill them, right?"

"Hmm-hmm."

"You were hospitalized, I believe in March and May of this year—2001—and the drownings occurred on June 20, so you had these thoughts . . . do you recall any other thoughts before that second hospitalization this year?"

"Uh, with one of the children, Noah," she said, referring to the hallucination she'd revealed for the first time in 1999 to Dr. Thompson.

"You had thoughts earlier of taking just Noah's life, but it was in the weeks after your second hospitalization when your depression increased and you started thinking about this in a clearer way?"

"Hmm-hmm."

"First of all, would you just tell me the names of your five children and their ages?"

"Noah, 7. John, 5. Paul, 3. Luke, 2. And Mary . . . was-s-s six months."

"Tell me your feelings toward your children. Did you love your children, were you angry at your children, what were your feelings toward your children?"

"I didn't hate my children."

"You loved your children?"

After a pause, Yates answered, "Yes. Not in the right way, though."

"All right. But as a mother, you stayed at home, you homeschooled them. Overall would you say that you loved your children?"

"Yeah." This time no hesitation.

"Now, you told me earlier there came a time when you felt you were being a bad mother. Could you explain that?"

"Well, they weren't developing right and, you know, in an academic sense, you know, righteous sense."

"Let me just repeat that, make sure I'm getting it. They weren't developing in an academic sense and a righteous sense."

"Uh-huh."

"And you were homeschooling. And you also told me you were teaching them right from wrong and they were doing some things that you felt weren't righteous. What were some of the things they'd do which showed you they weren't right?"

"Well, they, uh . . . just did a lot of silly stuff and didn't obey." The Woronieckis had found Noah (4), John (2), and Paul (1) poorly behaved when they'd vacationed with them in 1998. The owners of the homeschool center and bookstore called them their "model children." As Andrea became less present in her children's lives, Debbie Holmes saw the kids' behavior change to "self-centered, disobedient, deceitful."

"They didn't obey you when you told them to do things," Resnick repeated. "All right, you mentioned their manners before, can you give me an example of their manners?"

"Just . . . when Rusty's mom would visit, they'd not treat her well. They'd call her names."

"Be disrespectful?" Resnick asked.

"Uh-huh."

"You concluded that they're 'not righteous.' And you're a religious person and explain to me what you meant by their not being righteous."

"Well, they didn't do things . . . they didn't do things God likes."

"Okay. They didn't do the 'things God likes.' "

"Uh-huh."

"All right. You mentioned an aphorism from the Bible about a millstone. Would you say what that is?"

"It's better to . . . tie a stone around your neck and throw yourself into the s-sea . . . than to cause . . . to cause a little one to stum-stumble."

"Let me make sure I'm getting that. 'Better to tie a millstone around your neck and throw yourself in the sea' rather than to do what?"

"Cause someone to stumble . . . stumble."

Yates had studied this section of the Bible carefully. "Stumbling" was a reference to the Gospel of Mark, chapter 9, "The Full Revelation of the Mystery." The chapter concerns the temptations to sin. Michael Woroniecki quoted from it often. "Whoever causes one of these little ones to stumble, it would be better for him if, with a heavy millstone hung around his neck, he had been cast into the sea." There was more.

"If your hand causes you to stumble, cut it off; it is better for you to enter life crippled, than, having your two hands, to go into hell, into the unquenchable fire." The same thing with one's foot; the same with one's eye. According to Mark, anything was better than being cast into hell. A couple hundred words earlier, Jesus had dealt with a boy "possessed with a spirit which makes him mute." The boy's father begs for help. Jesus orders the "unclean spirit" out of the boy. A few convulsions later, the unclean spirit leaves for good. Jesus' disciples, who had seen others fail at exorcising the spirit, ask Jesus why they had not succeeded. "This kind cannot come out by anything but prayer," Jesus explains. As they leave for Galilee, he tells his disciples not to talk about what he'd done.

" 'Cause someone to stumble.' Okay, and when you say 'stumble' you mean that, like on the path to righteousness?"

"Yes."

"And so you thought that your children, all five of your children, somehow because of what you saw as your defective mothering, were not on the path of righteousness."

"Hmm."

"And did you feel then that it was good for them or bad for them, if you in fact threw them into the sea—or in a bathtub—in a very real sense? What were you trying to accomplish then when you did take your children's lives?"

"Maybe in their innocent years . . . God would take them up."

"It would be their innocent years and God would take them up? Is that what you said?"

"Be with him. Uh-huh."

"God would take them up to be with him in heaven? Is that what you mean?"

"Uh-huh."

"All right. And if you had not taken their lives, what did you think would happen to them?"

"Guess they would have continued stumbling."

"And then where would they end up?"

"Hell," Yates said, her voice cracking.

"In hell?"

"Uh-huh."

"All right. So in that sense, by taking them to God, and in heaven, did you feel you were doing what was in their best interest or did you feel it was not in their interest?"

"Thought it was in their interest."

"Okay. Another thing we talked about was what would happen to you. What did you think would happen to you if you took your children's lives?"

"I'd be punished."

"You'd be punished?"

"Uh-huh."

"All right. And tell me how Satan fits into that."

Five seconds passed. "In the punishment?"

"Right. You'd mentioned earlier that Satan was within you. Do you recall that?"

"Uh-huh."

"And explain how that would work then. So if you were punished what would happen? How would you be punished?"

"By being . . . uh, executed?" It was a question.

"Okay. So if you took your children's lives, you felt you were doing what was right for them but you did know that it might result in your own execution. And was that a good thing or a bad thing for you to be executed?"

"Probably a good thing."

"Why would that be a good thing, your being executed?"

"'Cause . . . I'm not righteous."

"Because you're not righteous? All right. And another way of phrasing that, that you told some doctor earlier, was that Satan was within you. Do you recall believing that?"

"Uh-huh."

"So at the time you took your children's lives you believed that Satan was within you?"

No answer.

"Do you remember that or you don't remember that?"

"I remember."

"You do?"

"Uh-huh."

"One other thing that you mentioned to Dr. Ferguson, the jail treating psychiatrist, was that if the State of Texas executed you, they would kill Satan because Satan was within you."

"Hmm."

"Do you recall sharing that?"

"Uh-huh."

"Okay. Can you explain that any further?"

"No."

"Okay. But you do recall thinking that way when you first came in the jail?"

"Hmm."

"And when you took your children's lives."

She nodded.

"All right. Now, just a couple of other things I want to bring out. You believed that you were a bad mother, is that right?"

"Hmm-hmm."

"And you also mentioned there was some, like, surveillance camera in your home which was showing you to be a bad mother. How long was that going on?"

She shrugged her shoulders. "I don't know . . . how—how long."

"Was it months or years before the killings of your children?"

"It was months before."

"For months before. . . . And who was behind that? Who would have put cameras in your house to monitor your mothering?"

Yates scratched at the bald spot on the crown of her head. "Somebody who just wanted to watch over them, I guess. I don't know who."

"All right. Would that have been like an agency to protect children—"

"Could be—"

"—or would that be Satan? Who was behind it, do you think?"

"Could be an agency."

"An agency, you think?"

"Yeah. I asked about it, and no one's answered me," she said, pressing her lips together.

"All right. All right. So there's no doubt in your mind now that there was surveillance cameras in your home?"

"I thought there was."

"Okay. And right now your thinking is—this is some three and a half weeks after your children's deaths—and right now you've got some doubts about some things, you're not as sure as when you first came here to the jail?"

"Hmm-hmm."

"All right. But the things we've talked about, you have—did you have any doubt about them at the time you were taking the children's lives?"

She leaned forward in her chair and started to speak, then paused. "Any doubt about what I did?"

"Yeah. That it was the right thing for the kids?"

She thought for five seconds. Blink. Blink. "Yeah, I had . . . doubt."

"You had doubt. Okay. So even though you did it, part of you was a little unsure?"

"Hmm-hmm."

"All right. Now the other thing you told me earlier was about [how] the TV talked specifically to you and your children sometimes, could you tell me a little bit about that?"

"Well . . . they'd ate some candy one morning and we had the TV on . . . cartoon . . . and—and just flashed a scene where the comic—the cartoon characters were talking to us . . . and they were saying, 'Hey, kids, stop eating so much candy.' It was just a flash and then back to the program."

"All right. So you concluded that the TV had this special message for you and your family."

"Hmm."

"All right, and were there other messages on your TV which commented on your mothering ability? Did you ever hear voices telling you that you were a bad mother?"

"No."

"You didn't. Okay. All right. Did Satan ever talk to you? Did you ever hear Satan's voice?"

"Think . . . when I was in the hospital last year or the year before, I was sleeping and I heard kind of a deep, growling voice, said my name."

"Deep, growling voice. Do you think it might have been a dream or was it—"

"I was awake."

"You were awake, for sure. And you heard a growling voice call your name?"

"Hmm-hmm."

"And did you ever hear anything else from Satan? Instructions from Satan over the course of the last few years?"

She paused to think. "Just what I mentioned earlier about harming Noah."

"All right. You heard Satan instruct you to harm Noah?"

"Yes."

"All right. And when was that?"

"When he was a few months old."

"So . . . it was shortly after he was born that you heard Satan instruct you to harm him?"

"Hmm-hmm."

"At one point, did Satan say, 'Grab a knife'? Do you recall that?"

"No."

"Don't recall that?"

She shook her head.

"To kind of summarize, after Noah was born, Satan talked to you about harming Noah. Then after Luke was born, this was 1999, you were depressed and hospitalized, and you thought of taking your children's lives—then, is that correct—in '99, or not?"

"I didn't think of it then. . . . Oh . . . yeah, I did, uh-huh . . ."

"You did think of it then? Okay. And then, in the last couple of months before June 20, you thought about it and that was after you concluded that somehow you'd ruined them and they were not righteous."

"Hmm-hmm."

"All right, is there anything else you want to add, Mrs. Yates, to the tape?" They'd been talking for nearly four hours.

She thought for a few moments. "I don't think so."

Andrea Yates's vacant gaze traveled from Resnick to the eye of the camera.[2]

BACK IN COURT, RESNICK rebutted the prosecution's assertion that Yates covered her children's dead bodies with the bedsheet to hide

---

2. *July 14, 2001, 3:54 PM. Videotaped evidence, time and date stamped.*

them. His opinion was that Andrea Yates covered the children out of respect, as she might have done when she was a nurse in a hospital. She called police to her house, told them she killed her children, and then led them to their bodies, he said. Those were not the actions of a woman who was hiding dead bodies under sheets.

Yates was, however, operating out of a psychotic delusion. Resnick attempted to explain how the psychotic mind worked. He gave an example of "rationality within irrationality." "A man thinks, 'My wife is poisoning me' and goes to the police. And the police say, 'You're crazy, go see a psychiatrist.' Eventually he kills his wife . . . within his delusional perception of the world." Yates's delusion was that she had to kill her children to save them.

According to Resnick, there are five classifications of parents who harm their children. This was not a case of spousal revenge: Andrea Yates believed Rusty Yates was a good husband. It was not a case of battered child syndrome: the Yates children weren't abused. It was certainly not an example of the children's being unwanted: Andrea Yates was a determined Supermom. Three of the five classifications did not apply, in Resnick's opinion. Yates, he said, did fit into the two remaining categories: "acutely psychotic" (no logical motive to do what she did— say, for insurance money) and "altruistic" (killing because she thought it was in the children's best interests). He classified the Yates children's killings as "altruistic."

"Mrs. Yates," he said, "had a choice to make: to allow her children to end up burning in hell for eternity or to take their lives on earth." By taking their earthly lives she achieved two good things: the children were happy through all eternity, and Satan was "eliminated for humankind. . . . She would give up her life on earth . . . *and her afterlife* for the purpose of eliminating Satan and protecting her children from the fate of eternal damnation."

In his opinion, even though she knew it was against the law, Yates did not know right from wrong and did what she thought was right through her psychotic eyes. Resnick's advocacy of her innocence was unreserved.

Judge Hill recessed the court until Monday, March 4, 2002, when psychiatrist Mohammad Saeed was scheduled to take the stand.

• • •

I HAD SPENT some of the early morning doing a stand-up, live from the Criminal Courts building, with CNN's Paula Zahn in New York. On Sunday, the *New York Times Magazine* had published an article I'd written about Rusty Yates. But what Zahn really wanted to know about was the mysterious minister, Michael Woroniecki, whom I'd been the first newsperson to locate and interview with my coproducer, Joe Delmonico, as a *Dateline NBC* exclusive. News junkies worldwide wanted to know what I knew about Rusty Yates and Woroniecki, but I wanted to know about a third man: Saeed. His grand jury testimony was sealed; Judge Hill's gag order protected him from the prying press. He was, potentially, indirectly responsible for the deaths of the Yates children.

First, Saeed's colleague, psychiatrist Ellen Allbritton, testified. Allbritton worked for the State 95 percent of the time and moonlighted at Devereux doing nighttime admissions and preliminary diagnoses. On March 31, she received a call from Nurse Martin, a nurse supervisor (no longer employed at Devereux). He had assessed a patient who needed inpatient care.

"When I walked in the room and saw her, I pretty much knew she needed to be in the hospital. . . . She looked very ill, mentally ill. She looked like—a shell." Allbritton immediately filed for emergency detention—"for safety of self and others," according to the detention form.

"Did she appear moot?" Parnham asked.

"Mute?" the doctor corrected.

An attorney wearing an orange sweater laughed. She was seated in the gallery next to another attorney, a silver-haired man in a gray suit. Both, in some combination, represented Saeed and Devereux (already involved in an unrelated wrongful death lawsuit) but refused to say so. The man scribbled furiously on a yellow legal pad, leaving wide left-hand margins.

Yes, Andrea Yates was "almost completely" mute. "I got very little information from her."

"That wasn't based on lack of trying, was it?" Parnham continued.

"No. . . . Typically, you start an interview with 'How are you doing? Why are you here? What's going on?' " When you get a blank stare,

Allbritton explained, you start asking yes or no questions. Andrea Yates could answer those, but only after a lengthy delay.

"So Mr. Yates was basically having to respond for her?"

"Yes."

"Did she give you any indication that she had the ability to have thought processes?"

"That was part of the problem with the evaluation," Allbritton answered. "I couldn't get enough information from her to decide . . . and that would lump her into the category of psychotic versus nonpsychotic . . . I can only tell you there are two different types of catatonic behavior. One is schizoaffective disorder and the other is schizophrenic disorder. She was nearly catatonic, but I didn't know which way." The definition of schizophrenia, Allbritton explained, is a difficulty with the brain processing thoughts. Associations routinely made in the brain "loosened" so that thoughts become delusions or hallucinations, unconnected to reality. For a schizophrenic, words one wants to say might simply vanish or become so jumbled he or she can't form a coherent idea to speak. For some, the unfamiliar collage of thoughts and words might seem to come from another person. [Schizophrenia does not, however, describe a split personality—the common misperception among lay people. Simply stated, it prevents a sufferer from being able to distinguish what is real from what is unreal.]

"And in this situation—you were unable, I take it—to evaluate her thought processes?"

"That's correct." Was Andrea Yates so depressed she didn't speak because of apathy, ambivalence, lack of energy, or lack of desire to tell anybody anything? Or, Allbritton considered, had Yates "advanced beyond that to 'in and out' psychotic?"

Parnham asked Allbritton to refresh her memory about her concern for Andrea Yates by looking at her chart notes for that March 31.

Allbritton thought she had written a note on the back of Yates's evaluation form. Usually she put an arrow at the bottom of the page to indicate additional medical comments. "In this case . . . I just vented to the nursing supervisor," she said. "What I wanted to write, I don't think would have been an appropriate part of a medical record. I was somewhat upset by the state of the patient."

Parnham asked whether Allbritton hadn't, in fact, been very upset.

"I was very upset, yes," she admitted, "because the patient was so ill and had obviously been ill for sometime longer than I was being given history for . . . and [I] wondered, really, why she hadn't [been] presented to our facilities sooner."

Parnham passed the witness to Owmby.

"Can I see the notes you're referring to?" Owmby asked.

"Emergency Detention Warrant, yes," Owmby remarked, perusing the document. "Basically you're taking away someone's rights. . . . They no longer have the right to leave the building."

"At least for this 24-hour emergency?"

"Right."

"What is the phrase that enables you to take away a person's right to, to commit them to a facility against their will?"

"Imminent danger to themselves . . . to others, and evidence of a disorder—mental illness—that will decline if not treated."

"You were unable to assess her thought process [but] you concluded she was a danger to the safety of herself. Did she say she had thoughts of suicide?"

"She denied it."

"Did you ask her about homicidal thoughts?"

"I think it was a pretty standard, are you going to harm yourself or others. No."

"And she said no?"

"No," Allbritton confirmed.

"What was imminent about that?"

"I wouldn't have trusted her to walk across the street. She might also not feed her children." Owmby asked how Allbritton could be so concerned when Yates denied serious illness. "The clinical presentation did not match the physical presence of the patient. We don't read minds, but we make clinical judgments."

Owmby had lost ground. He moved on to the Devereux patient intake packet, Defense Exhibit 25, page 291. The attorney in the orange sweater anxiously looked over the shoulder of the attorney in the gray suit as he grabbed a two-inch-thick black binder from his briefcase and flipped to find the corresponding page.

"The patient has the right to request to be discharged from the hospital?" Owmby asked.

"Yes."

"They [patients] have the right to be discharged within four hours of that request?"

"No, they have four hours in which a physician will reevaluate them and determine whether or not they should stay or go."

"I'm kind of confused," Owmby said. Owmby had a technique of feigning confusion that was quite successful with witnesses. Sometimes he really was confused. This deep into the case, for example, he sometimes had difficulty remembering that a psychiatrist was a medical doctor and a psychologist wasn't.

Possibly, the attorneys for Devereux and Saeed held their breath hoping Yates's defense team would not glance at the "Treatment Problem Sheet" (page DEV 0046) describing Yates's "problem #2" as "chemical dependency" and her discharge goal as "Pt. will verbalize sufficient coping skills to maintain ETOH/drug free life style." Her measurable objectives were listed in the exhibit as "Pt. will gain understanding of the disease concept of chemical dependency" and "Develop life long resources which can support life long abstinence from mind/mood altering drugs." The form suggested that Devereux was ill equipped to handle a patient like Andrea Yates, who psychiatrists agreed needed both mind- and mood-altering drugs for her own and her children's survival.

Owmby certainly wasn't going to bring it up and neither did the defense. This form, and others like it, have not been previously reported, nor specifically discussed at the Yates trial or pretrial hearings.

Allbritton testified that Rusty Yates said his wife had done well on Effexor and Wellbutrin in 1999 for four to six months. So, though she didn't usually prescribe medication, she prescribed those drugs. She was not aware that Yates had previously been psychotic and had taken Haldol. However, Nurse Bob Martin completed a Devereux intake report (the medical history presented to physicians simultaneously with a new patient) at 11:00 AM that day. Under the category "Previous Psychotrophic Medications" on page 5 of the report, Martin wrote the following:

Wellbutrin—effective 1999, dosage?
Effexor—effective 1999, dosage?

Zyprexa—ineffective, dosage?
Zoloft—ineffective (trial x 1 month), dosage?
Haldol—used briefly

If Rusty Yates hoped for validation and a demonstration of Devereux's failure during Parnham's redirect, he hoped in vain. The list of medications he had given the admitting nurse sat in the defense's treasury of unused exhibits, page DEV 0021, of Andrea Yates's medical records. Rusty's in-laws continue to believe that Rusty deliberately withheld from Allbritton the information that Andrea had previously taken Haldol.

Whatever Allbritton learned about Andrea's past treatment from Rusty or the records, Allbritton testified that following her evaluation of incoming patients, her routine was to leave written admission notes for a nurse to communicate to Saeed. "I don't talk to Dr. Saeed," she explained. Unfortunately, as testimony continued, Allbritton began to seem a bright light in Devereux's constellation of physicians.

Parnham asked why Allbritton had finished her written evaluation of Andrea Yates at 12:30 PM but had not signed the preliminary request for emergency detention until 3:00 PM. What had happened during those two and a half hours?

Rusty Yates, Allbritton said, did not want his wife committed. He wanted her to sign herself in, "and she didn't particularly appear to want to be at the hospital. She has to sign several different pages. She would start to sign something and stop and have to be retold what she was signing and she would make another mark and stop. Because of this there was certainly something going on that wasn't quite right. I ethically felt I had to file."

Meanwhile, in the far left front row of the courtroom, a sketch artist used binoculars to draw a picture of Andrea Yates.

MOHAMMAD SAEED RECEIVED both his undergraduate and medical school degrees from Karachi University in Pakistan. He moved to the United States in 1982 and began practicing psychiatry here in 1984. Some three or four months prior to the trial, he had stopped working in an administrative capacity as medical director of the Residential Unit for Adolescents at Devereux. He still had privileges at the hospital.

Parnham asked Saeed whether he knew Dr. Allbritton.

"I know of her," Saeed responded. He said he "was aware" that Dr. Allbritton had admitted Yates to Devereux on March 31 "because when the nurses . . . call, they most of the time indicate who saw the patient."

Parnham requested permission to approach, handed Saeed a copy of his testimony from a pretrial hearing three months earlier, and suggested Saeed "refresh" his memory. "I asked you, did I not, which doctor admitted Mrs. Yates?"

"That was your question," Saeed answered.

"All right," Parnham said, realizing he was going to have to do this the hard way. "Do you remember what your response was?"

"I can read it here. My response was, 'I do not know that doctor personally.' "

"Dr. Saeed," Parnham pressed, "is it a fact that you did not know that Dr. Allbritton was the doctor who admitted her?"

"That is quite possible, yes."

"I'm not asking about possibilities here, Doctor—"

"Objection!" Owmby to the rescue. "Leading the witness."

The attorneys approached the bench where Parnham asked permission to treat Saeed as a hostile witness. Judge Hill declined, noting "at this point he hasn't refused to answer a question."

Parnham picked up where he left off. "You don't even know who she is, do you?"

"I have saw [sic] her today for the first time."

"Did you introduce yourselves?"

"No."

One could grow old and die listening to Dr. Saeed. He belabored minor aspects of Parnham's questions, leading away from the questioner's intent without being "nonresponsive." His foreign accent explained away occasional communications difficulties and afforded Saeed the leeway of Parnham's inborn courtesy. Whoever prepared him to testify had done a bang-up job of it.

"Would you, Doctor, describe Mrs. Yates as being very ill?" Parnham asked.

"I would describe her that way."

"Would you describe Mrs. Yates as appearing to have lost a lot of weight?"

"I was aware of the history that she had lost a lot of weight."

"Would you describe her as having fair eye contact?"

"Very hard to recall," Saeed said. "But that could be a fair statement."

"Would you describe her as being 'unkempt'?"

"I wouldn't be surprised if I described her that way. . . . I have a notation here that . . . she was dressed in hospital clothes."

"Did she suffer from psycho-motor retardation?"

"Yes, that I can answer without a doubt. . . . She did suffer from severe psycho-motor retardation. I'm looking at this psychiatric assessment . . . of 3/31/2001 [dictated on April 2, 2002] . . . I have a notation here that she did not shake the hand. . . . She did appear slow in her mental processes. . . . I do not recall whether she was completely mute, but what I recall is that she was not answering all the questions."

"She did not respond to narrative questions?"

"That is correct."

"She could answer yes or no and nod her head, but she was not able to respond to a narrative question?"

"She gave me the husband's phone number. . . . I can't be 100 percent sure, but that's what I recall."

"What does not being able to respond to a narrative question trigger in the mind of someone like yourself, a psychiatrist?"

"A narrative question is, is more or less an open-ended question that requires, in my mind, answers in sentences. . . . He's [the husband] a very intelligent person, and he did provide me with a lot of information."

"Did you make contact with a psychiatrist by the name of Starbranch?"

"I don't recall having made contact, however, I recall that I had made attempts to call her on at least a couple of occasions."

"Please, if you would, take your time and check the records . . . and determine for this jury when your first effort was made to contact Dr. Starbranch."

Time passed. Saeed flipped pages.

"I know I have a notation here from her second inpatient treatment that we got consent from Mrs. Yates. . . . And the consent was faxed to Dr. Starbranch's office . . . I tried to call Dr. Starbranch. . . . I had made a couple of attempts and in one of the attempts I talked to Dr. Starbranch's office personnel personally, and I think that's what resulted in us getting the records [on May 9]."

"All those efforts that you expended . . . occurred relative to the second stay beginning on May the 4th, is that correct?"

"That is how it is documented."

"There are no records that would indicate any attempts made by you or your office staff to contact Dr. Starbranch between the dates of March 31 up until May 9?"

"It appears to be so."

With that answer, Saeed confirmed that after one failed fourteen-day stay at Devereux (when his patient had been so mentally ill that he filed to have her committed to a state mental hospital), six days into a *second* Devereux stay, with his patient's life in jeopardy, he had only *just* consulted successful 1999 treatment records from Yates's psychiatrist. *If only one thing had gone right.*

Parnham asked Saeed whether Yates had appeared nonfunctional when he saw her the first time on April 1.

"She appeared to be nonfunctional to a great degree, that is correct," Saeed answered.

"Did she exhibit an inability to form plans?" Parnham continued.

"I would agree with that."

Parnham asked whether Yates had been nearly catatonic.

"My recollection is that I did describe her as nearly catatonic."

"Did anyone, did Mr. Yates tell you, for instance, that Dr. Starbranch had placed his wife on an antipsychotic medication known as Haldol?" Parnham asked.

"I believe he did."

"When did he tell you that, Doctor?"

"My recollection is that he gave me that information when I talked to him the first time."

"April the first?"

"I believe so."

"In hindsight, would you say that if he told you on April first that she had previously been treated, had been determined to be psychotic, having been placed on Haldol, that it might have been prudent for you to try to reach Dr. Starbranch to get some information from her?" Parnham asked.

"Object to the form of the question," Owmby interrupted.

"Sustained."

"You didn't put her on Haldol at that visit, did you, sir?" Parnham persisted.

"No, I did not put her on Haldol."

"As a matter of fact, during the entirety of the first visit to Devereux she was not placed on Haldol?"

"She was not placed on Haldol," Saeed agreed, "but she was taking another [antipsychotic] medication called Risperdal."

"But it didn't work very well, did it?"

"I can't say that it did or did not."

"Did you sense a noticeable improvement in your patient?"

"Yes, I did see an improvement."

"As a matter of fact, you thought she had been greatly improved?"

"She was definitely improved."

Parnham wondered whether Saeed had received any correspondence from an insurance company regarding payment of benefits and "a precertification timeline" for Andrea Yates's recovery. In fact, he had. The letter was dated March 31, 2001, the day Rusty Yates had first taken his wife to Devereux.

"It says," Saeed read, "total days certified—fourteen."

"I take it there is no pressure on you or anyone associated with Devereux to get her rolling and get her out of there as quickly as possible—or was there in this case?"

"Not anything that I recall. I do not recall any pressure."

"And certainly, if there had been some type of pressure . . . you would have recalled that?" Parnham asked without a hint of sarcasm.

"I certainly hope so," Saeed answered.

"You saw improvement throughout her stay," Parnham said, referring to Saeed's patient progress notes. " 'She ate some solid food on 4/8,' " he read. "She's comin' round."

Saeed acknowledged that Yates was progressing toward her precertified release date.

"But [the chart notes of] the nurse who preceded you indicated that she 'refused nourishment . . . except taking fluids when taking medications . . . she remained depressed.' " How did Saeed explain the contemporaneous and contradictory observations between himself and his nurse? He didn't. Parnham seemed on a roll.

"Were you aware that . . . Andrea Pia Yates was being taken to daily drug therapy group sessions?"

"What I've been able to gather is that for the first few days . . . Mrs. Yates was not involving herself in the therapeutic groups," Saeed said, "but after that she started going to the groups. . . . Her participation was minimal and with encouragement."

"*Drug* group therapy?" Parnham asked, close to a reference to Yates's mismanaged care.

"All patients are expected to participate in the group activities," Saeed said. "It encompasses a broad treatment approach."

"You were aware she was being exposed to the drug therapy sessions, were you not?"

"I knew she was not being excluded from any groups."

"This young woman never ever had a drug problem. . . . Is there some benefit to either you as a physician or to Devereux . . . by having . . . a person that's possibly psychotic sitting in on therapy relative to narcotics addiction?"

"Object as to form of the question," Owmby interjected.

"Sustained."

"Do you know if Devereux gets any extra money as a result of how many heads they put in a room and watch folks, you know, with heroin needles in their arms?"

"Not to my knowledge at all," Saeed said.

Saeed remembered putting Yates on suicide precautions the first time he saw her. He hadn't changed her prescription from Risperdal to Haldol until her second inpatient stay, around May 4. He thought her filling the bathtub might be an indication that she was suicidal.

Saeed didn't indiscriminately prescribe "a harsh antipsychotic medication like Haldol, did he?"

No, he didn't.

"If she is doing so much better during that first inpatient stay, when she is on Risperdal, why do you change her medication to Haldol? . . . Why? . . ."

"Because she had deteriorated and her recovery or improvement could not only be attributed to one single medication. She was taking two antidepressant medications during that first hospitalization as well."

Where had Saeed gotten the information to change Yates's prescription from Risperdal to Haldol?

"Mr. Yates had described that during the past episode the patient was given 'some sort of cocktail' that included Haldol and Cogentin and she had recovered quite well with that. And Mr. Yates felt that that treatment would be effective."

George Parnham set Saeed up perfectly but did not go in for the kill. He pressed the point that Saeed spent too little time with someone as sick as Andrea, but did not focus on some of the most important of the hundreds of pages of Devereux treatment reports. Saeed wrote in Yates's charts almost every day (as required by Devereux Policies and Procedures Nursing, "Precautions," p. 4), and at least one Devereux employee believes that meant he physically saw her. However, much of what Saeed wrote may have been supplied to him by nurses rather than by his own assessment of his patient. According to the Devereux Special Intervention/Precaution Checklists (also required under Devereux Policies and Procedures Nursing, "Precautions," p. 5), assigned nursing staff observed Saeed visiting Yates for *one hour*—give or take a few minutes—during her twenty-four-plus days of confinement there. Another bewildering fact of Yates's treatment—or lack of it—unremarked upon until now.

BY TUESDAY, MARCH 5, when Resnick returned to the courtroom, Owmby had had several days to prepare for cross-examination. He began by questioning Resnick on generalizations he had made to nationwide press before having met Andrea Yates. Regarding his appearance on ABC's *Nightline,* for example, Owmby asked, "You couldn't comment, but broadly you guessed . . . she [Andrea Yates] would fit into the category of an altruistic killer, is that correct?"

"*If* her husband's account was taken at face value, yes," Resnick answered.

Owmby read from a *Cleveland Plain Dealer* interview with Resnick regarding the Susan Smith case. "You described Susan Smith as a 'gracious person' . . . you would not have any problem with her babysitting for your children. Do you remember saying that?"

"Actually, you *misread* the quote," Resnick said with charming candor. "The quote is accurate." Owmby asked Resnick to read the quote aloud accurately. In context, what the reporter had written about Resnick's opinion of Smith, who sent her car rolling into a South Carolina lake with her two young sons inside, was that she was not a danger to anyone's children but her own. "'I would not have any problem with her babysitting for my grandchildren. She loved her children,'" Resnick read.

"So the misquote was children versus grandchildren?"

"That's correct."

"Okay, I'm sorry," said Owmby, quickly moving on. What exactly was the evidence that made Resnick believe Yates killed her children to save them from hell?

Resnick cited an interview with Mrs. Yates that Dr. Ferguson had conducted in the presence of Sgt. Mehl. In the interview, Yates had said, "I am prepared to go to hell" and that the children "would burn in hell for eternity," because she was not raising them righteously, Resnick explained.

"Is that it?"

"Yes."

"Andrea Yates believed that the one, true Satan was inside of her?" Owmby asked. And more important, what had she said *before* she wound up in jail that supported Resnick's opinion?

"She believed if she said it [the idea of harming her children] out loud, Satan would hear it and make it happen," Resnick answered. "She told Debbie Holmes and her husband she was concerned she was possessed by Satan or a demon."

"A demonic influence?" Owmby carefully corrected.

"Yes."

"They share a belief system that includes demonic influence and the possibility of possession?"

"Yes."

Owmby was curious how psychiatrists could tell the difference between a shared belief and a delusion.

"Actually, a shared belief *can* be delusional," Resnick explained, "but if it is a religious belief, held by a large number of people, it's not usually considered a delusion."

"The Catholic Church constitutes a large number of people, don't they?"

"Yes."

In a few brief exchanges, Owmby had successfully insinuated that Resnick might believe the world's 1.06 billion Catholics were delusional.

A simple no was the least harmful route out for Resnick.

"Penal Code section 801 is the standard for legal insanity that's used in Texas?"

"Yes, it is."

"Sometimes referred to as the McNaughton Rule?"

"It comes closer to McNaughton than having an 'irresistible impulse,'" Resnick agreed. "In some jurisdictions, not Texas, in order to be found insane, one can either not know the wrongfulness of one's act or be unable to refrain from that act. . . . In Texas, it is limited to knowledge of wrongfulness."

Why didn't she kill herself rather than harm her children, Owmby asked.

In 1999 she tried to kill herself twice rather than harm her children, Resnick answered.

"We really should be examining the conduct on June 20th, right?" Owmby asked.

"Right, but you're asking the questions," Resnick answered.

IT WASN'T UNTIL psychiatrist Lucy Puryear came along that Andrea Yates trusted someone enough to tell her what she'd seen in those haunting 1994 visions involving baby Noah and a long, steel-gray knife: "lots of blood." After months of studying medical records and interviewing Yates, her family, and her friends, Puryear had concluded that in addition to postpartum psychosis and major depressive disorder, Yates had a "baseline psychosis disorder, probably schizophrenia." Schizophrenia is a poor prognosis psychosis.

Puryear's testimony for the defense began on Tuesday, March 5. The videotapes she had made with Yates on July 27, 2001, and February 4, 2002, were shown in the courtroom. When the videotapes of Resnick, Dietz, and Puryear were eventually made public by the Harris County clerk of courts under the Texas Public Information Act, the voice track on the earliest Puryear tape was missing.

Regarding Yates's final hospitalization under Dr. Saeed at Devereux, Puryear testified that the usual protocol for patients on suicide watch is for the patient to be off suicide watch for twenty-four hours before being discharged. Saeed had not followed the protocol.

Parnham also projected a slide of the Devereux suicide-watch chart for April 4, 2001. There were ninety-six separate entries—one entry every fifteen minutes around the clock—made by six Devereux nurses. The nurses placed a code opposite each fifteen-minute period to indicate what the patient was doing. For example, the code 7K indicated that the patient was visiting with her family in the hallway. On April 4, the 7K appeared three times—at 12:30 PM, 12:45 PM, and 1:00 PM—representing a visit about forty-five minutes long with her family members.

"What number is assigned . . . to represent visitations by her doctor?" Parnham asked Puryear.

"It's number 12."

"Do you know about how many times the number '12' is on the chart that day, representing visits by her doctor?"

"I could find it once."

Parnham shook his head in disbelief that Saeed had only checked on his patient once that day, at 2:00 PM, for about fifteen minutes. But Parnham left it at that.

In the suicide-watch charts for that thirteen-day hospitalization, from March 31 to April 12, the number "12" is entered three times (two of them on the same occasion). According to Devereux suicide-watch charts, attested to by the signatures of six nurses, it appears that Saeed spent approximately forty-five minutes total with Yates during the thirteen days she was so mentally ill he petitioned the courts to commit her to Austin State Hospital. What is worse, during the eleven-day hospitalization, from May 4 to May 14, immediately preceding the murders, Devereux suicide-watch charts indicate one entry of code "12," on May 10, 2001, at 1:00 PM. Fifteen minutes—give or take—that was it.

Parnham had pushed Owmby's case to the edge of a cliff. Saeed had testified that he spent "on an average in the vicinity of 30 minutes" assessing Andrea Yates, and some of his chart notes suggested visits with her. The defense did not attempt to clarify what Saeed had meant. One more shove might have sent the case over the edge if the defense had been able to establish that the suicide-watch charts confirmed only a few visits by Saeed with Andrea Yates. Even though records of Saeed's visits with Andrea were placed in evidence, the conclusions that might be drawn from the suicide-watch charts were never tested by the defense or pointed out to the jury, and until now, never mentioned in newspaper or magazine articles or television broadcasts.

Puryear testified that she understood that the Yates and Woroniecki families visited together and that the Yateses considered "the Woronieckis their spiritual leader. They could have conversations with him. . . . Once he told her she was going to hell and that she was quite upset by that and the next morning she apologized to him and acted humble and he forgave her."

Parnham reminded Puryear inaccurately of some lines from a Woroniecki poem: "The fruit of her selfishness she did now see . . . what becomes of the children from such a Jezebel." The poem spoke of "the fruit of rebellion," not selfishness, But he made his point. Copies of the Woroniecki publication *Perilous Times*, discovered in the Yates home, were filled with dangerous content for someone like Andrea, who, Puryear said, was delusional about religion. Religious delusions were common among psychotic people, Puryear testified, clarifying that a "shared faith belief is not psychosis."

Based on her own observations and the records she had studied from other physicians who examined Yates, Puryear concluded that Andrea Yates "was incapable of knowing what she did on June 20th was wrong." She played the "get out of jail free" card—the phrase that meant the difference between death or jail and supervised freedom. Yates was simply not in touch with reality at the time she drowned her children, Puryear insisted. She was psychotic.

"Dr. Saeed also had her on Remeron, an anti-depressant, at the very end of that time?" Parnham asked, leading Puryear back to a potential malpractice issue.

"There's a wrong diagnosis in there," Puryear disclosed. "She wasn't diagnosed with Major Depressive Disorder with psychotic features—it was a 'rule out psychosis' " diagnosis. Further testing should have been performed to reveal Yates's schizophrenia, she said. Treating her with medication for depression alone was a disaster. The defense rested its case in chief. On March 7, the prosecution began calling rebuttal witnesses.

• • •

PARK DIETZ KNEW how to enter a room. When the prosecution called his name and the doors in the rear of the courtroom opened that Thursday, March 7, he walked briskly to the witness stand. He was trim and impeccably dressed. Before he had uttered even a word, he had the *feel* of infallibility. "Hollywood Park," the newspaper called him. He'd never heard the nickname until he came to Houston. He thought Rusty Yates had made it up. He didn't live in Hollywood but in the polished community of Newport Beach, north of San Diego.

He was the $500-an-hour casemaker. Dietz's record of sanity evaluations was impressive: John Hinckley, who attempted to assassinate Ronald Reagan in 1981; serial murderer Jeffrey Dahmer; Melissa Drexler, the prom mom; Bryan Uyesugi, the Honolulu Xerox killer; Ted Kaczynski, the Unabomber; the Columbine High School killer teens' postmortem; the retrial of the Menendez brothers. He declined an invitation to work for the defense in O. J. Simpson's trial for the murder of his wife Nicole Brown Simpson, but worked on the civil matter. Dietz had begun testifying as an expert witness in 1977 and had given his opinion in a thousand cases by 1980—when he said he stopped counting.

It wasn't just Dietz's appearance that was impressive. He had credentials: Cornell undergrad; Johns Hopkins University School of Medicine; Johns Hopkins psychiatric residency; Johns Hopkins master's in public health; Johns Hopkins doctorate in sociology; resident and Chief Fellow in forensic psychiatry at the hospital at the University of Pennsylvania in Philadelphia as well as a fellowship in forensic psychiatry.

Dietz's first job after finishing his fellowship in 1978 was as assistant professor of psychiatry at Harvard Medical School. He was assigned to McClain Hospital and, through McClain, to Bridgewater State Hospital, a maximum-security prison for the criminally insane. He tried "without much success, to improve the quality of care" and during his third year there he was asked by the U.S. Justice Department to be in charge of the evaluation of John Hinckley, who stalked actress Jodie Foster and had almost succeeded in assassinating President Ronald Reagan.

Dietz moved on to become the medical director of the Forensic Psychiatry Clinic and medical director of the Institute of Law, Psychiatry, and Public Policy at the University of Virginia as an associate professor, and later a professor of behavioral medicine and psychiatry, teaching on both the law and medical school faculties. "During those years at Virginia, I also engaged in . . . a project for the U.S. Department of Justice that was the first study of threats and stalking and that led to general recognition of stalking as a problem," Dietz said. Early in his academic career, Dietz had written an article on how to prevent filicidal drownings of children for the *American Journal of Public Health.* He coauthored two books, *Autoerotic Fatalities* and *Psychotherapy and the Human Predicament: A Psychosocial Approach.*

Dietz left academia to go into private practice and spends 60 percent of his time working with his Threat Assessment Group, a company that specializes in violent-crime prevention and outwitting celebrity stalkers. He devotes the rest of his time to forensic case work—half criminal, half civil—under the auspices of his firm Park Dietz Associates.

Ten days a year Dietz consults for the FBI on open cases and attempts to close unsolved cases. "They don't always use it [the time] up, and sometimes they use more," he said. He also consulted for the trifecta–hit NBC television series *Law & Order.*

A search "to try to find the truth about matters" was how Dietz elegantly described his practice of the medical science, forensic psychiatry. Forensics is the enterprise where science meets the law.

Dietz was contacted on July 6, 2001, by the prosecution, sixteen days after Andrea Yates drowned her children. He told them the same thing he told anyone who retained him. "I'll only work for you if you agree to show me everything, that is not selectively hide things from me or just show me what you want me to see, . . . that you pay me for my time." . . . And "live with whatever I find and not try to influence my opinion." Nearly three months later, on September 26, the court signed an order authorizing Dietz to examine Andrea Yates. On November 6, the first of his four interviews with her occurred, four and a half months after the crime. Yates had been taking Haldol continuously. Before the interview, Dietz had examined a flow of medical records and police and legal documents pertaining to the case. The prosecution had chosen the strategy of calling Dietz as a rebuttal witness, saving their biggest gun for last.

"What were your findings as to the illness of Andrea Pia Yates?" Owmby asked Dietz.

"My own impression as opposed to diagnosis when I first met with Mrs. Yates was she was suffering from schizophrenia and . . . despite being on appropriate doses of antipsychotic medication, she was still showing what are called negative symptoms of schizophrenia and of being rather passive and her mood being flat," he said. Personally, he didn't "like the conception of schizoaffective disorder" (Resnick's diagnosis), and used it only in court because it's in the book [*Diagnostic and Statistical Manual of Mental Disorders*, Fourth Edition, Text Revision], the courtroom's medical bible.[3] "I don't really believe in it as a separate condition," he said.

In Dietz's opinion, schizoaffective disorder is a combination of schizophrenia and major depression with psychotic features. "I consider all three of those perfectly legitimate diagnoses for a doctor to give. One couldn't strongly disagree with any of them, and any one [of them] is a severe mental disease for the person who at the time they have it has got delusions or hallucinations or marked illogical thinking. Sometimes people with these conditions are in a good state of mind and not mentally diseased even though they have the condition, but when they are psychotic . . . then they have a severe mental disease."

Owmby organized his questioning around what Dietz called the " 'contextual factors' that help to explain Andrea Yates's decline and how it came to this." Dietz's company had produced a slide show for the jury titled "State of Texas v. Andrea Yates" as an audiovisual aid to his testimony. The jury left the courtroom while attorneys haggled over the admissibility into evidence of the slide presentation. Judge Hill allowed it.

Dietz first detailed Yates's 1999 stressors, external events that represented "changes or continuing problems for an individual. . . . Living in a bus with a family; three children, and a newborn and a husband, is a big stressor for someone. . . . It's tough for anybody to raise multiple small children. To be homeschooling them in a bus is, I think, something anyone would find quite stressful." In fact, Yates did not home-

---

3. *American Psychiatric Association,* Diagnostic and Statistical Manual of Mental Disorders, *Fourth Edition. Text Revision [herein after DSM-IV-TR] (Washington, DC: American Psychiatric Association, 2000).*

school in the bus. She had no school-age children until after Noah turned five in 1999 and the family had moved into the Beachcomber house. Neither Parnham nor Odom clarified the inaccuracy in cross-examination. "What was your next finding?" Owmby asked.

When Yates felt depressed and overwhelmed, she asked her husband for support, Dietz said. In Dietz's professional opinion, Rusty Yates's suggestion that his wife needed more rest gave "more than one meaning" to Andrea's choice of taking an overdose of her father's sleeping pills.

Owmby asked what Dietz's next finding was.

"Well, she's discharged from the hospital, from Methodist, and she has a prescription for Zyprexa," Dietz said. "Dr. Flack had been treating her there. She's given a prescription for an antipsychotic medication and she flushes it down the toilet without taking it."

Dr. Flack, medical records show, did not discharge Andrea Yates with a prescription for antipsychotic medication. He discharged her with a prescription for the antidepressant Zoloft and a referral to Dr. Starbranch. It was Starbranch who in July switched Yates from Zoloft to the antipsychotic Zyprexa—which Yates did flush down the toilet. "She would later say she didn't want to take it," Dietz continued. "She didn't think she was psychotic . . . didn't want to be thought of that way and resented someone calling her that." At the time, though, her doctors described her as mostly mute. So Rusty Yates spoke for his wife—even when his description was less than flattering. "Husband indicates that she [Andrea Yates] flushed the medications down the commode," one evaluating doctor wrote. Rusty Yates had also reminded nurses that his wife might "cheek" her medications.

Owmby pressed on. "The next significant factor, I believe that you found, was an incident with her husband and a knife?" he asked.

"Yes . . . Once again, when she's at her mother's house, there's a dramatic incident that leads to hospitalization. And in this case, the dramatic incident was with the knife rather than the pills," Dietz said. "So she's upped the ante."

"You said she'd upped the ante?"

"Yes . . . As a psychiatrist, I can't help but notice that she got help the first time only with an overdose. She didn't get enough help, so now she's going to do something more, which can get her more help. And, in fact, this time it not only got her hospitalized, it got her a house."

"And she was admitted to Spring Shadows Glen. And at some point during that time was when Russell Yates purchased the house?"

"Yes."

Andrea Yates attempted to kill herself for the second time on July 20, but after considering several properties she and her husband had cosigned a contract on the Beachcomber house on July 12, 1999—eight days *before* her second suicide attempt. Neither Parnham nor Odom introduced the contract signed by Andrea Yates into evidence or cross-examined Dietz about the misstatement Owmby elicited. "The house had been purchased by her husband while she was in the hospital," Dietz added later in his testimony. "She had never seen it," he volunteered. "She had no say in the decision of which house."

The next significant event Owmby asked about involved James P. Thompson, PhD.

". . . Dr. Thompson's report is the only thing in the entire record prior to the crime that suggests that Mrs. Yates ever had, ever gave, some basis for saying she had hallucinations."

"The only report prior to the crime?" Owmby seemed astonished.

"The only thing written by a mental health professional—well let me phrase that differently. There is [*sic*] some suggestive nursing notes . . . when she might be hearing voices. . . ." Thompson later called Dietz's characterization "a blatant manipulation" of the records.

The crowd in the courtroom was riveted, but had some of Andrea Yates's many nurses and other licensed health-care providers—medicine's second-class citizens—been present to hear Dietz's testimony, Judge Hill might have had to fend them off him with her gavel.

In both her grand jury and trial testimony, Dr. Starbranch, Andrea Yates's psychiatrist for much of 1999, testified that Andrea Yates "would rank in the five sickest—and most difficult to get out of psychosis—patients that I've ever treated." Starbranch had no doubt that Yates suffered both audio and visual hallucinations, but more than that, she was concerned for her patient's life. "It doesn't matter whether she's schizophrenic, bipolar, schizoaffective, or depressed," she later explained, "because all of those conditions can lead to catatonia and not eating and not sleeping, not taking in any fluids. When you're looking at a life threatening condition—which it was—you consider ECT." Which was why, in August 1999, Starbranch ordered evaluations for her patient by James P. Thompson, PhD, and Arturo Rios, MD, a psychiatrist who specializes in ECT.

"You note on the chart that ECT was recommended by Dr. Thompson and Dr. Rios?" Owmby continued.

" . . . Yes . . . They both recommended it."

"But she did not receive electroshock?"

"No, both she and her husband refused it."

"What was the significance of your finding there?"

"I think it was a very appropriate treatment to recommend, and tragic that it wasn't provided. Because, although we still don't know [the] effect it would have had, it may have had a dramatic effect on her."

The testimony did not reflect that Rusty Yates was reluctant to allow his catatonic wife to undergo the procedure without first exhausting less invasive alternatives. "Andrea couldn't agree or disagree," according to Starbranch. "She was incapable of making a decision." Fortunately, the Haldol Decanoate/Cogentin injections worked.

"You found it significant that Andrea Yates, as you put it, secretly went off medication; is that correct?"

"She had been followed by Dr. Starbranch after the discharge from Spring Shadows Glen," Dietz explained. "Dr. Starbranch had put her on Haldol and was continuing to treat her with antidepressants and Haldol, but then Mrs. Yates, unbeknownst to anyone, stopped taking all the medication in November of 1999 and kept going to Dr. Starbranch for some months after that, finally revealing in January of 2000 to Dr. Starbranch that she had stopped her medication."

Andrea had indeed "been blowing smoke" regarding compliance with most of her medications, but discontinuing the most important drug in her arsenal, Haldol, "wasn't a secret at all," Dr. Starbranch later recalled. "It [the injection] wasn't given in my office, but a nurse would give it, so we knew that she got the Haldol Dec."

Ultimately, the Yateses' health insurance declined to continue covering the antipsychotic injections. "We couldn't get the insurance company to agree to have a home health nurse go out and give it to her," Starbranch explained. "There's a note in my chart, 'October 14, 1999—Not getting Haldol Dec/Cogentin; conflict with insurance,' " Starbranch said. " 'Pt. wants to know if it's okay not to take it. Doing alright. Better.'

"So we said okay, don't take it [Haldol] at all, but take the Zyprexa." Unfortunately, Andrea had a history of noncompliance with oral medications. Notes regarding the discontinuation of Haldol injections and replacement with Zyprexa appeared in Starbranch's records for Andrea's November and December psychiatric sessions as well. On the November 11 visit, Starbranch reported that her patient was "doing okay" and her affect was "bright." "Will try lower Zyprexa," she wrote, and reduced Yates's antipsychotic dose by half—to 2.5 milligrams. Her recommendations noted, for a second time, that she had discontinued Haldol in October. She listed Yates's current medications as Zyprexa, Wellbutrin, and Effexor XR. A month later Starbranch again noted her patient's "bright" affect and made the same recommendations a third time: discontinue Haldol, continue Zyprexa, Wellbutrin, Effexor XR. "Husband may come to visit next time—Rusty," she added.

"She stopped taking Zyprexa, I didn't take her off," Starbranch said. "In December 1999, when I saw her in the office, the recommendation was to continue the Wellbutrin, Zyprexa, and Effexor. In January, she let me know she hadn't been taking them." "Husband says, he didn't like her doing this," Starbranch wrote in January 2000. Still, for the two months she had been off medication, Yates had done well—by Starbranch's own descriptions. At the end of the session, the patient, husband, and doctor had reached an understanding. Starbranch's recommendation read: "Wants to be off medications unless symptomatic. Husband agrees."

"Rusty really tries the best he possibly can," Starbranch added. "He really is a good person and he tries, but he's a computer jock and he's not as sensitive to things that were going on in Andrea—he could tolerate a lot of pathology in Andrea before he tried to get help—he just didn't see it. I think he's a very good-hearted man."

"I can't judge them," she continued. "They fervently believed that their religion was going to carry them through. They wanted to have as many children as God wanted them to have. We told them this was not a good idea.

"I said she was one of the sickest persons I had ever treated," Starbranch said, recalling her trial testimony. "I still say that."

The contextual factors Dietz identified in 2000 began in February with Andrea's becoming pregnant with her fifth child, Mary, against medical advice.

". . . You've explained, that good or bad, a pregnancy like that acts as a stressor?" Owmby asked.

"Yes," Dietz replied.

"Now, did she follow the advice regarding medication during and after pregnancy?" asked Owmby.

"No," Dietz said. "Against advice she got pregnant—"

"Objection," Parnham responded. "He's answered that question."

"Sustained."

"Did she get pregnant against medical advice?"

"Yes."

". . . After the baby was born, did you find records indicating she went back to the doctor to find out how to medicate and treat herself for her own problems after the baby was born?" Owmby asked.

"No, she didn't."

". . . I guess the next significant event was the admission to Devereux Hospital; is that correct?"

"Yes."

"And would you explain to the jury the context that—the significance that you attached to this contextual factor?"

". . . There's more than one version of how well she did between November and March . . . but everyone agrees she got extremely depressed after her father's death [March 12] and was functioning so poorly that she needed to be admitted again; and that's what led to the first Devereux admission."

"All right," Owmby continued, skillfully skipping over details of the Devereux hospitalization and the fact that Saeed had not ordered any diagnostic testing for his new patient nor had Dr. Starbranch been contacted for release of Andrea's prior treatment records. "She was released from Devereux and what was the next significant event that you found?"

"First of all, it's not clear how improved she was the first time she was released . . . but what gets her back to Devereux is the incident in which she's filled the bathrub with water."

". . . Now, I believe while at Devereux, again, ECT, electroconvulsive therapy, was recommended?"

"It was recommended by Dr. Saeed," Dietz said. "The advice was rejected. She never got ECT."

After her readmission to Devereux on May 4, Rusty Yates had been reluctant to allow his once-again-catatonic wife to undergo electric shock treatment without Saeed at least trying the injectable Haldol/Cogentin combination that had brought Andrea out of psychosis within hours two years earlier.

In Andrea's chart, Saeed filed handwritten progress notes dated May 7, 2001. "Husband was gravely concerned last evening because patient had not eaten anything even on his [Rusty's] request—which was unusual for patient. We discussed the options including ECT [a treatment not available at Devereux, League City]. They remain reluctant and want to try exactly the same treatment that got her better last time [1999]. We have faxed consent and will try to contact Dr. Starbranch."

According to Devereux records, Saeed's typewritten psychiatric assessment of Andrea Yates was dictated on May 6—a day earlier than he made his handwritten notes. The content was similar:

> The patient did not deny suicidal ideation, just kept staring into space and looked severely depressed, so a decision was made to admit the patient after discussing treatment options with patient and husband and I had mentioned in this situation, ECT is recommended. The ECT's risks and benefits were discussed with them. Her husband chose not to consider ECT at this point of time but agreed to rehospitalization. The husband reported that after the birth of her second youngest child the patient had gone into a similar episode of depression and had taken Zoloft for four weeks without any response. She was rehospitalized received some kind of injectable cocktail including Haldol and Cogentin. The patient was then started on Effexor and Wellbutrin and began responding at that point of time. The patient did not show any response to Risperdal and at this time we decided to try the Haldol again at the husband's request.

ECT has never again been mentioned in Andrea Yates's medical records.

"What could possibly account for this change between June 20th and June 21st?" Owmby asked.

"The biggest of all factors," Dietz said, "is that there came a time on June 20 when Mrs. Yates had killed all five of her children and even when those deaths are at the mother's own hands, it is an enormous stress . . . beyond any of our ability to imagine," he said. "And on top of that, she is arrested and handcuffed . . . separated from her family. . . . And she finds herself in a jail, and as I understand it, naked, and on suicide watch."

Owmby did not inquire about two additional stressors: the possible effects of sudden withdrawal from Haldol two weeks before the children's murders and Saeed's major dosage changes of Remeron and Effexor two days before the killings. As for June 21, it would be difficult for any psychiatrist to neglect to consider the chemical effects of instantaneous withdrawal from all drugs upon entering jail—especially on someone who had recently been medicated for psychosis as well as depression. But Dietz did not mention them.

As proof of his thinking, Dietz introduced the first of eight video segments that varied in length from more than eighteen minutes to less than one. All eyes were riveted on the projection screen for the first excerpt, referred to as Segment A. It was a little more than a minute long and had been taped on November 6, 2001. Dietz believed what Yates described in the segment exemplified "obsessional intrusive thoughts" that were less psychotic hallucinations than they were "thoughts and fear."

The video camera captured a three-quarter image of Yates sitting across from Dietz, the third psychiatrist to videotape her in the Harris County Jail. She wore a white T-shirt under her jail oranges. Her body was lifeless. The antipsychotic side effect is called tardive dyskinesia, reduction of normal body movement. Behind Yates, a black molded-plastic Eames-style chair stood empty in the corner.

Her bangs were too long. She needed to cut them. Scissors. No. Thoughts jackhammering in her head.[4]

On the tape, men's voices reverberate in the hallway.
"Had you thought of any way, at that point, that you might hurt the

---

4. A. Yates to L. Puryear, competency hearing, September 2001; conversation overheard by author.

children?" Dietz began. Thirteen vacant seconds passed before Andrea Yates answered his question.

"With a knife," she said.

"Had you pictured it?"

"In my head?"

"Yeah."

"The thought came over me, yes." A thought, not a picture, she corrected Dietz.

"What was the thought that came over you?"

Noah is inquisitive and bright—he probably could have been anything. He would have been a great doctor.[5]

"Noah getting hurt," Yates replied, nodding yes repeatedly.

"Noah, in particular. Any of the others?"

"Noah," she answered again softly through the relentless mind-jangling reverb of the jail's public address system.

. . . we were visiting Rusty's grandmother in a nursing home. . . . Her roommate called Noah over and started chatting. . . . Noah was . . . 3–4 years old and stood there calmly talking with her.[6]

"What did you think?"

. . . I could picture him wearing a lab-coat and holding a clip board.[7]

"I didn't see that," she said.

THE NEXT MORNING, November 7, 2001, around 10:00 AM, Park Dietz and Andrea Yates began again. Five-minute-long Segment B describes how Yates thought she was getting better in early May 2001, but her husband "worried" and took her to the hospital. Her mother's coax-

---

5. *Letter of A. Yates to author, May 14, 2003.*

6. *Ibid.*

7. *Ibid.*

ing, her husband's determination, and her brother Brian's strength got her into the car.

> I was thinking, who will take care of the kids? Mary wasn't taking the bottle very well, and I worried about her. . . . Maybe I was afraid.[8]

Dietz posed the question three different ways, and three times she told him filling the bathtub on May 3 was not part of a plan to drown the children.

Dietz continued with sixteen-minute-long Segment C covering possible plans, opportunities for carrying the plans out, and an interesting conversation about the film *Seven*.

"Were there any opportunities that came and went that you didn't do anything?" Dietz asked.

"No," Yates said. Dietz was aware that Rusty and Dora Yates had begun leaving Andrea alone with the children for an hour in the mornings following the 2001 Memorial Day weekend. Andrea's mother learned about the change at a family lunch on Father's Day, June 17, at the Cracker Barrel restaurant, three days before the killings.

"So the very first opportunity, when you were home alone with the children, was on the 20th?"

"Yes," Yates answered.

"On *every* day before that, had Dora been at the house by the time Rusty left?" Dietz asked carefully.

"Yes." Three times Yates had said she drowned her children at the earliest opportunity, but her answers didn't match the facts. Dietz rephrased the question. "That was the very first day that she was coming later?"

"No, I think she'd done it the week before," Yates said, reversing herself.

"Were there other days that you'd had an hour to yourself?"

"Yes," Yates said, once again answering contrary to what she'd said moments earlier. Satan had given her the idea to kill her children; the method was her idea. She couldn't remember the meaning of the

---

8. *Ibid.*

prophecy. "Do you remember having thought anything about the seventh deadly sin?"

"Yes." She rolled her tongue inside her bottom lip.

"Tell me about that."

"Well, I thought it was . . . I thought it was murder. . . ." Her voice cracked on the word. "And I felt I had done all the other sins and now this one would be the last one." She paused. "Just one of the sins." Her voice trailed off.

"This is a thought you had before drowning them—that this would be the last?"

"Yes."

"Do you know what the other deadly sins are?"

"Not all of them. Just gluttony, envy, greed . . ." Beat. Beat. Beat. "Lust . . . I forget the other two."

"Sloth."

"Sloth, yeah."

"And what else?"

"There's one more."

Ten seconds. "I can't remember." Silence.

"Where had you learned about the seven deadly sins?"

"Four-five-three. Four-five-three," the electric voice of the PA system screeched. Rata-tat-tat.

". . . I had seen a movie about it a couple years ago."

"Was the movie *Seven*?"

"Yes."

"Had that movie had any affect on you?"

"Not at the time, no."

"Were you thinking about that movie in June 2001?"

"Yes."

"What did you think about it?"

"That . . . I thought about what I was about to do and how it fit in there. The seventh deadly sin. That I would have done . . . all of them . . . after I drowned my children."

"So you saw it as a sin that you were going to commit?"

"Yes."

• • •

DIETZ ACKNOWLEDGED AN important fact about psychosis: that logical and illogical aspects of reality are not mutually exclusive. "So we can't always apply logic to it," he said. "There is no rule to say it must be logical or must be all illogical. It can be a mixture."

"But in this case . . . you are applying some logic to this thought—why?" Owmby asked.

"Because . . . she's concealing thoughts which we say are going on for a month," Dietz explained. "It is a plan to drown the children. She already knows that she's not going to do it when there are other people there. She admits that that's because they would stop her."

Dietz described Yates's fixation with *Seven*. She thought that killing the children would be sinful and that she would be committing the last of the Seven Deadly Sins. "Murder isn't even one of them. But she believed it was," Dietz said.

Apparently, Dietz, the prosecutors, and the defense attorneys were unfamiliar with the movie *Seven*. In the movie's penultimate scene, a courier delivers to a detective, played by Brad Pitt, the severed head of his pregnant wife. The detective receives the delivery on an empty road in a vast expanse of sand dunes. The film's conceit is that each of the seven murders exemplified directly, or provoked in another, the commission of one of the Seven Deadly Sins. The beautiful mother and unborn child had provoked the villain's Envy, and their murders, in turn, provoked the husband/father/detective's Wrath. Murder is not one of the Seven Deadly Sins, but it is the last sin committed in *Seven*. The detective murders his prisoner, played by Kevin Spacey.

A more diligent search might have led to a revealing explanation of Yates's vocabulary of sin. As a binge-and-purger she'd felt guilty of Gluttony (even during Mary's brief life), had been Envious of others, Slothful (Michael Woroniecki made certain she knew that), and had experienced Greed, at least as the Gospel of Luke explained it. Among the closing soliloquies in *Seven*, written by Andrew Kevin Walker, are these words spoken by the serial murderer: "We see a Deadly Sin on every street corner, in every home, and we tolerate it. We tolerate it because it's common. It's trivial. We tolerate it morning, noon, and night. Well, not anymore. I'm setting the example. And what I've done is going to be puzzled over and studied and followed forever."

• • •

ANDREA YATES BELIEVED she was not raising the children properly, Dietz testified when he took the stand again on March 8 for his
second day of testimony. She did not pay enough attention to them;
she feared they might get in trouble. "That's not delusional material,"
he said. "She's . . . guilt ridden about it . . . because she's depressed.
But it's true, if she stays that depressed and dysfunctional, she's not
going to be an adequate mother." Yes, Yates may have believed the
children were being tormented by Satan, or going to hell, "but she
didn't try non-lethal ways of protecting them and never mentioned
this until the day after the homicides." He said he would have expected someone with Satanic delusions to try to find nonlethal help
like calling the police, the FBI, sending her children away, even
suicide.

Why didn't Andrea Yates seek spiritual guidance from Rusty Yates
or Michael Woroniecki? Dietz asked.

Rusty Yates, of course, had abandoned the Woroniecki belief system back in 1998, and was not supportive of his wife's continued contact with the family. Rachel Woroniecki says Andrea talked to the
Woronieckis by phone when they were living at an RV park near Galveston in the month before Andrea killed the children. Neither the prosecution nor the defense had called Michael or Rachel Woroniecki as
witnesses or subpoenaed phone records. No one besides Andrea and
the Woronieckis knew of the call, not even Rusty.

Dietz pointed out that at no time prior to the crime did Yates say
she believed she was Satan. "There isn't psychotic material there," he
testified. "But there is a dramatic difference between what we know up
to and through June 20, . . . and everything we know through Dr. Ferguson's eyes [after]." Before the crimes, before Dr. Ferguson, "There's
nothing there about saving the children from burning in hell, . . . but a
number of things happen after the homicides."

Around 12:45 PM on that November 7, Yates began the longest
taped description she had given of the crime itself since her confession
to Officer Mehl. There is an unbearable softness in both Dietz's and
Yates's voices, overridden with clanging, jolting sounds from inside the
jail.

"When you got up that morning, on the 20th, did you know that was going to be the day?" Dietz asked quietly, gently.

"Yeah," Yates nodded, mumbling through thickened lips.

"When did you decide that?" Time. When did she decide? It was legally critical.

"The night before."

"Did you share that with anyone?" Was there a witness to premeditation?

She shook her head no.

"Had you talked to Rusty about the Seven Deadly Sins?"

"No," she said softly.

"Had you talked to him at all about Satan's presence?"

"No."

"Why not?"

"I was afraid."

"What were you afraid would happen?"

She paused. "I wouldn't do what I was supposed to do," she answered. "I couldn't do it with him in the house."

"And what would happen if you didn't do what you were supposed to do?" Dietz persisted.

"Children would still be alive," she said, nodding.

"And then what?"

"I was so worried about their souls with Satan around."

"Do I understand correctly that you were worried that if you told Rusty he would interfere and the children would still be in danger?"

"Yes," Yates answered promptly.

"Their souls would still be in danger from Satan?"

"Yes."

"So in the morning when you got up, did you try to act as normal as possible?" Dietz suggested. "You were trying to make sure he didn't think there was something unusual going on?"

"Yes," Yates answered simply.

"Because you knew that if he observed something out of the ordinary, he would interfere?" Dietz's question was ironically one of the most positive insinuations made about Rusty Yates since the drownings.

"Yes."

"So what'd you do that morning?"

"What'd I do?" she asked, sounding lost.

"Before he left," Dietz repeated, "what were you doing?"

"Oh . . . having breakfast," she answered, dry-mouthed. "Before he left, the kids were eating breakfast. . . . Rusty . . . left the house about . . . nine," she said, her voice trailing off.

"Did you feed Mary?"

"Yes."

"What did you feed her?"

"Formula," she said.

"What time were you expecting Dora?"

"Ten."

"Did you lock the house?"

"No."

"So the front door was unlocked?"

"It—it was already locked from the night before."

"What door did Rusty go out?"

"The . . . the . . . um. . . ." Yates's mind searched. "The garage door . . . I . . . think," she stammered.

"You mean the door that lets cars out?"

"It's a doorway . . . yes . . . that goes out to the garage . . . and . . . you have to give him . . . automatic garage door opener."

"So he was going out a regular doorway?"

"Regular doorway . . . where he also had to open . . . garage door."

"Oh. Had the back door been unlocked then?" Dietz was looking for detail and what Yates remembered.

"Probably."

"Did you pull the blinds—"

"No." There were no blinds.

"Or drapes?"

She shook her head.

"Did you take the phone off the hook?"

"No."

"Did you make any other special preparations?"

"I started to draw the water."

"Is there a stopper in the bottom of the tub?"

"Yes."

"How do you activate it?"

"It's a loose one," she said, indicating with her left hand. "It's rubber . . . stopper . . . that you pull out. It was attached to the faucet."

"So you put that in, filled the tub, what temperature were you trying to make it?"

Yates shook her head slightly, indicating that she had no intention regarding water temperature. "It was . . . it was whatever it was set at . . . the cold water."

"It was cold, it wasn't warm?"

"It was cold."

"Was there any reason for that?"

"No."

"What were the children doing while you were filling the tub?"

"They were eating breakfast . . . getting dressed."

Dietz cleared his voice.

"Was the television on—or the radio?"

"No." She was almost inaudible.

"Had you eaten anything?"

"Cereal earlier."

"Anything else to prepare?"

She shook her head and grew somber.

"What were you wearing?"

Her lower lip quivered. "Clothes," she said plainly.

"You'd already gotten dressed for the day?"

Yes, she nodded.

"Had you showered?"

"No."

"Did you usually shower in the morning?"

"Yes."

"Why didn't you that day?"

"I don't know," she shrugged.

"Was that usual for you not to shower?" Deitz asked, trying another route to the matter.

"I might sometimes shower later in the day."

"Had you taken your medication?"

"In the morning time? Yes." She hesitated. "I think I did."

"But you were no longer taking Haldol?"

"Yes."

"And had you been taking all the medicine that had been pre-scribed for the last three weeks?"

"Yes." This is one detail Yates would continue to be adamant about.

"Since you were out of the hospital, you took everything you were supposed to?" Dietz asked again.

"Yes."

"Did you have any additional thoughts that morning that you hadn't had before?"

"No."

"Any thoughts you didn't tell me about?"

Did you know that Walt Disney was an atheist?[9]

"I was just thinking about the children."

Dietz paused in the questioning.

"Do you know if you had any thoughts that morning about a prophecy?"

That's why "magic" is a theme often portrayed in his movies.[10]

Yates shook her head no.

"Were you still thinking about the Seven Deadly Sins?"

Participating in idolatry is prohibited: "the acts of the sinful nature are obvious: sexual immorality, impurity and debauchery, idolatry and witchcraft . . ."[11]

"Yes."

"You used the phrase that you were 'supposed' to do this. What did you mean by that?"

"Well, it needed to be done for the children's sake . . . I felt," she said unsteadily.

---

9. *Letter of A. Yates to author, postmarked January 6, 2003.*
10. *Ibid.*
11. *Ibid.*

"Was there any doubt about that in your mind?"

"No. . . . I didn't think anything about doubt."

"I warn you, as I did before, that those who live like this will not inherit the kingdom of God" (Gal 5: 19–21). For example, allowing children to watch "addictive" Disney videos zillions of times . . .[12]

"How certain were you that it needed to be done?"

"I just thought it needed to be done."

"And the benefits to the children would be what?"

"Eternal life—in heaven."

"Who would pay the cost?"

"Who would *pay*?" she asked, confused.

"I mean, would somebody have to pay a cost for that?"

"You mean my cost?" she asked, gesturing to her chest with her left hand.

The cowardly, the unbelieving, the vile, the murderers, . . . the sexually immoral, those who practice *magic arts* . . . their place will be in the fiery lake of burning sulfur (Rev. 21:8).[13]

"Yes."

"Yes, it would probably cost," she agreed.

"What would that cost be?" Dietz persisted.

"You mean like jail time or . . . punishment?"

"What were you thinking?"

"Probably punishment."

"How did you think you'd be punished?"

"Jail."

"So you thought you'd be arrested and put in jail?"

"Yes."

"Did you think there'd be other punishment for you?"

"I wasn't thinking anything else."

"But you did think it was illegal?"

---

12. *Ibid.*
13. *Ibid.*

"Yes," she answered. After more than four months of practice and legal coaching, she had given the answer most detrimental to herself.

"Did you feel the conflict?" Dietz's throat seemed dry.

"Doing it, not doing it?"

"Yes," Dietz said.

"No," she nodded. "I set it in my mind to do it."

"Was there an earlier time when you thought a conflict about it?"

"Yes."

"What had the conflict been earlier?"

"Same."

"Same as what?"

"Same . . . as when I had a conflict before."

"And what was that? What conflict was that?"

"Doing it . . . or not doing it."

"What were the factors weighing on each side?"

"Well, doing it . . . not doing it . . . you take the risk that Satan would get the kids."

"What about for you?"

"What about for me?" Yates had trouble with this question.

"If you did it or didn't do it, what were you thinking would happen to you?" Dietz asked gently.

"Probably if I did it . . . it'd be . . . I would get in trouble."

"And if you didn't do it?"

"They'd still be with us."

"Who?"

"The children."

"How did you resolve that conflict—"

"Didn't—"

"How did you make up your mind?"

"I just decided that [it] needed to be done."

"Do you know when you made that decision?"

"The night before."

"The night before was when you became certain?"

"Yes," she nodded.

"But you'd been planning for about a week?"

"Yes."

"Or was it a month?"

"A month, yes." A night, a week, a month. Yates agreed with whatever Dietz was saying.

"Do you recall any other thoughts you were having around that time?"

Fourteen seconds passed. "Just . . . just . . . being ready for the drowning."

Dietz didn't pursue the question of readiness. "Were you thinking about being a bad mother?"

"Yes."

"What were you thinking about that?"

"Probably if—if—if they remain here, um, I would have . . . a harder time dealing with them since Satan was involved." On the word "Satan," Yates moved forward and back in her chair.

"Satan was going to make them more disobedient?"

"Yes."

"Is that right?"

"Yes."

"Did you feel that you had damaged the children somehow?"

"Yes," she said more rapidly.

"What was that?"

"I seemed like I might have ruined them . . . to learning new things . . . or their behavior . . . starting to regress . . ."

"So what did you think you had done to ruin them?"

Ten seconds. "Not being a good mother and . . . and . . . and not being affectionate with them or spending time with them. . . ."

"Was there some point at which you thought you had made some of the children retarded?"

Yates scratched her upper lip with her left hand. It was the most rapid movement she had made in the interviews. "I felt like some were expressing it in that way . . . Luke wasn't talking very clearly at that point . . . and the other kids . . . behaviorally . . . were slightly off."

"And you thought that was your fault?" Luke was the baby she had been nursing when she had taken the Trazodone overdose.

"Yes."

"And that it would continue to worsen?"

"Yes."

"Did you think that Satan was doing it?"

"He does tempt people, yes . . ." Seconds passed. "And if you're weak, you can't overcome a temptation." This was perhaps the most enlightening insight into her thought process that Andrea Yates had volunteered in the interviews.

"And you were weak then?"

"Yes."

"Was he tempting you?"

"No."

No? Why no? Dietz reworded. "Did you sense the presence of Satan that morning?"

"Yes."

"How did you experience that?"

"Urging me on."

"How?"

Yates was beginning to space out. "Just helped me set up the tub . . . and getting ready."

"Did you feel encouraged?"

"Yes," she mumbled.

"Did you hear anything encouraging you?"

"No, just thoughts."

"What were those thoughts?"

"Telling me to—to go ahead and do it."

"Anything else?"

"No."

"Tell me what you went ahead and did," Dietz said at 1:18 PM.

"Drowned them . . . I drew the water . . . and Rusty already left for work that day . . . and I went in the bathroom and I sat Mary on the floor . . . and . . . while I was filling the tub . . . Paul came in and he sat on the tub and he said . . . he said . . . , 'Mommy, are we going to take a bath today?' " She used Paul's vocal inflection. "And he asked me, and I didn't answer him—," she continued, crying out the word "him." "And I put him in the water," she said, crying softly, "for a couple minutes . . . and when it was too much . . . I came . . . I took him . . . and took him down on that bed . . . our bed. And I went back in the bathroom and John wanted in." She paused. "So I put him in . . . for a couple minutes. And Luke was close by. . . ." She came to a dead stop. "And I put him in . . . and I moved John on the bed. I put Luke on the bed. And I called for Noah . . . from the kitchen," she continued, her voice rising. "He came to me, and I let him in the bathtub." Now Yates had to think. Something was wrong. "Before . . . before . . . Noah I did Mary. Mary was still in the tub when he came in. And he said 'Mommy, what's wrong with Mary?' " she said, imitating Noah's voice.

"One-oh-nine-three . . . one-oh-nine-three," the voice on the scratchy public address system called.

"So I put him in the tub." Heartbeats passed. "And I called the police . . . to come to the house. And I called Rusty to come home." She stopped, blinking slowly several times.

"You said you read?"

"Sorry?"

"You said that you read?"

"I read?"

"Did you read something to the children?"

"No."

"Did you put Jonathan [*sic*] and Luke in the bed at the same time?"

"Yes."

"Where was John when you were drowning Luke?"

"In the tub."

"So they were both in the tub at the same time? And then the same thing happened with Mary and Noah—"

"Yes."

"They were both in the tub at the same time?"

She nodded.

"Did the children struggle?"

She nodded again.

"Every one of them?"

"Except Mary," Yates gasped, in tears. "And she wasn't strong enough." Tap-tap-tap. Tap-tap. The familiar sound of Yates's sewing machine foot against the interview table had returned. "Noah the most because he was the biggest."

"Did he say anything else to you?"

She stiffened her upper lip, but it was like trying to stop rain. "He came up out of the water and said something," she cried. ". . . That . . . I didn't know what it was, like 'I'm sor'—and I didn't hear the rest. I didn't know if he was saying 'I'm sorry' or what—"

Segment D stopped there.

In the three minutes that intervened between tape Segments D and E, Andrea Yates acquired a tissue. The gallery was still.

"Why did you call the police?" Dietz asked, trying to establish whether she knew she would be arrested and put in jail.

"Because I had to."

"Why?"

"Because of what I did."

"Why was it the police you called?"

"That's who you call."

"When what?"

"When you did something wrong."

"Did you think you'd done something wrong?"

"Yeah," she said sadly, her chin dropping to her chest.

"Before you did it, did you think it would be wrong to do it?"

"Unh-unh." She shook her head no.

"When did you think it was wrong?"

"When I called the police."

"Before you did it, did you think it was the right thing to do?"

"Yes."

"And why is that?"

"It was my feeling that . . . that they . . . wo— would be tormented by Satan if I didn't."

"But if you did, then what?"

"Then they wouldn't be . . . tormented," she said.

"Well, afterwards, why did you think it was wrong?"

She waited. "Because I did what I did."

"But had you done the right thing or the wrong thing?" Dietz persisted.

"I thought that it was the *right* thing," Yates said, blowing her nose in the tissue and seeming as close to frustration as she had the entire interview.

"Well then, what do you mean when you say you'd done something wrong?"

"Killing your *children*." Sniff. Sniff. And then an open stare.

"As you drowned each one, did you think that it was the right thing to be doing?"

She nodded yes, rocking her full body.

"When the police came, do you remember what you told them?"

"When they came, I opened the door, and told them I killed my children. And led them down the hall to where they were."

"The police report indicates that the police asked you if you'd ever tried to kill the children before," Dietz said. "You said you'd been close to it, but stopped, and it [the report] goes on to say about two months ago you filled the bathtub with water and you were going to drown the children, but you didn't carry out the plan. That's a little different from what you told me. You told me you weren't prepared to drown the children that time."

Yates nodded agreement as she listened to Dietz. She agreed with what she'd told him.

"You told me you filled the tub because you saw the water truck. Which of those is correct?"

"I-I-I didn't do it, because I knew they were coming home . . . coming home . . . that time."

"Dora was home," Dietz pointed out.

"Yes." Yates wasn't making sense.

"But were you going to do it then?"

"No."

"And the police wrote that you said that you weren't a good mother to your children and you wanted to be punished, and that you were prepared to go to hell for what you'd done—"

"Yes . . . I told the police off-officer?"

"Yes. Which is what you just mentioned to me."

Yates nodded.

"Why did you think you'd go to hell for it?"

"It was wrong," she replied in a monotone.

"So beforehand, you thought it was a sin to do it," Dietz said. Andrea Yates had just said that *before* she killed the children she thought her actions were right. "And afterwards you thought that what you did was illegal and you needed to call the police. You thought it was wrong and you would go to hell."

She said nothing.

"But at the same time, you're saying that you thought it was a way to save the children's souls . . . from Satan."

To this statement she replied, "Yes."

It was complicated, Dietz thought. What he heard was that Yates knew the drownings were sinful and illegal, but on the other hand, she saved the children from torment and their souls from Satan. She knew she was doing the right thing for the children. Twenty-seven seconds of quiet passed. Even the hallways outside the interview room were silent. Yates said nothing.

"How did you think Rusty would judge this?"

"He'd think it was bad."

"How did you think society would judge it?"

"Bad."

"How did you think God would judge it?"

"Bad."

"Was there some standpoint from which it was good?"

"My thought," she said.

"That it would save the children's souls?"

"Yes."

JOE OWMBY PRESSED Dietz for his opinion on the difference between Andrea Yates's mental state on the day of the crime and the days immediately following the crime, when she was under the care of Ferguson and Osterman.

Dietz described a "dramatic difference." Yates was "grossly psychotic," according to Ferguson and Osterman, when they began treating her, he said. "She is either hearing growls and voices or . . . having what's called an illusion. . . . She talks about a prophecy. She talks about being Satan and Governor [George W.] Bush executing her and a host of other things that are very sick, psychotic thoughts and her memory for that period of time is impaired. . . . When people asked her what she remembers about a prophecy, she's puzzled. . . . We know she was in that state from June 21st. . . . The question is, was she in that state on June 20th when she did these crimes?

"We don't find nearly as much evidence of that kind of extreme sickness or gross psychosis on June 20th as we have for the period beginning June 21st. That's not to say she wasn't sick on June 20th, because she still had the beliefs about the cameras and had recently thought the television was speaking to her."

There was a big window for Parnham and Odom to explore reasonable doubt here. And to challenge Dietz on neglecting to mention effects of sudden withdrawal from medication. They didn't.

So it was the killings themselves that had driven her crazy. On June 21, she was too sick to be sentenced to die for her crimes; twenty-four hours earlier, she was healthy enough to pay with her life. The prosecution cued up forty-three-second-long Segment G.

"At the time, you didn't feel you were struggling against Satan?"

"No."

"You felt he had taken over?"

"He was nearby. Early on, I didn't think he was in me."

"When did you first think he was in you?"

"When I was arrested."

"So you didn't feel that he was in you while you were drowning the children. It was afterwards."

"I felt his presence," she disagreed.

"When?"

"When I was doing it."

"His presence—or that he was in you?" It was like asking how many angels could dance on the head of a pin. But to Dietz, this was the fine point on which Yates's guilt or innocence rested.

"His presence."

Wrong answer.

"Were you able to form an opinion relative to the sanity of Mrs. Yates under the Penal Code, under 8.01, at the time of this offense?" Owmby asked after placing Park Dietz's written summary of his opinions into evidence as State's Exhibit 239.[14]

"I don't offer an opinion on the ultimate issue of sanity, . . . but I do

---

14. *The Harris County District Attorney's Office refused a request to make State's Exhibit 239 available under the Texas Public Information Act, citing possible handwritten notes in the margins relating to confidential aspects of the prosecution's case. The Attorney General of the State of Texas upheld the refusal.*

have opinions on the defendant's knowledge of wrongfulness at the time of the offense. . . . My opinion with reasonable medical certainty is that at the time of the drowning of each of the children, Mrs. Yates knew that her actions were wrong in the eyes of the law . . . in the eyes of society . . . in the eyes of God. . . . Mrs. Yates may have believed the killings were in the best interest of the children and that the ends— saving the chidren—justified the means, which was to wrongly and illegally kill them."

Park Dietz's direct testimony was cut short on Friday, March 8, at lunch hour. Judge Hill released the jurors, instructing them to return the following day at 9:30 AM for an unusual Saturday session. Hill then heard a defense motion to block the showing of a $45,000 animated videotape re-creation of the drownings that the prosecution planned to introduce into evidence. Hill granted the defense's motion. The tape was never shown. Court adjourned at 1:45 PM.

Saturday's cross-examination of Dietz was full of sound and fury, signifying little, or so it seemed that day. But a few words exchanged between Parnham and Dietz would alter lives and linger over the Yates case.

"You are a consultant, are you not, on the television program known as *Law & Order*?" Parnham asked Dietz under oath.

"Two of them," Dietz answered.

"Okay. Did either one of those deal with postpartum depression or women's mental health?"

"As a matter of fact," Dietz said, "there was a show of a woman with postpartum depression who drowned her children in the bathtub and was found insane, and it was aired shortly before this crime occurred."

BY MONDAY, MARCH 11, there had been a sea change. The attorneys on both sides saw the finish line. Speculation had been that the trial would go to the end of the week. Puryear was recalled to rebut Park Dietz.

Andrea Yates's "frontal lobe was impaired to a degree that would make her unable to have abstract thought at that time [June 20]," Puryear said, disagreeing with Dietz's suppositions about what Yates was thinking as she drowned her children. "She wasn't thinking anything," Puryear said flatly. There was plenty of evidence that Yates was psychotic both before and after June 20. Not to mention that, in Puryear's experience, frontal lobe impairment didn't appear—or clear up—overnight.

"Was that itself [saving her children] a delusion?" Parnham asked her.

"Absolutely."

Owmby got straight to the money on his cross-examination of Puryear. "I'm not charging door-to-door," Puryear said, referring to her travel time. She received $250 an hour, less than her out-of-town male counterparts. "So far, I've been paid $7,500." Owmby suggested that Puryear was giving away her services because she was sympathetic to Yates. He asked about her studies treating depressed women with "fish oil."

Puryear explained that although she was studying the effects of omega-3 fatty acids, found in oily fish such as tuna, salmon, herring, and sardines, she did "not recommend it as a sole treatment" for patients with mental illness. An analysis of 11,271 pregnant British women showed that signs of major depression decreased with increased consumption of omega-3 fatty acids during the third trimester of pregnancy. One of the researchers, Dr. Joseph R. Hibbeln, noted that the beneficial results began in the third trimester and continued as long as eight months after childbirth.

Owmby moved from fish oil through "the Woroniecki cult" to *Law & Order*. "You know she watched *Law & Order* a lot, right?"

"No."

Owmby's implication was that if Park Dietz and Rusty Yates knew, how could a thorough expert not know, particularly when the information established motive and premeditation? "Did you know that in the weeks before June 20," Owmby continued, "there was a *Law & Order* episode where a woman killed her children by drowning them in a bathtub, . . . [t]he diagnosis was postpartum depression, . . . the person was found insane, not guilty by reason of insanity."

Puryear acknowledged she hadn't been aware of any possible *Law & Order* connection. For the first time in her testimony, she did not seem in command.

"If you'd known that," Owmby said, ". . . would you have investi-

gated whether she got the idea somehow she could do this and not suffer hell or prison?"

Puryear supposed she would have asked about the show. There was no objection as to relevance from the defense table. Her patience with Owmby's needling seemed to wear thin.

Owmby had a hypothetical for Puryear about her opinion that Yates's motive appeared to be "doing right." What if the defendant's delusion was based on a cultlike teaching she adopted from someone who thought the United States was the Great Satan?

"I have no idea what you're talking about."

"Really?"

"No, I can't follow you."

Owmby tried three more hypotheticals.

"You don't understand mental illness," Puryear finally said impatiently. "Psychosis and delusion is something that is so real it's as real as the fact that the jury is in this courtroom. I'm sitting in this chair, and you are asking the questions. It's crazy to everybody else."

"Believing the United States is the Great Satan isn't crazy?"

"You are taking things out of context and asking me questions that don't make any sense."

"We don't have any other questions for this witness."

Parnham appeared for damage control. "Dr. Puryear, I have one last question and . . . you've testified about your standing in the medical community. And you're up there at the top, aren't you?"

Puryear did not answer the question. Parnham withdrew the question.

The defense rested.

ON TUESDAY, MARCH 12, after having heard more than three weeks of testimony from more than forty witnesses and viewing more than three hundred exhibits, the jury heard nearly two hours of final arguments. Owmby began at 9:34 AM with an eleven-minute reminder to the jury of Texas Penal Code section 801, governing severe mental defect. The state must prove beyond a reasonable doubt—not beyond all possible doubt—that Andrea Yates had known what she did was wrong. He refreshed jurors' memories about the McNaughton rule. "The standard is strict for a reason." He appreciated the opportunity to prosecute the deaths of John, Noah, and Mary Yates for the State of Texas.

Wendell Odom spent nearly half an hour recapping the testimony of witnesses. "I know you are restless and moving around," he told jurors, "and I know you're tired of hearing me talking. But I have a confession to make. I'm scared to death right now. I'm more scared than I've ever been in a courtroom. I don't know if what I know is in evidence. I just don't know, and that scares me . . . because there might be a wrong result. How many times are we going to say that this is just mental illness . . . stick our heads in the sand? All I ask you to do is use your common sense." What Odom was really asking for was jury nullification. That jurors vote with their conscience, not necessarily with the law. All he needed was one vote, one person who thought as he did, to hang the jury.

Parnham continued the defense's final argument by telling the jury that he and Owmby agreed on one thing: "This about prevention . . . the world is watching. Please, please do not allow that horrific set of circumstances—and the deaths of Noah, John, Paul, Luke, and precious Mary—take your eye off the . . . issue that you must come to grips with—mental illness. . . . If this woman doesn't meet the test of insanity in this state, then nobody does. Zero."

Kaylynn Williford had the penultimate word. "According to Dora Yates and according to Rusty Yates 'she was getting better.'" For two years, Andrea had been harboring the idea, Williford said. She made the choice the night before. "Mary was the easiest. This is where, ladies and gentlemen, I want you to look at the loving act of a mother. She picks up the phone and calls 911. 'I need the police.' She doesn't disclose that she has just saved her children and that the 'great Satan' is in her. She says to the policeman, 'I killed my kids.' . . . How do you punish someone for having to live in a bus? . . . Each of these children fought and struggled for their lives. They did not want to die. Andrea Yates took that control over her life that day. She . . . wasn't doing this . . . except for a motivation that only she knows. . . . Andrea Yates is responsible. She knew it was wrong in the eyes of God, wrong in the eyes of the law. Do what is right. Look at the evidence. Don't be confused." The mom with two young children of her own demonstrated a precision unequaled by her three fellow attorneys.

Owmby spoke last, filling out the nearly one hour of the state's closing arguments. "There is no women's mental health, there is no men's mental health," he said. "There is the treatment of people who have mental illness. Men who kidnap children and hold them hostage deserve the same treatment as a woman who drowns children in a bathtub." After invoking Dietz's opinion that "at the time of drowning of each child, Andrea Yates knew it was wrong." Owmby talked about motive. "Everything still seems to be reasonable until Russell Yates introduces these concepts of religion from Michael Woroniecki." He reminded the jury that according to one social worker, Rusty Yates was critical of his wife, said hurtful things, and that the perfect mother thinks that if she weren't perfect he'd leave. He scored points but didn't leave well enough alone. "She watches *Law & Order* regularly, she sees this program," he explained, "there is a way out. . . . The only time Andrea Yates gets attention is when she's in a hospital. She leaves those children for him to see. . . . She takes not just her children, they belong to us. Every time you see a child laugh, it will stab your heart, because you'll remember this trial."

It was 11:40 AM. Rusty Yates, wearing an orange plaid, button-down shirt, had been allowed into the courtroom for final arguments. He sat next to his mother. Color rose in his face as he rocked. The cruelest thing he had ever personally witnessed was his wife being forced to listen to those closing arguments, he said. After only a few minutes, he'd stopped trying to count the lies. Following an hour-long lunch recess, the jury began deliberations.

No one imagined that a verdict would be returned in less than three and a half hours—not even half the time it had taken the previous jury to find Andrea Yates competent to stand trial. The only testimony the jurors requested for review during their deliberation was one large-print poster of the Texas insanity statute and a tape recorder to play Yates's confession and 911 tapes.

At 4:59 PM, Andrea Yates, wearing a gray blouse and white cardigan, entered the courtroom with Parnham trailing close behind. As Judge Hill silently scanned the verdict, Yates stood with Odom at her left, hands clasped behind his back. Parnham stood to her right and wrapped a protective arm around her waist. Many rows back, Rusty Yates sat with his elbows on his knees, his face turned toward the floor.

Judge Hill read the verdict aloud. "We the jury find the defendant,

Andrea Pia Yates, guilty of capital murder as charged in the indictment."

Odom rocked slightly on his feet; Parnham looked down. Andrea
Yates lifted her face to Odom. Rusty Yates hung his head between his
legs and sobbed. As Andrea Yates was led away, her eyes searched for
her mother.

The speed of the jury's verdict suggested that the death penalty was
not far behind.

JUST AFTER EIGHT on the night of the guilty verdict, my cell phone
rang. It was Rusty Yates calling from George Parnham's office. The
lawyer wanted to speak to me. He sounded desperate. It was about
Law & Order.

Since March 9, when Park Dietz testified about a *Law & Order*
episode and Joe Owmby began to spin a theory that Andrea Yates had
found a blueprint for escaping a bad marriage and tiresome kids by
watching her favorite television show, I'd been curious about the accu-
racy of Dietz's testimony. That *Law & Order* was Yates's favorite program was certainly true. Rusty Yates had told me so (and Andrea later
confirmed the fact herself). But it was doubtful that there had ever
been an episode in which a mother drowned her children, claimed
postpartum depression, and was acquitted, as Dietz testified. I didn't
believe such an episode existed.

I had greeted Dietz outside the courtroom before he testified. I
had written scripts for *Law & Order.* Dietz was a technical adviser to
the show and I'd consulted with him myself on one episode I wrote.
Writers treasured him for his grasp of medicine and the law and for
having enough imagination not to constrain their ripped-from-the-
headlines dramas with stultifying real-world limitations. *Law & Order*
was closing in on *Gunsmoke* as the longest-running dramatic series in
television history. Its sister shows, *Special Victim's Unit* and *Criminal
Intent,* were also network staples. Dietz had worked with writers on
hundreds of plots; it wasn't unthinkable he'd made a mistake. I telephoned the show's creator, Dick Wolf. He confirmed what I suspected.
Such an episode was "never written, never produced, and certainly
never aired," he said.

At the time I confirmed the mistestimony, I was covering the Yates trial for executive producer David Corvo of *Dateline NBC. Dateline's* format didn't lend itself to the Dietz story, but Corvo passed the Dietz information along to the *Today* show and *Nightly News with Tom Brokaw.* When NBC passed, I suggested the story to colleagues at other networks and finally to *New York Post* stringer Steven Long, who had been covering the trial.

Long interviewed Dick Wolf by phone and dictated the story to the *Post's* rewrite desk, hoping his scoop would run the following day, Saturday, March 9, 2002, the day Dietz was cross-examined. "They [the rewrite desk] barely acknowledged what I was telling them," Long recalled. "It seemed to go over their heads at the time, as if they didn't watch TV." The story never ran—anywhere.

The prosecution's key witness had erred in his testimony. Not only had the jury heard false testimony from Dietz on direct questioning but Owmby had used the testimony to impugn key defense expert Lucy Puryear and again in his closing arguments to drive home his theory of motive. Earlier that day, awaiting the verdict outside the courtroom, Rusty Yates heard me talking through notes for a *Salon.com* article. How could a mistake of such magnitude go uncorrected? Whatever I thought of Andrea Yates's guilt or innocence, fiction had been made fact in a court of law. Dietz's mistestimony was not simply a curious intersection of television and the law, it was grounds for a mistrial.

That was why George Parnham had called. It was a matter of life and death, he said. He had tried unsuccessfully to get through to Dick Wolf and NBC. He said he needed a witness to testify to the nonexistence of the episode in the penalty phase of the trial, when jurors would determine Andrea Yates's sentence. Did I know a *Law & Order* actor who might fly to Houston and testify the following day? I told Parnham an actor would be legally useless to him, but that I thought Dick Wolf would do the right thing.

I put Parnham in touch with Wolf, who initially planned to fly to Houston and testify Thursday morning, March 14. That morning before court, Parnham called me frantically. Did I know where Wolf was? I didn't. Next, Wolf called me to say his and USA Studios' attorneys had decided to resolve the matter directly with Dietz, Parnham, Odom,

Owmby, and Williford. Court began that morning with extensive side-
bars and whisperings regarding the missing witness.

Eleven other witnesses were called by the defense to plead for Andrea Yates's life: Joe Lovelace (of the National Alliance for the Mentally
Ill), Molly Maguire-Stefano, Robert Holmes, Debbie Holmes, Marlene
Burda Wark, Patrick Kennedy, Rusty Yates, Reverend Fairy Caroland,
Dora Yates, Dr. Lucy Puryear, and Andrea's mother, Mrs. Kennedy,
who said, "I'm here pleading for her life. I've lost seven people in one
year." The emotional wear and tear showed on Parnham. The prosecution called no witnesses.

When court resumed Friday morning, March 15, 2002, at 9:53, just
prior to seating the jury, there was a dramatic turn-around for Parnham, who made an oral motion for a mistrial. He revealed the identity
of the mystery witness. He said that in lieu of Mr. Wolf's testimony, at
7:00 the previous night, attorneys for USA Studios completed research
of their *Law & Order* archives and determined that "Dr. Dietz was
mistaken" in his testimony. There had been no episode of *Law & Order*
similar to the Yates crime. Parnham and Owmby met and agreed that
Owmby had innocently relied on the evidence of his chief expert, who
had given testimony that was inaccurate.

"We ask the Court to consider a motion for mistrial," Parnham told
Judge Hill. His grounds were "false evidence." He further requested a
mistrial of the verdict and punishment. "There was no testimony in the
course of this case concerning an objective blueprint for a plan to be
tried and acquitted . . . other than the testimony about the *Law &
Order* episode," Parnham said. "We do not believe . . . the jury can, at
this point, segregate what they already know," Odom added. "Harm has
already been done."

Judge Hill disagreed. She denied the motions, but directed that
Parnham present a stipulation to the jury. The stipulation revoked
Dietz's earlier testimony and added new testimony to the record that
"no episode of *Law & Order* and/or *Law & Order: Criminal Intent*
as described . . . was ever produced for the *Law & Order* television
series."

(After the trial, when the focus of my *Dateline* coverage turned
away from the attorneys and toward the jury's deliberation, I apologized to Owmby for not conducting the interview with him I had

planned. "That's okay," he said. "I've made a big enough fool of myself in public for one week.")

At 10:33 AM Judge Hill charged the jury in the penalty phase of the trial. There were only two choices: death by lethal injection or confinement in the Texas Department of Criminal Justice for life (forty years of actual time served). The jury, she said, should base its decision on whether the defendant's background and character mitigated against death, as well as on the likelihood of her future dangerousness.

Odom argued that Yates was only a threat if she had more chidren. She could not get pregnant in a prison setting, he said, and would be almost 77, well beyond her childbearing years, when eligible for release.

Parnham hammered at the false testimony. "Didn't happen, guys," he told jurors. "That show never existed. Our chief witness, Dr. Lucy Puryear when asked, 'You know she watched *Law & Order* a lot, right? If you had known that . . . would that have changed the way you went about interviewing her?'" Parnham shook his head. There was no evidence that there was an "objective reality" (i.e., premeditation) other than the falsely presented *Law & Order* evidence. The jury softened perceptibly. Parnham closed with a paraphrase from John Donne's "Devotions upon Emergent Occasions": "The life, or death, of any man diminishes me for I am a part of mankind, therefore never seek to know for whom the bell tolls; it tolls for me. It tolls for all of us. For we are a part of this system, and we are a part of mankind. Just take that back to the jury room with you. I want her to live. Thanks."

ANDREA YATES MADE choices, ADA Williford told the jurors. Wrong choices. "I want you to take one piece of evidence back with you," she said, "take State's Exhibit 242 [a poster of the five children]. . . . This crime is a crime of ultimate betrayal," she concluded. Andrea Yates was a mother who killed her children and deserved to pay the ultimate price: death.

Owmby wavered. He assured the jury they'd be doing the right thing voting *either* way. Superficially, his remarks seemed an odd turn. Harris County prosecutors are among the most aggressive in the country. District Attorney Chuck Rosenthal had been emphatic about pursuing the death penalty in the Yates case from the outset, brushing away criticism of how he'd charged the crime. But did Owmby realize a life sentence could be better for the State? He was an experienced prosecutor who'd made a big mistake. If the jury sentenced Yates to death, his big mistake might assure her a successful appeal; the State would be back at square one. "I wasn't thinking that way," Owmby said later. "I did not think at that point that the Dietz issue was a significant appellate issue. By that time the jury knew what had happened in a general way. There may have been higher scrutiny if it had been the death penalty, but I wasn't thinking that way."

At 1:40 PM, after a thirty-five-minute deliberation, the jury returned a verdict that Andrea Yates was not a future threat to society, thereby recommending a life sentence. Yates smiled weakly at her attorneys, but to this day is confused about how and why her life was spared. Shielded from news and public contact, she knew little, if anything, about the intense scrutiny her family endured. Relief preceded grief for Yates, her husband, and their families. Two days earlier, Rusty Yates had been prepared for only one verdict: not guilty by reason of insanity. Like his wife, he'd been insulated, but in a different way. Judge Hill had not allowed him to sit through the trial. Thus, he knew little more than did the general public about what took place in court each day. He was dead certain that American justice would triumph; his wife wouldn't be jailed or executed but would receive years of mandated psychiatric care under the court's supervision. By March 15, life in prison seemed like a prize. Judge Hill thanked and released the jurors, and adjourned the court. George Parnham found me in the corridor outside. "You saved her life," he said.

> What have you heard about Dr. Park Dietz's claim that I got my idea for my crime on an episode about a woman who took the life of her child after she gave birth to it (or some months later)?[15]

A press conference took place on the Preston Street side of the courthouse. District Attorney Chuck Rosenthal spoke, as well as ADAs Owmby and Williford, Rusty Yates, Parnham, and Odom. With the

---

15. *Letter of A. Yates to author, postmarked January 6, 2003.*

automatic expiration of Judge Hill's gag order (retroactively determined by Special Prosecutor Mac Secrest to be unconstitutional), sources close to the case were finally free to end the embargo on information that flowed to the public about Andrea Yates. At Total Video, one of Houston's full-service remote television facilities, news agencies lined up for their piece of time with each of the principals.

On Sunday night, Rusty Yates and his family were bundled off to New York City on a chartered jet and ensconced in suites at the Stanhope Park Hyatt Hotel on Fifth Avenue, just opposite Central Park and the Metropolitan Museum of Art. Katie Couric's staff had won the war for Yates's first posttrial interview. They narrowly beat out ABC's Diane Sawyer. Rusty and his mother and brother Randy Yates as well as his aunts Kathy Crisp and Reverend Fairy Caroland appeared live on NBC's *Today* show for much of its first two hours, 7–9:00 AM Eastern Standard Time, Monday morning, March 18, 2002. Their scheduled appearance was promoted heavily during the weekend. At the same time, an interview of Mrs. Kennedy and some of Andrea's siblings—prerecorded in Houston with reporter Cynthia Hunt of the ABC affiliate KTRK-Channel 13—appeared on *Good Morning America.*

"With no family members or national media present," reporter Carol Christian of the *Houston Chronicle* wrote, "Andrea Pia Yates stood before a judge who officially sentenced her to life in prison Monday. In an anticlimactic finish to her monthlong trial, Yates glanced at the gallery, but her only close supporters were her jail psychiatrists, Drs. Debra Osterman and Melissa Ferguson, in the back row."

An unfortunate story appeared in the *Wall Street Journal* under the byline of Daniel Henninger on March 22, 2002.

> Once you've seen and listened to Rusty Yates on TV's talk shows, it's not hard to see why so many women want to lynch him. This column was going to comment on the social and psychiatric issues raised by the Yates case and guilty verdict. But the case itself—with its arguments over psychosis and major depression—seems intellectually austere compared with trying to explain the psychopathologies of American television. . . . Earlier that same day in Houston, a judge sentenced Andrea to life in prison. Rusty was on Larry King. The disjunction—Andrea hearing she was going away forever, her husband

talking with Larry—was hard to process. There was more. About an hour later, another cable wave rolled in, offering a replay of Rusty being interviewed by Katie Couric. But wait, isn't Katie Couric on in the morning? Wasn't Rusty's wife in Houston, being formally sentenced to life about when Katie Couric had him talking in New York about his support and love for Andrea? . . . There are moments—and watching Rusty, Larry and Katie was one of them—when one wants to go out to the street, stare up at the stars in the dark sky and admit, I don't get it anymore. It's also getting hard to know who to get mad at first.

It was possible to blame the family of Andrea Yates for some things, but not for speaking out on its first legal occasion to do so in nine months. Both the Yates and Kennedy families had been with Andrea in court every day.

"At 9:10 AM all parties announced ready, the court proceeds with sentencing of the said defendant, Andrea Pia Yates," Court Reporter Jennifer Slessinger typed into her steno machine on Monday, March 18, 2002. "The jury having returned the answer of 'no' as to Special Issue No. 1, you are hereby sentenced to life in TDCJ-ID [Texas Department of Criminal Justice–Institutional Division]," Judge Hill said. "Good luck to you, Mrs. Yates."

CHAPTER 14

Slow Guilty

From the moment Judge Hill released the jury from service on Friday, Mike Kosner, Sarah Longden, Robin Oelkers, and on-air reporter Dawn Fratangello worked at warp speed on a *Dateline NBC* segment focused on the Yates jurors. The piece would air in little more than forty-eight hours. By 7:35 PM Saturday, cameras were rolling on four jurors in a darkened banquet room in the Renaissance Houston Hotel at Greenway Plaza, next door to the Houston Rockets' home basketball court at the Compaq Center.

Melissa Ryan, Erlinda Bernal, Jill Swinney, and Roy Jordan had been sequestered at the Double Tree Hotel at 400 Dallas with eleven other jurors and alternates (who were excused before deliberations) throughout the trial—twenty-eight days out of their lives. With the maximum news saturation the Yates case received, there was little news they could watch or read, and they weren't supposed to discuss the case among themselves. How had total strangers passed their time together? They watched movies like *Shrek* on Pay Per View. The jury police nixed *K-Pax* halfway through, when the word "Haldol" was mentioned. Roy Jordan, a former Air Force recruiting officer, had brought along a number of DVDs, including *The Matrix; O Brother, Where Art Thou;* and *Seven.* All three were taken away for being referenced at trial: *O Brother, Where Art Thou* because of a Satanic character and "hounds from hell" described by Andrea Yates; *Seven* because of its Seven Deadly Sins. About *The Matrix,* Ryan said none of the jurors could remember why.

The Matrix was one of Rusty Yates's favorite recent movies. The matrix is a computer-generated dream world, built to distract human beings as they are changed into the equivalent of computer batteries. The few rebels who escape are waiting for the Second Coming—a savior. Near the end of the film, the hero, Mr. Anderson (aka Neo), played by Keanu Reeves, lies spread-eagled on subway tracks before an oncoming train. "Hear that, Mr. Anderson?" the indestructible villain Agent Smith yells. "That is *the sound of inevitability.* That is the sound of your death." *The sound of inevitability* was a crowd-pleaser and became a running gag in the Yates household. The older boys learned the phrase, and soon it described everything from an undeniable bedtime to the thud of their father's footsteps before an inescapable tickling. Andrea Yates, too, spoke of *the sound of inevitability* to jail psychiatrists after she murdered her children. No one understood the symbolism except Rusty. Quarantined outside the courtroom, he had no idea his wife had mentioned the phrase to jail doctors until I asked him months later. By then, the phrase had been drained of humor.

"WE JUST MADE the right decision," social worker Jill Swinney said in the *Dateline* piece. "It was an emotional final vote. We knew what we had to do." Her fellow jurors agreed. It had been fairly simple. "There's no doubt in anyone's mind she was mentally ill," Swinney explained, "but that wasn't the question asked us. Did she know right from wrong? That was the only thing we talked about in deliberation. . . . That confession tape to Officer Mehl was crucial."

And so it was. Andrea Yates's confession on June 20, 2001, had legally determined her fate. Parnham and Odom understood that their client had made a routine statement to police when she was arrested. That wasn't unusual. Two weeks later, after several requests, the DA's office provided them with a copy to which they listened carefully. "That was when we went, Oh, shit," Odom remembered. "It wasn't so much the statement as the voice, what was said, and how it was said."

Through nearly nine months of reporting the Yates case, I remained certain the verdict would be guilty. In Texas there is another expression for the insanity defense: "the slow guilty plea."

Two people I sought opinions from were seasoned veterans of

Texas justice. One was a hardworking Dallas civil attorney, Edward Brandt III, who had offices in a Dallas shopping mall and never made headlines. The second was headline-maker Burl Osborne, Chairman of the Board of the Associated Press and publisher emeritus of the *Dallas Morning News*. Insanity defenses, as a matter of record, do not fly in Texas, they agreed. Life was the bone of mercy that might be thrown to Andrea Yates in view of what had shaped up to be a well-documented and nasty case of mental illness.

After courtroom exposure to Yates's medical history, the press corps listed toward sparing Yates to a lifetime of judicial supervision in a mental health facility. But the jury was powerless to select that fate for Yates, or to be informed that it was an option. A Texas judge automatically imposes it, but only after a jury first finds that by the "greater weight of believable evidence" that the defendant should be acquitted. Unlike many states, Texas has no "lack of common knowledge" clause in its penal code requiring a judge to charge the jury that, if a not guilty verdict is reached, hearings regarding the defendant's present mental condition will automatically be held and involuntary commitment to a state psychiatric facility will be imposed by the presiding judge, who remains in charge of the defendant's freedom for the rest of the defendant's natural life.[1]

Owmby believed jurors knew better. "I don't think anybody in today's world believes that that person is going to walk out of that courtroom. . . . I just cannot see you getting twelve reasonably intelligent people to believe that a guy, that they found doesn't know the difference between right and wrong and has killed someone, is going to walk out of that courtroom unsupervised unless they find him guilty." Owmby raised a prickly question. How much do you tell a jury? "Do you allow me, as a prosecutor, to argue that unless you find this person guilty they may be out on the street in ninety days? This sword cuts both ways."

Jurors in Andrea Yates's capital murder trial had taken less than half the time to find her guilty than a jury (of eleven women and one man) had taken to find her competent to stand trial the previous September. The jury in the competency hearing spent eight and a half hours in

---

1. For example, *New York Criminal Procedure Law*, Article 300.10.

what is generally a rubber stamp procedure. "If you can walk, you're competent," one court watcher told me, describing Texas competency hearings. When the competency jurors delivered their verdict, some were visibly shaken. The initial jury poll, reported for the first time here, was eight for incompetence, four for competence. Over the course of deliberations, the vote became unanimous for competence.

What was the clear difference between the two juries? The jury that delivered the guilty verdict was death-qualified; all prospects unwilling to impose the death penalty are automatically eliminated in a Texas capital murder case, substantially skewing the jury toward conviction and away from a "not guilty by reason of insanity" verdict, according to some legal experts.

In 1968, Harvard University law professor Alan M. Dershowitz brought to the U.S. Supreme Court a California murder case that addressed the imbalance he believed was inherent in death-qualified juries. He told *Houston Chronicle* columnist Thom Marshall, "The high court granted review, but then decided to duck this issue, leaving it for another day." Today, Dershowitz believes that Yates's defense attorneys should make the death penalty jury-selection tactic part of Yates's appeal. "Perhaps the courts finally will declare this practice unethical, even unconstitutional," he has said.

Shortly after Andrea Yates began making world headlines, Marshall asked a DA from another Texas jurisdiction whether he would have pursued the death penalty in the case. "No," the DA told him, "without hesitation or qualification." The exchange highlighted the disparity of justice meted out between jurisdictions, particularly in cases of mental illness. Had Yates received less media attention or committed her sensational crime in another jurisdiction, she might be in a mental health facility today instead of prison.

IN A TEXAS capital murder case there are two choices of punishment: death by lethal injection or life in prison. Effectively, juries make up their minds on the punishment at the time they render a guilty verdict, according to noted Houston criminal defense attorney Dick DeGuerin. In 2003, DeGuerin successfully represented New York real estate scion Robert Durst in the 2001 death and dismemberment of Morris Black in Galveston, Texas. The jurors answer the questions put to them by Texas law: Did a preponderance of the evidence show that Andrea Yates knew the nature and quality of her act when she drowned her children, and did she know it was wrong?

The first vote the Yates jurors took among themselves was anonymous. The tally was 10–2: guilty. Roy Jordan was surprised. "I was thinking I might be the only one to say guilty," he recalled. After some discussion, the guilty vote grew to 11–1. Juror Ronald Jones was the lone holdout. His discomfort with the guilty verdict increased over time, particularly around the issue of Park Dietz's false testimony. After the trial, Jones was still so troubled that he wrote to Judge Hill about his misgivings.

Jurors were "shocked and confused" over Park Dietz's testimony regarding *Law & Order,* according to Swinney. Swinney had believed the prosecution's blueprint for crime theory. "I thought it [the *Law & Order* episode] had to be more than a coincidence," she explained. "It *was* shocking," Ryan agreed. "False evidence may well be the grounds for appeal," she said. Jordan, too, thought an appeal was inevitable. In the highly charged politics of Houston's District Attorney's office, and despite Dietz's assertion that the error was an innocent mistake, it wasn't unthinkable that the errant evidence might also become grounds for a grand jury investigation. In fact, in September 2003, a Harris County grand jury reviewed the matter and ultimately declined to indict Dietz in connection with his mistaken statements about *Law & Order.*

The jurors also agreed that Yates could have had better doctors. "The last doctor that she saw, some people blame more," said juror Erlinda Bernal, an air-conditioning technician. The jurors all felt Yates should never have been released from the hospital. Because she committed the crimes in such a brief window of time, they agreed there had been some premeditation. However, they also agreed that she would never have committed the crimes if she hadn't been mentally ill. "The medical community has to take a hard look at itself," Jordan emphasized. But malpractice, or poor practice, was not the issue before these citizens. "I feel bad for her, I do," Swinney said. "But she still knew it was wrong."

Was it a revenge killing? The jurors hadn't thought so. "They [the prosecution] tried to give us a motive," Jordan said, "but we don't know what her real motive is."

"There's more to her motives than what we saw," Swinney agreed.

"Yes, I thought, 'a way out' had a lot to do with it. . . . There has to be more there."

> I guess it bothered me the jury didn't think I was mentally ill and I was offended they thought there was a "hidden motive." But it was . . . a terrible case and I am grateful the jury didn't give me the death penalty.[2]

ON APRIL 3, 2002, George Parnham and Wendell Odom filed a one-page Notice of Appeal of Andrea Pia Yates's "conviction and sentencing March 18, 2002, for the offense of Capital Murder."

Although seeking an appeal was an obvious source of redress for the Dietz error and pro-prosecution jury, the big question wasn't justice. It was money—a real-life barricade that characters in television dramas seldom experience. No appeal, criminal or civil, can be filed without a printed transcript of the complete court proceeding, an expense that can be prohibitive, if not punitive. The transcript of the Yates trial was twelve thousand pages long; to get a copy, one had to pay $60,000 (eventually reduced to $49,000) to the court reporter attached to Judge Hill, Jennifer Slessinger. The men and women, like Slessinger, who dutifully record every word of every trial on their stenotype machines are civil servants on the public payroll. However, they are not required to produce electronic or printed copies of trial transcripts without being paid privately or, in the case of a prosecution appeal or a defendant's indigence, by more public funds. In other words, they moonlight, selling a product the public has paid them to *type* but not to produce. Seen in this light, Court TV's long fight for cameras in courtrooms, with instantaneous electronic transcriptions, seems an inalienable right.

In every trial I've covered, it was possible to order pages of a transcript from a court stenographer and receive them in a matter of days. With Slessinger, over the course of the trial, I ordered copies at her price of $5 per page (higher than stenographers' prices in Westchester,

---

2. *Letter of A. Yates to author, September 12, 2003.*

New York, for example) no fewer than five times—in person, in writing, and over the telephone. I brought the difficulty to the attention of Judge Hill, her court coordinator, and the Harris County communication coordinator. Though Slessinger finally promised to fill my request on one occasion, I never received a page of transcript.

During the same time period, she produced, at the request of the District Attorney's office, transcribed testimony of John Bayliss, RN, Dr. Phillip Resnick, Dr. Eileen Starbranch, Dr. Mohammad Saeed, Russell Yates, Dr. Gerald Harris, Dr. Steven Rubenzer, and Officers Frank Stumpo, Robert King, and Eric Mehl. According to documents obtained under the Texas Public Information Act on July 25, 2003, Slessinger billed and received $4,800.80 beyond her base pay for the services.

Harris County seems to have singular difficulties with producing trial transcripts. In a recent bribery and conspiracy trial (the VitaPro case) of former State Prison Director Andy Collins and Canadian businessman Yank Barry, a court-ordered reconstruction of 950 pages of transcript contained, again according to columnist Thom Marshall, "393 words or phrases inaccurately transcribed, 42 inaccurate dollar amounts, names and numbers; 334 omissions of parts of trial events, and 29 incorrect attributions of statements made by the trial judge, attorneys or witnesses."[3]

Equally daunting was the record of the Court of Criminal Appeals —once an august body respected for its intellectual honesty but now an embarrassment—to which Andrea Yates would ultimately apply if her appeal were granted or denied by the First Court of Appeals. Marshall spoke for many citizens when he wrote:

> This is the same body that saw no problem with a dozing defense lawyer in one case you might recall. It is the same body that remained unswayed even after DNA results cleared a man in another case.
>
> And it is the same body that has not acted on an appeal filed six months ago for a man caught up in a bogus drug case in Dallas, even

---

3. *Thom Marshall*, Houston Chronicle, *October 2, 2002.*

though the prosecutor agrees the conviction should be overturned and dismissed.

The outcome of her [Andrea Yates's] appeal may not make much difference to Andrea Yates. But it might make a lot of difference to the rest of us.[4]

It is little wonder Andrea Yates's family came to regard the price of a transcript as a sledgehammer wielded by the Court against their appeal. The transcript remained unavailable a year and a half after the trial ended. In early October 2002, Rusty Yates paid Slessinger $15,000 toward the transcript. Another $15,000 was paid anonymously. I learned that the anonymous donors were Debbie and Robert Holmes, who have since been repaid $10,000 by Andrea's mother. The final payment to Slessinger was made in April 2003 by George Parnham himself, who advanced the money against Andrea Yates's M. D. Anderson Pension Fund, valued at $19,000 (after early withdrawal penalties). He, too, was repaid.

With Slessinger's bill satisfied, the First Court of Appeals ordered her to produce and file the transcript by June 10, 2003, with no further extensions. Even so, on June 6, Slessinger applied for another extension. Her motion had neither been granted nor denied four weeks later. Finally, on July 10, the First Court of Appeals issued its unpublished Order: "The motion for extension of time to file the reporter's record is *denied*. Unless the reporter's record is filed on or before August 10, 2003, the Court will take appropriate action which may include the initiation of contempt proceedings against the court reporter. It is so ORDERED."

Though the Court had ordered no further extensions after June 10, on August 12 the First Court of Appeals informally allowed Slessinger ten more days to comply because of computer-related difficulties. August 22 came and went—no transcript. On September 10, I followed up on a Texas Public Information Act request with Ted Cruz, Solicitor General of Texas, regarding the lack of commercial availability of the Yates trial transcript. The next day, Slessinger emailed me that the tran-

---

4. *Ibid.*

script was available for sale at a dollar per page. The transcript was filed with the First Court of Appeals on September 11. Odom had thirty days to write the appeal—the clock began ticking on the filing date. Parnham and Odom, who had ordered the document, learned it was complete on September 13, when I told them. They received their copy later the next week. They requested and received additional time to file their brief because of the size of the transcript. On October 3, an electronic copy of the transcript was advertised for sale on Ebay. Asking price: $3,500.

CHAPTER 15

Heartbreakers

I drove out to Dr. Mohammad Saeed's office in Dickinson, Texas, on August 2, 2002. He wasn't expected until 3:30 PM, but his assistant gave me directions to 305 Pine Drive. The directions were to take Exit 19 (Farm Road 517E) off I-45 South. It was the Heartbreakers strip club exit. Behind the billboard advertising Heartbreakers was another equally large but taller billboard that read "Jesus Heals the Brokenhearted."

> I think I know what it's like for a heart to break. But alas, "The Lord heals the broken hearted." (Ps. 147:3)[1]

People who haven't traveled Texas by car seldom realize its size: it is bigger than the next four largest states (excluding Alaska) combined. With few exceptions, the highways are excellent, often lined with scrub oaks that seem forever stuck at twenty feet tall and at intervals gas and food stops or strip malls. Hundred-foot-tall poles advertising Whataburger, Taco Bell, KFC, Exxon, Conoco, Pizza Hut, Wal-Mart, Home Depot, Shell, Hobby Lobby, Garden Ridge, Bally Total Fitness, Holiday Inn, Motel 6, Super 8, Best Western, XXX Men's Club, Brake Check rise like blimps in the 360-degree Texas sky. Mobile homes, prefab homes, RV sales sites, and fireworks stands ("Buy one get five free—open all year") sometimes alternate with grazing cattle, fields of

---

1. *Letter of A. Yates to author, received July 13, 2003.*

baled hay, and cell phone towers three Olympic-size swimming-pool lengths in height. Churches, RV parks, and pawn shops are ubiquitous. In downtown Houston, premier Phillip Johnson skyscrapers tower above Dubuffet sculptures lolling on street corners. The symphony, theater, museums, Angelika Film Center, Houston Ballet, and the opera are top-notch. Increasingly, Houstonians are drawn to live in the converted downtown lofts of their city's cultural mecca. The line between upscale and down is hazy almost anywhere you go.

After a left turn at the Heartbreakers underpass, I made another quick left into a parking lot behind a cigar and liquor store and an Enterprise Car Rental outlet, looking for Dickinson Medical Clinic. There it was. A low, white, single-level section of strip mall. Strip-mall medicine. Along with urban medical centers—and downtown Houston has the world's largest—it wasn't unusual.

I pulled into a parking spot and entered from the sidewalk through the glass door marked 305 into an anteroom with three reception areas. Saeed's was the most prominent. There was a hand-lettered sign above a picture window on the partition that enclosed his waiting room. The sign requested that the privacy of patients be respected—that only patients, and those escorting them, enter the door to the waiting area. Strange privacy, as the sign announced to passersby that the people who could readily be viewed through the picture windows were indeed patients and their escorts. This day, privacy wasn't an issue. Both the anteroom and the waiting room were empty.

I asked the bearded, bespectacled older gentleman inside about seeing Dr. Saeed.

"I'm the one who just called on the phone," I said. "I'm interested in possibly seeing the doctor. May I have a card?"

He handed me one. "Dr. Saeed isn't in today until 3:30 PM. You'll have to wait and just see if he can fit you in. What's your name?" he asked, sizing me up.

"Suzanne," I said. "How many people would I have to wait for?" The man counted nine names on a yellow legal pad list.

"What's the earliest day he can fit me in?" I asked. The receptionist flipped through the pages of the appointment book. I saw that most patients were scheduled at fifteen-minute intervals from 3:30 to 6:30 PM. A few were scheduled at thirty-minute intervals.

"I could fit you in Monday or Tuesday, if you're willing to wait a little while for the doctor to see you."

"How long will it take—how long will the doctor spend with me?" I asked.

"I don't know," the receptionist replied. "The first time, maybe forty-five minutes, maybe an hour, maybe more."

"I'm not really sure I want to do it yet," I said.

"You have to make up your mind," he answered.

He asked whether Monday or Tuesday was better. I told him I'd be on vacation that week. That I wanted to think about seeing the doctor and I'd call when I got back.

"Make up your mind," he said again, not pleasantly.

"By the way," I asked as an afterthought, "how much is it?"

"One hundred fifty dollars for the first visit. A hundred for follow-up visits."

I CALLED DR. SAEED's office on August 28, 2002. "I'm following up on scheduling an appointment with Dr. Saeed," I told the fellow who'd told me to make up my mind—twice.

"What insurance do you have?" he asked.

"PHCS," I said.

"We'll have to get precertification from your insurance company. Can I have your card?"

I told him I would pay on my own.

"The doctor's not in today, and Thursday and Friday he's booked."

"I plan to pay by check," I continued.

There was a pause. "A check will be fine, because I don't take credit cards. You know the amount?"

"Yes, you told me $150 for the first appointment."

"And then $100 for follow-up," he said. "You can bring cash or a check.... Next week I have the 3rd or 5th or 6th."

"Tuesday, the 3rd."

"What time?"

"I'm flexible."

"Tuesday is the only day he comes at noontime. He's supposed to come at 12:30 PM." The man suggested 2:30 PM.

"How many patients before me?"

The man counted. "Four. One more patient at two o'clock who is coming for the first time and three old patients. If you have to sit here I guess you will not mind it, because I cannot figure out how much time he is taking with each patient."

> There is one thing I must clarify. I have read in more than one publication that I stopped taking my anti-depressant and/or anti-psychotic medications. This is not true, If you look at my medical records from Dr. Saeed, I was given the anti-depressants Wellbutrin and Effexor and the anti-psychotics of some sort.
>
> First he prescribed Risperdal while I was at Devereux hospital, then he ordered Remeron for about 2 weeks and finally he had me on Haldol. . . . Anyway, I continued to take the medication prescribed when I was discharged home. Then the Friday or Monday before the accident I was taken off the Haldol.[2]

AT 2:07 PM on September 3, 2002, I arrived outside Dr. Saeed's office for my 2:30 appointment. As I gathered my things to go inside and wait, the man I had seen testify at Andrea Yates's murder trial exited his office building. Saeed wore a tan suit, a deep blue shirt, and blue tie with red and yellow detail. He studied papers as he crossed the parking lot. Then he got into a white BMW 525i station wagon with wire wheels and drove off. The car could have used a wash.

When I entered, the waiting room was empty, same as my last visit.

"Is the doctor here?" I asked the receptionist.

"He will be," he answered. "Sign in, please," he said gesturing at a sign-in sheet pressed to a drug company promotional clipboard.

I noticed that three patients had signed in ahead of me, one at 12:15, two at 12:45. All three listed copays of $20 or less in the copay column.

---

2. *Letter of A. Yates to author, postmarked January 6, 2003. Medical records and trial testimony say that on June 4, 2001, Yates was "tapered off [Haldol] over the next three or four days." The drownings occurred two weeks and two days afterward.*

The receptionist gave me a standard patient information form to fill out. I completed it and handed it back. The names of twenty patients were neatly written on the yellow legal pad on the man's desk. The times for their appointments were noon to 6:30 PM that day.

At 2:20, Saeed walked back in. At 2:30 he called my name. Dr. Saeed spent a full hour with me. He was not what I expected.

Saeed knew medical terms and medications, side effects, and dosage levels that many doctors, in my experience, hadn't known. He was not overly eager to prescribe medication.

When he asked my occupation, I explained that I was a freelancer. He nodded. I explained my complaint—that I had trouble settling in to work and was not as productive as I'd like to be. I did not have trouble concentrating once I got into a thing, but I had difficulty at the beginning, that I was more likely to be distracted when I was working alone in a room than at, say, Starbucks. In short, I described conventional behavior for a writer. Maybe I had attention deficit disorder? An adult colleague of mine had been diagnosed with it and I'd recently read an article about it in the *New York Times*. I wondered, could I have it?

Dr. Saeed asked whether I felt the problem required medication or could I deal with it cognitively by making lists and finishing one item before advancing to the next. I said those techniques certainly helped, and I used them. He handed me a questionnaire several pages long designed for children. Many of the questions had to do with grade school and the classroom. Saeed suggested I extrapolate to my adult life and answer the questions as best I could.

After reading my answers, he said he wasn't inclined to prescribe Ritalin in what was a mild case at worst, but suggested trying me on Wellbutrin to see if it helped. Saeed said Wellbutrin was a more modern drug than Ritalin, sometimes used successfully with ADD. It is not in the same family of drugs as Prozac, Paxil, Celexa, and Zoloft. He wrote me a prescription for thirty 100-milligram Wellbutrin tablets to be taken once daily—no refills. I never filled the prescription but I independently confirmed that the dose was appropriate. He suggested not taking the drug after 5:00 PM because it could cause insomnia. He also suggested returning to see him in two weeks and at one month intervals thereafter.

When I left he thanked me for coming. I shook his hand. At the appointment desk I made out a check for $150. I asked the receptionist his name. "The same as the doctor," he said.

"Are you his father?"

"Yes."

AT THE TIME of Andrea's trial, Saeed had already been named in an unrelated wrongful-death suit against Devereux (which was settled in 2003). In April 2002, Andrea Yates's mother and brothers, Brian and Andrew Kennedy, Harris County residents, filed a complaint against Saeed with District Attorney Rosenthal. The complaint alleged that Saeed improperly managed Andrea Yates's medications and discharged her from Devereux while she was delusional. "We feel that Dr. Saeed's actions of excessive, harmful treatment, and his lack of action to warn about the endangerment of the children, made him negligent in his duty to protect the children," the complaint alleged. Senior prosecutors investigated the allegation and found Saeed not criminally responsible in the children's drownings. The statute of limitations for a civil suit against Saeed expired in June 2003. Dr. Saeed did not respond to my requests to interview him concerning his treatment of Andrea Yates for this book. To this day, some staff who worked with Dr. Saeed when Andrea Yates was a patient at Devereux, including Janice Clemens, RN, a former Devereux program director who handled much of Saeed's Devereux correspondence, say he is a good doctor.

THE FIRST TIME I met the Woronieckis in person, I had asked Michael and Rachel how Sarah, 22, and their next two eldest children, vital and engaging young women, planned to navigate the challenging waters of Christian marriage. They confided that there were no appropriate mates for their daughters in today's secular society. Doing the work of Jesus would be their fulfillment. For Sarah, I knew the choice was a conscious one. The Woronieckis did not discuss with me the futures of the boys, the three youngest members of the family.

In August 2002, I received a small manila envelope postmarked Bridgeport, Texas, from Sarah Woroniecki. It contained a typed two-page, single-spaced letter from Sarah describing her family's recent mission to El Salvador. Her letter was a well-written, thoughtful journal sprinkled with personal insights about the nature of self-pity and the manifestation of God's Spirit in her life. She earnestly described her fear for my salvation. There was also a postcard of the Mayan Indians of the Mam tribe in Los Todosanteros, Guatemala, from David and a note on black paper with silver ink from Elizabeth, signed with x's and o's in the shape of hearts.

In a handwritten P.S., Sarah wrote, "I'm also including a little tract I wrote awhile ago. I thought you'd be interested in reading it." The "little tract" was an eighteen-page short story in the O. Henry style, called "Nowhere in America," about a reporter from New York on a deadline. The reporter, a woman, had driven to the Midwest to re-search an article about an impossibly perfect town. The reporter found the town exactly as it had been rumored to be: manicured lawns, clean sidewalks, friendly people, intact families, no poverty, no disharmony. Its single flaw, she discovered, was a man who lived on the outskirts of town, a Woroniecki-like "See-er." The townspeople called him crazy.

The more time the reporter spent with the See-er, the more she began to see cracks in the beauty of the town. Whenever she saw the townspeople while she was in the See-er's company, she was able to see into their true natures, not filled with love but with "hostility, rejection and hatred." As the See-er and the reporter passed a giant mirror for sale on the sidewalk, the reporter glimpsed her own reflection and

gasped with an inner horror. She was hideous. She had known it must be true, but to see it was more than she could bear. She was indeed a horrible monster. One of the worst. With long mangy hair, a turned up nose, and tiny, beady eyes, she couldn't stand the sight of herself. Her hands were scaly and with only four fingers they clenched and unclenched in horror. She stepped out of the See-er's light and looked again. There was the person she had known all her life looking back at her. Where had this . . . this other thing come from? At that, latent memories rose unbidden inside her. Times she had done things she never would have imagined possible. Times she had said things she had not known she was capable of saying. These memories rose as if to give proof of the existence of the monster inside of her.

Sarah's story had a happy ending, echoing its beginning words, but with a couple of twists:

> There's this town I heard of once, located on the border of New York and New Jersey. . . . There's only one flaw in this perfect, little town. A crazy woman lives there. They say she says she sees monsters, when they say at all. . . . By the way, I never did get my story written.

AROUND THE SAME time, a former Woroniecki disciple sent me a 1994 videotape of Sarah's father explaining the responsibilities of parents. Rusty and Andrea Yates owned a copy of the tape and had watched it. Woroniecki told his viewers that ingraining good character in children at an early age was the responsibility of a father and a mother—"a submitted woman who's got the fear of God in her heart for what her Mother Eve has done and her nature is culpable of doing and [knows] that hell is right on the doorstep waiting to bring you in. . . . Jesus said man—all man—is wicked, but Jesus does single out one group—children. He singles out children, and he says, 'And whoever receives one such child in my name receives me. But whoever causes one of these little ones who believe in me to stumble, it is better for him that a heavy millstone be hung around his neck and that he be drowned in the depth of the sea.' " Woroniecki paused.

" 'You mean, Jesus, you're saying to *kill* yourself?' " he asked rhetorically, eyes dead ahead into the camera.

"Yeah," Woroniecki answered. "That's reality."

CHAPTER 16

A Sinister Stew

I s Andrea Yates bipolar?" I asked Margaret G. Spinelli, MD, the world's leading expert on infanticide. "Most new onset postpartum psychosis diagnoses are bipolar unless proven otherwise," Spinelli replied matter-of-factly. Those eleven words formed the most depressing sentence I had heard in the two years I studied the Andrea Yates case. Five children were dead, a million-dollar trial was over, a dozen psychiatric witnesses had spoken, the world had listened. If Spinelli was right, convicted murderer Andrea Yates was in prison, still being treated for the wrong disease.

"George Parnham called me on June 22 or 23," said Spinelli, director of the Maternal Mental Health Program at New York State Psychiatric Institute and assistant professor of psychiatry at Columbia University College of Physicians and Surgeons in New York City. Parnham made a plan to fly to New York to meet with her; they had begun discussing her fees. Of the thirty-five cases in which Spinelli had been employed as an expert psychiatric witness since 1994, all but eight had been settled out of court. Spinelli reviewed Andrea Yates's medical records, but her meeting with Parnham never happened. The day after she and Parnham first spoke, she broke her neck in a car accident in upstate New York. She was forced to cancel her meeting with Parnham, but advised him by phone from her hospital bed, "Just make sure you have someone who won't leave out the neurohormonal stuff." There was forensic evidence that Yates's brain was organically damaged when she killed her children, Spinelli said. But there was no forensic evidence that her damaged brain was capable of cognition—that is, organically *able* to determine her actions were wrong.

I first spoke to Dr. Spinelli in January 2003, just after her $49.95 textbook *Infanticide: Psychosocial and Legal Perspectives on Mothers*

Who Kill was published by American Psychiatric Publishing, Inc. The book includes contributions by sixteen international experts and was awarded the Guttmacher Book Award from the American Psychiatric Association and the American Academy of Forensic Psychiatry.

Bipolar mood disorder, also known as manic depression, is a brain illness that compromises the brain's ability to regulate its own chemical functioning. The disease begins in adolescence or early adulthood (though some cases with adult onset had been documented), affects between 0.5 and 1.6 percent of the total population, and often runs in families.[1] Andrea Yates's brother Brian had been diagnosed as bipolar. The DSM-IV-TR describes a skeletal picture of the disease, whose symptoms include a classic "waxing and waning" between depression (minor or severe) and periods of "mania" that include high energy, elated mood, grandiosity, non-stop activity, little need for sleep, rapid talking, racing thoughts and ideas, delusions, hallucinations, paranoia, fearful thoughts, poor judgment, shopping binges, promiscuity, or illegal behavior.[2] Patients in early stages of the disease are often considered charming, charismatic, and capable.

Research indicates that infanticide frequently is committed by women diagnosed with bipolar mood disorder, major depressive disorder, or major depressive disorder with psychotic features, who often are biochemically pushed into postpartum psychosis by childbirth. Among 120 women admitted for hospital treatment of PPP within ninety days of giving birth, 80 percent suffered from mood disorders. Schizophrenia—Andrea Yates's most recent questionable diagnosis— was the underlying disorder in only 3 percent of the PPP cases. The highest risk for repeat PPP was among women with bipolar mood disorder, at 21.4 percent.[3]

The DSM-IV-TR, too, cautioned about the increased danger. "The

1. *Deborah Sichel, MD, and Jeanne Watson Driscoll, MS, RN, CS,* Women's Moods *(New York: HarperCollins/Quill, 2000).*

2. Diagnostic and Statistical Manual of Mental Disorders, *Fourth Edition, Text Revision, pp. 422–423.*

3. *R.E. Kendell, S. Wainwright, A. Hailey, et al., "The Influence of Childbirth on Psychiatric Morbidity,"* Psychological Medicine *6 (1976):297–302; R.E. Kendell, D. Rennie, J.A. Clarke, et al., "The Social and Obstetric Correlates of Psychiatric Admission in the Puerperium,"* Psychological Medicine *11 (1981):341–350; R.E. Kendell, J.C. Chalmers, and C. Platz. "Epidemiology of Puerperal Psychoses,"* British Journal of Psychiatry *150 (1987):662–673.*

risk of postpartum episodes wih psychotic features is particularly increased for women with prior postpartum mood episodes but is also elevated for those with a prior history of Mood Disorder (especially Bipolar I Disorder). . . . There is also some evidence of increased risk of postpartum psychotic mood episodes among women without a history of Mood Disorders with a family history of Bipolar Disorders."[4]

Talking to Dr. Spinelli was like learning that the world is round. One regretted instantly the valuable hours, days, weeks, years, spent contemplating a four-cornered, flat world.

THE PHYSICIAN SELECTED by Dr. Spinelli to write the textbook chapter on neurohormonal mechanisms is perinatal psychiatrist and clinician Deborah Sichel, MD. Dr. Sichel, a native of South Africa and a former instructor at Harvard University Medical College as well as former director of Hestia Women's Health Center in Wellesley, Massachusetts, was also consulted by George Parnham before Andrea Yates's trial. Sichel had testified as an expert witness only three or four times. She gave a favorable opinion in a Vermont case where a woman who had been found guilty of killing her child had made a motion to be removed from prison to another setting. "There was a very odd outcome," Sichel said. "The judge actually said to me, 'I don't believe much of what you've said.' " Then he ruled in favor of Sichel's opinion and granted the motion.

Dr. Sichel had called Parnham and offered help, no charge. Parnham flew to meet her in her Boston office. They talked for most of one morning and part of an afternoon. Sichel, too, was clear in her opinion about Andrea Yates: "I hate to say this," Sichel said to me, "but this tragedy was completely preventable—and I know that if I had cared for her [Andrea Yates] this would never have happened." It was her view that Yates had *never* been diagnosed or medicated correctly, including up to that very moment in January 2003, as Andrea Yates sat in Rusk Penitentiary.

---

4. Diagnostic and Statistical Manual of Mental Disorders, *Fourth Edition, Text Revision, pp. 422–423.*

"Just listening to a family member's story about the life of his partner easily gives you the diagnosis," Sichel said, referring to *Time* magazine's interview with Rusty Yates. "Because the person is so ill, they are
often unable to articulate what is going on—and so you [the psychia-
trist] miss all the relevant points." Too many psychiatrists use what
Sichel calls "psychiatric jargon" that sick patients, in particular, are
unable to understand. Asking a patient whether she has ever been
manic or hypomanic, for example, struck Sichel as "quite ridiculous.
Most people have no idea what manic is . . . and you will never get an
accurate history using those terms." Sichel believes in talking to as
many family members as possible and forming a mosaic of what a
patient was like from childhood and a timeline of the beginning of the
illness.

When Sichel offered her help, Parnham sent Andrea Yates's videotapes and her complete medical records to her, including her psychiatric treatment at the Harris County Jail, along with descriptions in the
press by friends and family about Andrea as a teenager. Based on these,
Sichel told me, "Andrea's [teenage] diagnosis is bipolar 2, and [it]
changed into bipolar 1, or the classic manic depressive illness that most
of us know about." Bipolar 1 is the most serious form of manic depressive illness. "This means," Sichel explained, "she had clear symptoms of
mood swings with classic periods of depression, alternating with periods of increased activity. . . . This is not an uncommon scenario—it is
not reported in the literature, but we have documented at least twenty-
four cases in which this has happened."

In other words, according to Sichel, though Andrea Yates's periods of depression were classic, her periods of mania were not. Sichel
had noted mania that manifested itself simply as a period of increased
energy relative to the depression. In high school, college, and adulthood, Yates's friends spoke of times when she just "disappeared." "At
those times," Sichel said, "she was depressed, stayed in her room at
home, and contacted no one. When she came out of those periods,
no one asked her where she'd been." Similarly, when she was valedictorian of her school or a competitive swimmer at the highest
citywide level, these accomplishments were simply accepted. Perhaps
her high performance took place during manic periods, Sichel suggested.

"According to her husband," Sichel said, "she once swam around an island. Most of us would say, 'Oh, that's great,' but in the context of Andrea Yates, this was clearly one of her increased energy periods. Her husband describes her as a great mom—which she was. She adored her children—but again, there was evidence she was having mood swings, which sounded like they were getting worse. She took her children's education seriously—took them riding when she was teaching them about horses . . . would get up early in the morning, swim about eighty laps, come home, bake elaborate cakes from scratch, cut up enough oranges and apple pieces for her kids plus the kids in the park, stay up late making costumes for her children and her friends' children. This is not normal behavior—it is over the edge—but unfortunately in this crazy world, when women function like that, it is applauded, not seen as abnormal."

Sichel theorizes that when bipolar 1 patients become depressed after childbirth, a number of biological sequences in the brain, including increased cortisol levels at the end of pregnancy, hormonal changes after delivery, and an acute drop in estrogen among women vulnerable to these changes, trigger a much more serious and dangerous illness with psychotic symptoms, including delusions.

Sichel was absolutely clear that not having more children after Andrea's psychosis following Luke's birth "would not have protected her from getting severely ill again. She had the biology to get very ill, as we see, and it may not always occur related to birth."

"I was very unimpressed with the defense team's so-called experts," Sichel said, "because they put words into her [Andrea Yates's] mouth which she could not explain, and suggested things to her which, again, she was not able to explain. They latched onto the wrong diagnosis [postpartum depression/psychosis], and then changed it halfway though the trial [to schizophrenia], which is a disaster for the defendant, because it just indicates to the jury that the psychiatrists do not know what they are doing."

Sichel's review of Yates's medical records revealed something else to her. "There wasn't one time the issue of bipolar illness came up. What they diagnosed consistently was depression with psychotic features . . . and that is really a different illness [from what she has]. What happens is that they don't realize that this is actually bipolar and they end up treating it with antidepressants [without a mood stabilizer], which worsen the illness."

Though positron emission tomography (PET) scans of schizophrenic and bipolar brains differ from those of normal brains, there are no conclusive tests to distinguish between the two diseases. Brain science hasn't advanced that far. Like a culinary art, the proof is in the pudding. If lithium or the lithium family of drugs works, the patient is bipolar. Successful drug therapy is crucial. Repeated relapses into psychosis cement dangerous pathways in the brain. "Remeron and Effexor . . . we only use those two drugs in a situation when we really know that this is just depression," Sichel said.[5]

Parnham and Odom relied on well-qualified medical professionals and experts in whom they had every reason to trust. The defense did not want to place a fourth diagnosis, bipolar—in addition to PPP, major depression with psychotic features, and schizophrenia/schizoaffective disorder—before the jury and risk confusing or alienating jurors.

Could a woman who had been as depressed as Andrea drown her five children in less than an hour? "No one knows for sure," Sichel said. "But perhaps [taking] a combination of those two medications [Remeron and Effexor] which we call 'rocket fuel,' because—they shock somebody out of depression but have a capacity to make them manic— they [patients] end up having strength that is mind-boggling. . . . I've seen a manic patient pull a radiator out of a cement wall. They can pick up cupboards. They can pick up desks and throw them across the room. So it's not inconceivable that she was able to do this in that space of time. . . . The children's struggling would have been useless."

Stephen M. Stahl, MD, chairman of the Neuroscience Education Institute and professor of psychiatry at the University of California at San Diego, coined the term "California rocket fuel" in his book *Essential Psychopharmacology of Depression and Bipolar Disorder.*[6] Dr. Stahl notes that the combination of Remeron and Effexor is a "powerful antidepressant combination" for depression, but can activate bipolar disorder or psychosis in some patients. "It could be like putting gaso-

5. *Email of Deborah Sichel to author, December 2002.*

6. *Stahl, Stephen M.*, Essential Psychopharmacology of Depression and Bipolar Disorder *(New York: Cambridge University Press, 2000).*

line on a fire. . . . It doesn't happen all the time, so some people actually do this erroneously over and over again and don't get burned . . .
when you do see it, it can be catastrophic—like this . . . it's a medical
mystery that's completely solvable."

Sichel's diagnosis was not surprising to some of the experts who testified at trial. "Unfortunately, with disorders like schizophrenia, schizoaffective disorder, and bipolar disorder," Dr. Puryear said, "if somebody
showed up in the emergency room sick, all of those three diagnoses
would look exactly the same on any given day. So you look at them and
you put them in a category and the category would be psychotic. And
then you try to figure out which of the psychotic disorders best fits
this person. And that's based on [patient] history. There's a lot of
thought that schizophrenia, schizoaffective disorder, and bipolar disorder are on a continuum. With schizophrenia, psychosis would be the
predominant symptom. With bipolar disorder, mood symptoms would
be predominant, but you could also be psychotic at times. Schizoaffective disorder is in the middle—you have psychosis and mood symptoms
about the same amount of time.

"If somebody was holding a fire to my feet and said pick a diagnosis
[today], I'd probably pick schizoaffective," Dr. Puryear said, moving
away from her trial diagnosis of schizophrenia in consideration of
Yates's recent stability on lithium. "One, because the psychosis she had
was much more than you usually see in bipolar disorder," she said. And
two, "schizoaffective disorder is both a psychotic illness and a mood illness. The treatment is an antipsychotic and a drug like lithium." The
same drug combination is used to treat a bipolar patient experiencing a
psychotic episode.

Dr. Resnick had given the diagnosis of schizoaffective disorder at
trial. "I'm not strongly wedded to the diagnosis," he said later. "Lithium
is the appropriate treatment for either disease." He readily pointed out
his specialty is forensic psychiatry, not psychopharmacology. But his
opinion is that if Andrea Yates remains free of psychosis for at least two
years on lithium alone, her diagnosis would be "pure" bipolar, rather
than schizoaffective disorder. "He hedged" on Yates's diagnosis, Resnick said of Dr. Park Dietz, his sometime colleague and adversary in
the Yates case. Dr. Dietz's opinion at trial was that technically either
schizophrenia or schizoaffective disorder were appropriate diagnoses

for Yates's mental illness. Dr. Dietz declined to be interviewed for this book without the opportunity to review the manuscript so that he could comment prior to publication on any passages that mention him.

Dr. Puryear agrees that "any antidepressant such as Effexor and Remeron given to somebody with a bipolar disorder—if you're not also giving them a mood stabilizer—can flip them into mania." Like Dr. Sichel, Puryear believes that Wellbutrin is the antidepressant least likely to trigger mania in bipolar patients.

"I think about Andrea sometimes and get incredibly sad," Dr. Puryear said. "But the thing that comes out of this that's redeeming is an opportunity to educate and make change. It [the Yates tragedy] has advanced the cause of women's mental health forward by fifty years." Houston benefactors have established a $50,000 Yates Children Memorial Fund (YCMF), devoted to women's mental health education, under the auspices of the Mental Health Association of Greater Houston. House Bill 341, known as the "Andrea Yates Bill," authored by Representative Carlos Uresti, was enacted into Texas law on September 1, 2003. The law requires health care professionals treating pregnant and postpartum women to inform patients of a range of related mental illnesses. Dr. Puryear's self-help book on mental health during pregnancy and postpartum includes a chapter on Andrea Yates and is scheduled for publication in late 2004.

IN HER JULY 2, 2001, *Newsweek* column, Anna Quindlen hit a collective nerve, "Every mother I've asked about the Yates case has the same reaction. She's appalled; she's aghast. And then she gets this look. And the look says that at some forbidden level she understands." Cynthia Schroer and another mother, a Harvard-trained lawyer who suffered emotional difficulty following a complicated childbirth, do not blame Rusty Yates when I talk about the inevitability of his divorcing his imprisoned wife.

The two women discussed Schroer's delusional thinking in psychosis. During her "break" with reality, many people took on the form of the goddess Psyche, Schroer said. In Greek mythology, Psyche's test was to say no to whoever reached out to her. During her two-week hospitalization, Schroer remembered a woman in withdrawal from heroin on a gurney reaching out to her. Schroer said no. Another woman pressed her face against the single window in the door to her hospital room. She was being watched. Schroer remembered being in her hospital room in a locked ward when a cleaning woman came in to empty the trash. "I'd like to have a vacation from my babies, too," the woman muttered to her.

Schroer told the head nurse that there had been a woman emptying trash in her room. The nurse said it was routine.

"It really happened?" Schroer's friend asked.

"Yes."

"Are you sure?"

"I don't know," Schroer admitted. When she thought about it, what difference did it make? When she was psychotic, what was real was no different from what was not. During one brief visit to a community room during her hospitalization, she remembered seeing a television news report about a Mexican priest smuggling guns from Texas into Mexico. She thought she recognized the priest. That fact? Real. The priest was someone she had known.

It had taken a friend who had suffered with mental illness to teach Schroer's husband that his wife needed to be in a hospital. After her own experiences, Schroer had no problem understanding how the family members of Andrea Yates's, through lack of knowledge or denial, did not recognize her illness. When she recovered from the psychosis she experienced postpartum, Schroer went back to graduate school and got a master's degree. She organized postpartum support and education groups in five hospitals. Only one had shunned the program out of fear of liability for participants who might harm themselves or others.

ANDREA YATES'S CASE is not without precedent in New York, a Model Penal Code state. On May 30, 1990, 36-year-old Maria Amaya used a kitchen knife to slit the throats of her four children, ages 3 to 11 years, as they slept. She then drank lye and slit her throat in a failed suicide attempt. Amaya had a history of mental illness and had failed to meet her husband at her psychiatrist's appointment that day. He returned home to find his wife cradling one of their dead children on a blood-soaked bed.

Amaya spent two years in the County Medical Center prison ward, then in a maximum security state hospital, undergoing esophageal reconstruction and psychiatric care. In 1992, she was found fit to stand trial. According to three-term Westchester District Attorney Jeanine Pirro, psychiatrists for the defense and the prosecution agreed that Amaya was mentally ill. Her not guilty plea was accepted by the prosecution and the court and she spent two additional years in court-ordered psychiatric treatment at the lower-security Rockland Psychiatric Center in Orangeburg. By May 1994, psychiatric reports described her as a model patient who took her medication, functioned well, worked in the Center's kitchen, was appropriately saddened by what she had done to her children, and recognized that she would never again live with a man or have children.

On June 14, 1999, New York State Supreme Court Justice Alfred Weiner ordered Amaya to attend a mental health outpatient program for five years, living on-site at the Rockland Psychiatric Center in a dormitory-style residence for recovering mentally ill patients. The non-profit Rockland Hospital Guild affiliate, Community Link Up Experience, provided round-the-clock supervision for her. Both the *New York Law Journal* and Westchester *Journal News* reported, "Today, she [Amaya] is free to work and enjoy other activities."[7] Six days before the third anniversary of the Yates killings, on June 20, 2004, Amaya's term will be up. A judge will order her to continue in her current setting or release her into part-time, less-structured supervision. Community reaction to her potential partial release is mixed. District Attorney Pirro herself prefers the Texas law to New York law, thinks the insanity defense should be eliminated, and plans to oppose Amaya's release.

"THE EASIEST THING to do is say, Listen, she's a product of this crazy religion, she's got a major mental illness, she's as pure as the driven snow, she's absolutely wonderful, poor kid," psychiatrist Paul McHugh said from his Baltimore office. The case had gotten under his

---

7. *Pollet, Susan L. "Courts Address Mothers Who Kill,"* New York Law Journal, *May 31, 2002; Caren Halbfinger, "Local Slayings, Yates Case in Stark Contrast,"* Journal News, *March 17, 2002, p. 1A.*

skin. "Maybe it's all right for someone with two X chromosomes to kill her children, but it's not all right for someone with an X and a Y," he said. "It is still an evil act. . . . We as a population should do what we can to make it clear how appalled we are by this behavior and ultimately treat this woman and decide what further should be done." For twenty-six years McHugh was the head of the Psychiatry Department at Johns Hopkins Medical School. Author Tom Wolfe credited McHugh with jolting him out of a post–heart bypass depression and dedicated his second novel, *A Man in Full,* to him.

It "often happens, a person says to me, 'Dr. McHugh, I was arrested while driving while intoxicated. Go to the courts and tell the judge I'm an alcoholic and therefore shouldn't be punished.' I *want* people to be arrested and punished for driving while intoxicated—whether they are alcoholics or not. I'm prepared to treat some of them, but the behavior itself deserves reprobation.

"Forensic psychiatry has worked this out very well," McHugh said. "The McNaughton rules, which have been around since the 1800s, hold that an insane person is one who doesn't know the nature and quality of her acts and doesn't know they are wrong. That's the standard—the psychiatric judgment—that entitles Andrea Yates to the insanity defense.

"There's an aspect of *her* mind that got her to do that evil thing," McHugh continued. "It is a 'distorted will' that she had—distorted by her mental life." Psychiatrists call the mind's ability to do this the "pathoplastic" feature of psychosis. That is, "I can have a hallucination about my mother, but I can't have one about your mother," McHugh said.

"We psychiatrists never say, 'If she had been a member of my church or read my poem she would never have done that.' . . . People use whatever atmosphere they grow up in to do whatever they're going to do. There's something wrong with us, not anything else.

"To the simple question, Can psychotic people find the energy to do vile things, particularly things to their relatives, the answer is yes," McHugh said. "The idea of believing that you've contaminated your children is not uncommon amongst patients with serious psychotic depression. . . . It's a terrible and evil act, but crazy people have done equally evil things . . . like hold onto two kids and jump off high buildings.

"After the fact, is she somebody you want to let be around children again?" McHugh asked. "No. Can we predict these things? Nobody really knows. She didn't seem to be a danger before." Was that the bottom line? "Probably not," McHugh said, "but that's something else, not psychiatry."

McHugh believes that mentally ill offenders should receive the best medical care available. "What should be done about her behavior and what consequences should be paid for that behavior, I think, is something we all struggle with . . . the idea of what would be appropriate reprobation—psychiatrists aren't a great help. . . . I don't think 'hanging them high' [the death penalty] is an appropriate solution."

Joe Owmby, too, had given the insanity defense some thought. "I don't know what the right answer is," he says. "This is a decision that people like to put off on the judicial system. . . . *You* guys [citizens] have got to tell us, we're going to follow the laws that exist as they are right now. If there's something different that we should be doing, you're going to have to tell us. . . . The debate is going to get worse, because psychology is moving ever closer to . . . claiming the ability to attach an organic cause to every instance of violence . . . very close to arguing there is no free will."

Many societies distinguish between infanticide and other violent crime. More than 22 nations use forms of The British Infanticide Act of 1922 (amended in 1938) which requires mothers who demonstrate postpartum mental "disturbance" to be charged with manslaughter, not murder. Instead of prison sentences, the majority of women convicted of infanticide receive sentences of probation with required counseling. Carving out a class of crime related to female biology was literally a step foreign to Americans. It tread perilously close to the national debate on abortion.[8]

Texas Attorney General Greg Abbott, a former Harris County District Court Judge, went on the record with this carefully worded statement: "Justice is about both deterrence and punishment, balanced in a legal system that ensures fairness for both the accused and victims of crime. Our system of justice must protect the safety and security of society as a whole by ensuring swift and certain punishment for wrongful

---

8. *Ibid.*, p. 9.

conduct while working to rehabilitate those who have committed crimes."

THE SHINY RAZOR wire that runs along the top of the twelve-foot-high fences between guard towers at Rusk Penitentiary looks better than the razor wire between some of the classiest apartment buildings on upper Fifth Avenue in New York. Guards joke that it isn't very sharp—occasionally prisoners scramble over it unscathed. Their stories may be apocryphal, but on Highway 45 leading north to Dallas, there is a state road sign that cautions: Prison Area Do Not Pick Up Hitchhikers.

> Description of my "house" (really, that's what they call these cells and they'll ask you where do you live, and that will be house #312). Size 7 or 8 x 7 or 8 square—cinderblocks with cream colored paint, concrete gray floor with various amounts of lint and "snow bunnies."[9]

Andrea Yates's cell has two long, narrow windows with a view of the yard and Rusk's Building 5. She has a steel sink and toilet. Her mother lectures her to buy Dial soap from the prison store for her face instead of using lye soap, which causes her to break out.

> Twin bed, smarty pants![10]

She has three shelves to store things and, like the other inmates, is allowed one netted grapefruit bag as well. One day prison guards collected her things and filled five bags full. When she told her husband, he shook his head because he remembered the stuffed drawers in their Beachcomber house.

> Dx: Pack-rat-ism.[11]

---

9. *Letter of A. Yates to author, May 14, 2003.*
10. *Ibid.*
11. *Ibid.*

CHAPTER 17

Eternity

Wendell Odom wondered: Could he do it? Was he lawyer enough—writer enough—to craft an appeal that wouldn't somehow screw up Andrea Yates's chances when her case eventually went before the Supreme Court of the United States? To the detriment of the client. Never do anything to the detriment of the client. The words law school had drilled into him in a hundred different ways, a hundred different times, went through his head.

A difference in opinion had developed between Parnham and Odom. Parnham believed Odom's sluggishness about committing to write the appeal once the transcript was complete was attributable to his doing the work pro bono. Odom worked for money; he'd always been upfront about that. But to Odom, the issues were time and Andrea Yates's best legal interests. Odom hadn't worked with his partner on the Clara Harris case. Dr. Harris, a dentist, received a twenty-year sentence for killing her husband by running over him three times with her Mercedes. For a brief time, before Harris was transferred to Gatesville maximum security prison, Yates and Harris had been in the same unit at Rusk Penitentiary. The standing joke was, "What do Andrea Yates and Clara Harris have in common?" Answer: "Post-Parnham depression."

Parnham was hanging on to Yates for reasons Odom didn't fully understand. Parnham had never quite made it into the top ranks of Houston defense attorneys. His failure puzzled colleagues who had. He'd famously won an insanity case in Texas in 1992—ironically, against Rosenthal, then an ADA. But years earlier, he'd missed grabbing the brass ring when he represented Melvin Dummar, a man who claimed he had billionaire Howard Hughes's authentic last will and testament. On the night before the verdict, Parnham turned down a settlement offer rumored to be worth $6 million (Parnham denies specifics of the offer and its proffer). The will was determined to be a fake. Not only might Parnham have squandered a big win and a small fortune but his name was, however briefly, associated with Dummar.

On September 26, 2002, when the *Houston Press* published its "2002 Best of Houston" awards, who was named Best Lawyer? George Parnham. "Along with defense cocounsel Wendell Odom Jr., Parnham brought a soothing calm into the chaos," the citation read. "His matter-of-fact demeanor, wisdom and insight combined for a textbook performance of professionalism under intense fire. . . . With the world watching and weighing the local caliber of justice in this worst of crimes, Parnham carried away a rare sense of quiet dignity for both the defendant and the system."[1]

Whether trial lawyers Parnham and Odom had the resources and experience to write an argument involving major constitutional issues in 120 days, the max they could expect with extensions, had little to do with any newspaper award. There were other lawyers—such as David Sterling, with the powerhouse firm of Baker Botts behind him, or Mike Tigar, an American University Washington College of Law professor— who did. Their names on a legal brief might be as persuasive to jurists as Andrea Yates's name was infamous to the public.

Parnham was loyal to Yates. He visited her in prison, wrote to her, lifted her spirits. He gave away legal time for which other lawyers would have billed. In late April 2002, Andrea Yates signed over the life rights to her story to George Parnham, creating an uproar that reached to the Texas Attorney General's office in Austin. Houston's Victims Assistance Center saw the transfer of rights as a possible end run around Texas law, which prohibits convicts from making money from their crimes. The statute is identical to the "Son of Sam" law, named for the case of a 1977 New York serial killer, which the U.S. Supreme Court struck down in 1991. Parnham said any proceeds would be used to

---

1. Houston Press, *September 26–October 2, 2002, p. 34.*

cover Yates's legal expenses and to provide funding for the Yates Children Memorial Fund for Women's Mental Health Education (YCMF), administered by the Mental Health Association of Greater Houston at 2211 Norfolk, Houston, TX 77098.

Parnham had made no secret of looking for commercial projects that might pay for the trial transcript and fund an appeal of his client's conviction. He said he consulted the State Bar of Texas before accepting the rights assignment and was satisfied that the action was legal and ethical. Parnham and *People* correspondent Gabrielle Cosgriff circulated a book proposal promising access to Parnham's personal stash of defense documents. His story didn't sell to New York publishers. Later, Parnham signed a book option agreement with field producer Jenna Jackson of CBS's *48 Hours*. Jackson and Dan Rather planned a book with a foreword by Rather and a documentary-style television interview of Andrea Yates.

> Mr. Parnham came to see me on Monday. . . . He is doing a book with Dan Rather and some writer. I hope it reflects the truth.[2]

According to Rusty Yates, by December 2002, Parnham had given preliminary consideration not only to Dan Rather but also to Mike Wallace of *60 Minutes* and to NBC's Katie Couric for a coveted, prison interview with Andrea. But Andrea herself nixed any potential interview.

> I don't want to appear to be seeking fame because of the tragedy.[3]

RUSTY YATES BLINKS less than most people. He has a hard time looking people in the eye. "I always have," he said. "I'm not worried that they'll see good in me—you can see a person's soul when you see their eyes—it's kind of like touching someone or invading their privacy."

He is unblinking in a figurative way as well. He rarely ducks tough questions or uncomfortable situations. He might rock back and forth

---

2. *Letter of A. Yates to R. Yates, postmarked November 14, 2002.*
3. *Letter of A. Yates to author, postmarked January 6, 2003.*

on his feet or physically inch away when someone stands too close. But he is forthright and even-tempered. He says what he has to say and moves on.

During the trial, he'd successfully maintained the position that Andrea would be found innocent. He had fantasies of having more children with her after she was successfully treated in a mental health facility and released on the proper medication. He worked his way through various fixes for their damaged lives, such as surrogate motherhood and adoption (horrifying Andrea's family, attorneys, and Houston psychiatrists) before giving in to reality.

In two years, he'd become familiar with courtrooms, prisons, national publicity, and the fact of being hated by people who didn't know him. "I knew I couldn't handle it if Andrea was found guilty," he told a friend, "but I did. I keep waking up every morning and I seem to be putting one foot in front of the other."

By the time I met Yates for dinner at a Rice Center restaurant six weeks after the trial, he'd begun to reflect on the legal realities. "That full range of punishment Chuck Rosenthal talked about was 'life' or 'death,'" he said, indignant. The press in general, and the *Houston Chronicle* in particular, just "didn't think. . . . They tell people what they want to hear, not what they need to hear." He hadn't lost everything over a period of years, as it had once seemed. He'd lost it in an irretrievable instant. "It was like I came up to the house and the weather was maybe a little cloudy," he said, "and suddenly my wife and five kids were struck by lightning, and I was still standing there. The only one left. All the bad happened that one day and there was no way to turn back the clock." He struggled to find words to describe his feelings.

All he wanted to do now was "make things as right as possible." He was doing that with a website he'd established in memory of his children, yateskids.org. The website has received more than 800,000 hits since November 10, 2001. He received seven thousand emails before he stopped counting. Seventy-five percent of them were positive, many from people struggling to understand. About the other 25 percent he said, "I have a theory, my 'Virtual Mob Theory.' In a charged situation where 'the mob' is acting on bad facts and wants a quick remedy, the leaders come from hate radio and hate TV. It's like a modern-day lynching—'Let's string up that husband of hers.'

"Here's a simple perspective," he said. "It's called the Constitution. Judge Hill gave power to the state to silence anyone they wanted, by simply threatening anyone who talked to the press with going to jail. The Constitution doesn't guarantee a right to a 'fair' trial, it guarantees a right to a 'public' trial. The defendant requested to have the trial televised. How many times is that denied?

"The way I look at Andrea is as a child that I've lost custody of to a mother [the penal system] I don't like or trust," he said, his knee bobbing under the checkered tablecloth.

Yates is allowed two two-hour visits per month with his wife at Rusk Penitentiary, one noncontact visit behind a thick Plexiglas window over a telephone-type intercom and one contact visit in a small room near the prison's entrance, where he can give his wife a hug or hold her hand. He always brings her a Snickers bar and a Dr Pepper—she likes the combination of their tastes. Andrea's mother, family, and Debbie and Bob Holmes visit on alternating weekends. Her mother-in-law, Dora Yates, visited Andrea for the first time on July 20, 2003.

In the months of his first visits to Rusk, Rusty's contact visits ended with a parting hug and a reflexive, "Let's go home now." To which Andrea answered, "Okay, take me home." They smiled, but mostly hurt.

Andrea still believes that one's time on earth is short, and then she will be together with her kids and Rusty again in eternity. Some days she can believe that her husband has forgiven her. That her brain is sick. That she can be redeemed even after the horrible acts she committed and for which she believes she should be punished. Other days she denies her illness. On those days she believes she has to die and go to hell before her children will be allowed into heaven.

On Saturday, August 31, 2002, I began a series of trips to the penitentiary with Rusty Yates. We met that morning for the three-hour-plus drive from Houston to the East Texas town of Rusk, stopping at Catfish King for lunch.

Rusty spoke of his recent conversations with Andrea about her delusions. "I mean," he said, "we say it's a delusion, but to her it's a memory. . . . She was talking about the kids and she was saying she didn't think the kids were developing properly. I mean, she *still* did think that. I asked her, 'Did you think that before you were sick?' She said no. And I said, 'That tells you something.' "

He worried that his wife couldn't identify these false memories. He envisioned her dropping them "in a bucket with a 'not real' tag on it. 'These things weren't real. These things were your sickness.' " No one was working with her to sort those things out, he said. "That's not good. She needs to be able to separate those things out to help her recover." In prison, she receives one group therapy session with a counselor per week. A psychiatrist visits every other week to adjust her medications.

When he'd asked her back then if she wanted to go back to work part time, she'd answered, "I'm a mother now." Looking back, he wished he'd made the decision for her. "More of a separate identity apart from being a mother would have been good. I don't know if that would have prevented what happened. She still would have gotten sick. But it might have been good for her—for everyone."

Andrea has high standards for herself, he said, and feels a lot of guilt when she doesn't meet those standards. Michael Woroniecki's "Live as we do or perish" mentality hadn't been good for her. "If I had it to do all over again, I think I've learned a lot from Michael Woroniecki and gotten a lot, it's helped me a lot—but I think I probably would never have introduced him to Andrea. . . . The downside for Andrea was too great. She grew up with that same sense of shame and same high standards, and I think that hurt her. What she needs is somebody who can work on the most positive encouraging sides and say, 'Andrea, you're a great mother. Look at your beautiful children. They're so fortunate to have you as a mother'—not 'If you screw up, you might as well have a millstone hung around your neck and be thrown into the sea.' She's looking at that [scripture] as if one of the kids took a candy bar in the checkout line at the grocery store, she's ready for hell."

He recalled Andrea's telling him about her father teaching her how to parallel park. "She had to park like a hundred times. It was over and over and over and over again. And it was never, 'Nice job, Andrea. Good job, Andrea. Do it again. Do it again. Do it again.' And the way she put it, she said, 'He took the joy out of everything.' You have the no-nonsense mom from Nazi Germany and the strict Catholic father, and you're the fifth [child], kind of the forgotten baby, in a way." Because of the large age gap between her and her siblings, he said Andrea used to think her conception had been an accident.

I waited in the visitors' center during his two-hour visit with Andrea and then listened to him on the drive back to Houston. There was a marked change in his mood. "She's doing pretty good," he said. "She made a facial gesture."

Rusty had moved to a gated rental apartment. He had given their dog Blackie to a family with a large acreage. He had told Andrea a story about Blackie redeeming herself after a dog fight by scaring off a water moccasin that threatened to bite her new owner's child. "Andrea got a kick out of that. She just laughed. She seemed better today than from the last visit. . . . I asked her if she was having any problems with her thinking. She seemed coherent. But what's tough is to see her more like her old self. You know? That's tough for me."

Every time the Andrea he had known resurfaced, he wanted her back. Which brought up "the black cloud" issue, as he called it. "You can't protect your family from a psychotic person. You just can't. We could take a walk one day and she could throw herself in front of a truck going down the street." She could poison him or burn the house down. She'd done it to him before, hurt him more than anyone could ever hurt him, with no warning of what she had been contemplating. Even if her appeal were to succeed and she got out of prison, what assurance did he have that she would tell him—or even recognize—if her thoughts began to go awry again?

"I have always loved her," Yates said. "I will continue to love her. And care for her." But the future? That was a difficult hurdle even for Rusty Yates.

WHEN I AGAIN accompanied Yates to Rusk on September 28, 2002, he worried that as Andrea's mental health improved her grief might jeopardize her life.

"In pretty much every respect, she's had it harder than I have. I mean, she's been isolated from all the media and attacks, where I've been in the middle of it. We both lost our children, but it was by her hand. We lost each other, but she's in prison and I'm free. We both dealt with serious mental illness, but it was she who was sick. We both went through this ordeal of the trial, but she was the one on trial. Across the board, it's been harder for her. She's more private than I am and everything in our life has been displayed in front of the world. That's just one more thing she has to deal with.

"I tend to judge people by what their heart is in the matter—what their intentions are. Andrea looks at *what* happened. I don't think she needs forgiveness because her heart was never bad. Whereas what she did was so horrible, *she* will never be able to forgive herself.

"But just because there's this horrible tragedy doesn't mean somebody has to hang for it, you know? It is a tragedy. Let's take appropriate action, and let's learn from it. That's all I'm asking.

"But people can't get past what happened. 'Oh, you don't care about the kids because you don't want Andrea to be punished,' they say. That's absolutely not true. I love the children. I desperately miss them. And I don't blame Andrea."

We stopped for lunch at Barnhill's Mesquite Grill. Rusty's face has become so familiar from television and newspaper photos that fellow diners now frequently give him a friendly hello, thinking he is someone they know.

We pulled up to the prison gate at 12:55 PM. Rusk is bucolic. The tiny shingled guard shack allowed vehicles in and out of the prison grounds. The guard's dog lazed in the sun as his owner listened to KOUI 106.5 FM radio. The vast, freshly mowed lawns that surrounded the Skyview Units were green even in the Texas heat. Monarch butterflies flitted past.

The visiting rooms for the no-contact, two-hour visit Rusty was entitled to with his wife that day were occupied until 2:20 PM. With visiting hours ending at 5:00, he was anxious that he wouldn't get his full two hours with Andrea. We sat at a table in the Skyview/Hodge Units' Texas Department of Criminal Justice Family Visitor's Center putting together a Hasbro jigsaw puzzle. It was a still life of a vase of daisies next to a red water pump against a forest background. The dozens of prisoners' friends and relatives who had passed through the homey, white frame house at the prison's entry gate had assembled the easy puzzle pieces. The couple of hundred pieces left were impossible: solid black with no color clue to where they belonged. For ten minutes I placed and replaced pieces without success.

Across the table from me, Rusty's gaze settled over the puzzle, his chin resting on his folded hands. Several more minutes passed before he picked up a single puzzle piece and, remarkably to me, put it in its place. Rusty Yates solves puzzles by looking at them. He memorizes the shape where a missing piece belongs, then surveys the unplaced puzzle pieces and knows by sight when there is a fit.

RUSTY CONTINUED TO struggle with the "black cloud" issue. He had taken off his wedding band while assembling an IKEA wall unit for the study in his new apartment. "It didn't feel right to put it back on," he said. He was now a member of Clear Lake Church of Christ's singles group. After two years without his wife, his loneliness had driven him to discuss their future, including his temptation to adultery.[4] As much as Andrea now wanted her husband to be happy, she also wanted to be his wife until death parted them. Rusty wished he could have it both ways: a new wife who could share his life, and Andrea, the only person who shared his loss. He still needed her. Since her imprisonment in March 2002 he had never missed a visit. He especially cherished contact visits, where no artificial barriers intruded on their conversation. One of his fears about divorcing Andrea was that he would no longer be legally part of her family and would lose his contact visits with her.

Not wanting to upset her when he visited, he meant to put the ring back on but forgot. He knew she noticed. "She kind of stared at my hand," he said. "It was a contact visit and we were holding hands." Neither mentioned the missing ring. Her ring was stowed away with the belongings taken from her in Harris County Jail. Even while hospitalized and psychotic she had refused to take it off until the criminal justice system intervened.

"It kind of hurt me [not wearing the ring], this time," he said afterward. "We had a good conversation, but I remember Andrea saying something about the fact that we'd be married ten years in April [2003]. And it'll be ten years and that ten years may never come. That's what's sad. Because on the one hand she seemed kind of excited and on

---

4. *Letter of Bob Holmes to author, September 7, 2002.*

the other hand she's saying, Well . . . she'd like to see me have a family . . . see me happy. It's really hard for both of us. For both of us there was never ever any kind of question like that. We were going to be married the rest of our lives. . . . That's what makes it so hard. Makes it such an impossible situation."

> Maybe sometimes I do wear rose-colored glasses regarding my husband. . . . Sometimes I doubt his sincerity regarding his "belief" that "this would not have happened had you not been sick." He says it in a mechanical way. I'll ask him what was I like when I was sick? "Oh, like you usually are, just quieter."[5]

"This counselor I see was talking about how she counsels people, and invariably when they're angry about something, she'll ask them, 'Well, what are you afraid of?' And then she'll bring them around, and there's like an underlying fear to our anger. I never really made that association before. But it makes perfect sense, because when I've seen how angry people have gotten, it gets back to . . . the little security blanket that we have that says our life is in our control. If we act responsibly, then nothing bad will happen to us. If we're careful, we'll be safe. If we're good, nothing bad will happen to us. . . . The fact that Andrea's mind became so sick that she did something like this . . . we identify very closely with our mind, our own person. If our mind can become so sick that we could do something that is contrary to what we would ordinarily do, or do something this horrible—that's scary.

"Andrea and I have always gotten along. We never fight. And we love each other. We enjoy our time together and all. I would say, in that respect [sexuality], we're probably different. She kind of seems ashamed of her body in a way. And you never know if that's how she was brought up or what, but it's like she seems almost seeing her body like being shameful and sex is kind of that way. It's almost like enjoying that would be guilty—painful somehow. For me, it's like I always thought of it [sex] being a part of our relationship. It's an important part. To enjoy each other and pay respect to that part of our relation-

---

5. *Letter of A. Yates to Bob Holmes, August 5, 2003.*

ship. Probably our needs were different. We came to a kind of middle ground, so you live with it—if that makes sense."

Did Rusty know whether Andrea had had negative sexual experiences in her childhood or past? "Personally, I kind of questioned it all. Inside the church, it wouldn't at all surprise me if there was something going on. But I can't—I don't know."

By October 20, 2002, Andrea's prison psychiatrist had tapered her off her antipsychotic medication, Haldol. He began increasing her dose of the antidepressant Effexor in anticipation of the holidays. Andrea's letters to Rusty and to her friends Debbie and Bob Holmes had begun to ramble. She sent real estate listings and classified ads from the Lufkin, Texas, newspaper describing how wonderful it would be for them to move nearer to her. She told Debbie that she wanted her to be the one to pick her up when she got out of prison. She imagined the three things she would do that day: visit the children's graves, eat a slice of pizza, and swim.

Rusty says when I swim, I am more graceful in the water than on land.[6]

Rusty Yates visited his wife in prison on his routine visiting days, Saturday, December 21, 2002, and January 4, 2003. Andrea "worried him a little," especially on January 4. He thought she was manic. She'd written him two letters totaling twenty handwritten pages. A Jehovah's Witness was teaching a Sunday morning Bible study at the prison on—of all the books of the Bible—Revelation. "Revelation!" Rusty exclaimed. "Not the Scripture for people in her state to work on. . . . Her whole world has fallen down around her, and she's headed down some areas she shouldn't go down. I'm not surprised she's manic." He had come to recognize three topics on which his wife was easily set adrift: religion, politics, and prison reform.

On January 6, 2003, Yates called his wife's prison psychiatrist—"only the second time I've called"—and discussed his concerns. By then, the psychiatrist, Dr. W. Lee McNabb, had raised Andrea's dos-

---

6. *Letter of A. Yates to author, May 14, 2003.*

age of Effexor to 300 milligrams daily, the same dose she had been given when she was taken off Haldol and killed her children. McNabb was considering prescribing mood-stabilizing medication from the lithium/Depakote family of drugs, consistent with bipolar disease, for the first time in her medical history. He hadn't done it yet.

In mid-January Andrea returned to the same level of psychosis as when she drowned her children. Though he came to understand that his wife was bipolar, it hurt Rusty to consider that some of the things he most admired about Andrea also defined her illness.

She lost her prison privileges. Through good behavior, she had worked her way up to mopping floors and laundering uniforms, grateful to be busy six or seven hours of the day. Now she was back to spending twenty-three hours a day alone in her cell. The pattern would repeat itself eight months later, in September 2003, when Andrea began refusing food, liquids, and medications and slipped once again into psychosis—shortly after she stepped into a bathtub for the first time in over two years.

> I got baptized this week. . . . Another woman and I were escorted to the Hodge Chapel. When we entered, I saw the baptismal <u>tub</u> and as I got dressed to enter the water, I started crying (you know the last time I saw a tub and you can imagine how self-conscious I felt surrounded by 6–7 grim faced officers). Well, at first I felt bad, but later I figured the Lord realized my tears were of sorrow.[7]

"Her biggest problem is denial," Rusty said after his January 25, 2003, visit with her. "She doesn't believe she was sick. She just thought she felt good."

"You don't think I'm sick, do you?" he said she asked him.

"Well, yeah, I do," he said. "Do you?"

"Well, maybe," she said. She smiled and waved her arms overhead in self-parody. "Manic is good."

Once again, she was prescribed Haldol. It took many months for her to find her way back to the level of clarity she had before the re-

---

7. *Letter of A. Yates to author, September 12, 2003.*

lapse into psychosis. Letter writing became difficult, her vision was blurred, mild dyskinesia returned.

> Where in the world is the month of February? Where is it? Look
> under your couch or that pile of clothes. . . . I have lost the entire
> month.[8]

During her recovery, McNabb prescribed lithium for the first time in her four-year-long illness. It worked.

> Recently I have been diagnosed as bipolar and the doctor started me
> back on Haldol, Cogentin, Effexor and Lithium. I seem to be stable.[9]

AT 8:45 AM on Saturday, February 1, 2003, Rusty Yates answered the phone in his apartment near NASA. "There's this thing happening on TV right now," he said. "I'm trying to . . . are you watching? The *Columbia* is exploding."

I switched on my television set. Nearly seventeen years to the day of the 1986 *Challenger* crash, the Space Shuttle *Columbia*, destined for a 9 AM landing at Kennedy Space Center in Florida, roared through the East Texas sky in thousands of pieces. "It's the flight with the Israeli astronaut," Yates said. "They've been up there sixteen days. . . . I'm just trying to figure out whether I need to get in to work. I'm not really responsible for any of the systems on the orbiter except a TV system, and that wouldn't cause it. It's basically a glider at this point. If you came in early or wrong during reentry, there's not much you can do."

Sheriff Thomas Kerss of Nacogdoches, Texas, appeared on the television screen. He anticipated a deadly debris field encompassing all one thousand square miles of his county. He warned viewers that some shuttle debris might be surrounded by a toxic brown fog that kills its victims within forty-eight hours by sealing their lung linings.

Rusty decided to go to work. "They [NASA] lost communication [with the orbiter]. If they need me to help, I want to be there." Then he

---

8. *Letter of A. Yates to author, March 8, 2003.*
9. *Letter of A. Yates to C. Schroer, June 29, 2003.*

wavered. He didn't want to miss the visit with Andrea he was scheduled to make that day, a nine-hour round trip that included two hours of visiting time. He compromised. After driving to NASA and confirming that none of his systems were involved in the disaster, he picked me up at the parking lot of Fingers Furniture Store on Southwest Freeway. From there, we drove northeast toward Rusk, ground zero of the *Columbia* disaster. A Pinnacle 2 white golf ball rolled around inside the dashboard cup holder.

WORDS THAT FORMED a familiar verbal collage streamed over the SUV's radio: "We are suffering for the events that happened this morning . . . when we lose family members it is devastating to us . . . mustn't rush to judgment . . . a period of mourning was necessary . . . a period of getting together helping each other, supporting each other . . . not many scenarios that could lead to this kind of tragedy . . . a terrible and instant tragedy . . . no reason to foresee this would happen . . . some horrible malfunction with rocket fuel . . . would probably like to turn back the clock . . ." The phrases were similar to ones spoken by Rusty Yates on the days after his children's murders. How could he function, people wondered? Why had he seemed so oddly composed? For more than eighteen years his job at NASA had been avoiding disasters and cleaning up after those he couldn't prevent. The post-*Challenger* days had been the worst years of his career, he said. When Andrea had gotten sick in 1999, he was still tired from *Challenger's* aftermath.

Rusty Yates had dealt with his family tragedy in the way NASA dealt with company tragedy. Within an hour of his children's deaths, NASA extended him privileges accorded families of fallen heroes. A grief counselor was dispatched to Beachcomber Lane, the same grief counselor who later treated family members of the *Columbia's* lost astronauts. But the language used to describe astronauts killed while exploring space didn't fit the circumstance of five children killed by their mother. Perhaps this was one reason Yates seemed to attract less than his share of sympathy.

"Safe today, alive tomorrow" was not necessarily true, Yates said he had learned at NASA and at home. "There's a 1-in-1,000 chance of getting postpartum psychosis," he said. "It *can* happen to you. Period. Victims are among the [mathematical] set of people who don't think it will happen to them. So look out, because you're next."

We drove on. Yates's thoughts ricocheted between his personal life and the ongoing crisis. "The one department that's responsible for the orbiter is headed by my boss," he said. "I feel for him." During the time the *Columbia* astronauts had been in space, another colleague had reviewed anomalies in flight data that fortunately were harmless. As with the *Challenger* disaster, Yates said, he and his coworkers had to "find out what happened, fix it, and move on." We watched the road for shuttle parts and brown fog.

He wondered over the shuttle program's future. "I'd love to fly," he said. "Most of the stuff we do is 3 in 10,000. If those were the odds, I'd probably do it." In the orbiter, he told me, the odds of dying are 1 in 400.

"If I gave you a 1-in-400 chance in an orbiter, would you do it?" he asked.

"Yes, definitely," I said, "if space travel was what I had a passion to do."

"I wouldn't," Rusty said. "One in 400 is too risky. Would you do it for a hundred million dollars?"—roughly one-fifth of the cost of an orbiter flight. He wasn't convinced that I comprehended the odds against my safe return. I nodded yes. "How about if I gave you a gun, and I put a bullet in one of four hundred chambers and spun it, and I told you to put the gun to your head and pull the trigger. Would you do it then?"

"Probably," I said, as we passed Land's End RV Park, Second-Chance Mobile Homes, Repo Depot, and VFW Post 8568.

Yates quickly calculated the odds equivalent of a 99.9 percent survival rate. "One in 10,000 would do it for me," he said.

Pieces of the *Columbia* fell on the metal roof of Rusk Penitentiary that day. From the room where he and Andrea visited, Rusty saw the familiar orange marker flags placed by shuttle recovery teams. He tried pointing them out to her, but she couldn't see them. She explained that she'd "gotten a little rough" with her ten-year-old designer eyeglasses and was awaiting a standard prison-issue "Drew Carey pair."[10]

---

10. Letter of A. Yates to author, March 8, 2003.

The weekend Rusty visited during the Columbia tragedy, he had to tell me. He pointed out two places in the yard where Space Shuttle debris had fallen. It was so sad. . . . But the program will go on.[11]

ON THE DRIVE back to Houston, Rusty Yates's Alpine car stereo resonated with mainstream heavy metal: Nirvana's "Mary, Mary . . . everything is my fault," a song of apology; Judas Priest's "Breaking the Law," whose siren sound never failed to make Rusty's mom believe her son was getting a speeding ticket; Soundgarden's "Black Hole Sun," System of a Down's "Chop Suey!," with its lyrics about "when angels deserve to die."

In the months to come, Rusty spent seven weeks in a Kennedy Space Center airplane hangar fitting pieces of the *Columbia* back together using the same skill he had used assembling Guild puzzle 550. The largest single piece of shuttle NASA recovered was the size of a tabletop.

We drove a while longer through the darkness.

"I wonder if there is a capacity of grief?" Yates asked. "You can only handle so much?"

ON A SUMMER weekend in 2003, Rusty Yates and fifteen volunteers from Clear Lake Church of Christ, where Andrea Yates's name had been on the prayer list since the tragedy, made a final assault on the renovation of 942 Beachcomber. The large white dress box containing Andrea's wedding gown, the one Rusty had promised to remarry her in on their twentieth anniversary, had disappeared from the middle of the living room floor. So had the fragile china teacups and saucers, and the intricate cross-stitch needlework Andrea had done. Rusty put them in a climate-controlled storage unit, along with keepsakes he'd saved of the children. The church group hauled off water-stained carpeting and spackled the walls for painting. A general contractor replaced the plumbing fixtures in both bathrooms. An interior decorator who belonged to the parish had selected paint colors and fixtures.

---

11. *Ibid.*

Yates had sold the Chevy Suburban that conjured up memories of the silly faces he made at his kids through the side window every time he gassed up. The van was so impregnated with the children's scents that Mrs. Kennedy's German shepherd, Senta, came running expectantly whenever Rusty drove up. Yates had chosen a silver 2003 Subaru Forester as the SUV's replacement.

Some things hadn't changed. The infamous Woroniecki coach still sat on fifty-one cubic yards of concrete that Rusty had poured to make a driveway strong enough to hold it. In time, Rusty would donate the bus to charity—if he could ever get it started. Mrs. Kennedy still brooded over whether her money had gone to a driveway instead of a houseful of furniture and new appliances for her successful and cherished youngest child. The wooden bicycle rack Rusty had built stood at the head of the driveway, blocked from view by the bus. Five small bicycles and tassle-handled tricycles of graduated size were still parked there, ready for children to drive them off amid noisy challenges and near collisions.

At the end of the day, Rusty Yates hired a handyman to smash to pieces the white porcelain bathtub in which his children had died.

"PEOPLE ARE ACTUALLY telling us what is driving them to do what they're doing. But we don't accept it," said Patrick Kennedy, a California oil-terminal storage manager and the brother to whom Andrea described herself as closest spiritually.

"Who told Andrea . . . that her children were going to go to hell? She knew that their sins and all of our sins are paid for already, I talked to her for months, years, before that [the drownings]. And somehow she was convinced that those children were not saved. . . . What in the world convinced her, all of a sudden, that Jesus didn't die on the cross for all her sins? That she had to take it upon herself to bring salvation to those children? She knew better than that, but something convinced her that that wasn't the case.

"I don't want to sound like a religious fanatic or whatever, but I do read Scripture almost every night and I believe in everything the Lord says through Scripture, and to me it's not going to stand up in court or anything, but even after she got treated, she still saw these things. She told me that. . . .

"We believe everything in Scripture but the demonic possession part. . . . [T]hat's my opinion. People are probably going to think I'm nuts, but when you look at the horrific impact these illnesses—if that's what you want to call them—have on children, to me that's what Satan wants. He wants to see children harmed, he wants to see families broken up, that's what he's getting out of this. I have a hard time understanding why that would have happened to Andrea, but I'm not going to lean on my own understanding for that. All I can do is pray for her."

TWO YEARS TO the hour that her daughter drowned her five grandchildren, Jutta Karin Kennedy took a white rag out of the plastic grocery bag she'd brought from her home, dampened it with water, and polished the gray granite marker on their graves. She cleaned the monument, etched with the images of Mary, Luke, Paul, John, and Noah, every week.

The day was 90 degrees and sunny, same as it had been the past two June 20s. Senta—named for the female protagonist in *The Flying Dutchman*—romped on the easement sloping toward a narrow creek. Senta was the last Christmas gift Andrea had given her parents before the unthinkable, unmentionable, unprocessable *it* had happened. "She [Senta] goes everywhere with me. She's the only child I have now," Mrs. Kennedy reflected. Of course, her son Brian still lived with her. Together with Andrew, the oldest, named for his dad, he was at that moment varnishing kitchen cabinets at their home near the corner of Glenview and Bliss.

> Mom wrote she met you at the cemetery. And Rusty said he saw you and Mom. . . . Mom tends to the gravesite; picking up stray grass, wiping the headstone.[12]

Rusty Yates had been given seven graves—six together and another in an adjacent plot. Andrea had repeatedly asked that she be buried next to the children. That way, at the Last Judgment, when everyone

---

12. *Letter of A. Yates to author, June 13, 2003.*

was resurrected body and soul, she could see her children again. Rusty told her whichever of them died first would be buried in the plot with the children. Or he'd take the adjacent spot, especially if he ever got remarried.

I sat with Mrs. Kennedy on a stone bench under the nearest shade tree, talking. She was 74 and looked years younger than she had during her daughter's trial. I asked her if she ever felt guilty. There was a long pause. "Sometimes," she said.

She noticed her son-in-law drive up some distance to our left. He got out of his car and approached his children's graves alone. Senta ran off to greet him. Without seeing Mrs. Kennedy, Rusty didn't recognize Senta and looked about for the owner of the dog. Eventually he walked toward us. I wondered how Mrs. Kennedy explained her son-in-law's sticking with her daughter through the murders of their children, a costly trial, and public ridicule. How two years later he continued visiting her every other weekend.

"You want to know the truth?" she asked.

"Yes."

"I think he's waiting for you to finish the book."

Though his relationship with Mrs. Kennedy and her family had become strained by the Kennedy family's criticism, Rusty Yates stood and talked for twenty minutes, offering to show us one of fifteen color photocopies Andrea had requested he make and mail to her. The copies were of an 8-by-10 self-portrait done in crayon. In the drawing, Andrea is smiling broadly and wears a delicate crucifix around her neck. Rusty wondered whether she'd done it from memory, as there are no mirrors or jewelry in prison.

The doctor's been weaning me off of Haldol, so the effects of the "anniversary" were more profound.[13]

Since her mother first brought Andrea photographs of her children in Harris County Jail, she'd been asking for more. Recently, she'd asked for family videos. Rusty made a tape and sent it to her prison therapist

---

13. *Ibid.*

for consideration. "I hope they let her see it," he said. "When I watched it after the tragedy, twelve armed guards couldn't have pried me away."

He wasn't as certain about having more children as he once had been. "You kind of don't want to think of replacing your children," he said. He didn't know what to do about his divorce either. Maybe there would be a solution neither he nor anyone but God could foresee.

> This is an inspirational verse: "For I know the plans I have for you," declares the Lord, "plans to prosper you and not to harm you, plans to give you hope and a future [Jeremiah 24:11–13]."
>
> Sincerely,
>
> Andrea[14]

---

14. *Ibid.*

ACKNOWLEDGMENTS

"Are You There Alone?" would not have been possible—as shopworn as that expression may be—without the support of Jan Cobler and her late mother, Rita Cobler, who founded Cobler's bookstores of Houston and was a patron of authors during her lifetime and after. The editing and encouragement of Mary Pat O'Malley; Carolyn Keck; Katie Bolton; and Sharon Powers were invaluable; as were the suggestions of Ellen Brockman (my consigliore); Amanda Vaill (who told me to write chronologically); Tom Stewart (who told me to organize by chapter); Tom Wolfe (who told me to write a short book); Charles Warner (who told me to write); Susan Calhoun and Charlie Moss (who saw me through various endings, including the one to this book); Julia Bradford; Jesse Kornbluth; Karen Collins; Harriet Higgins; Kathryn Hammell; Michael Gross; Elise O'Shaughnessy; Bobbie Seril; Priscilla Rattazzi; Sandi Mendelson; Dr. and Mrs. Lawrence Inra; Catherine Fedeli, MD, PhD; Jane Salmon, MD; Susan Levine, MD; Murk-Hein Heinemann, MD; Joan and John Jakobson; Suzanne Jones Maas; and Peggy Cooper Cafritz; each of whom made unique contributions.

Special regards are owed to the insightful and daring Amy Gross, editor-in-chief of *O, the Oprah Magazine,* and editor-at-large, Gayle King, who joined in my enthusiasm for shedding light on the darkness of the Yates trial, with the support of editors Dawn Raffel, Sudie Redmond, Derryale Barnes, and, of course, Oprah Winfrey, whose name opens both doors and minds.

At NBC, I am indebted to network news director Neal Shapiro (again and again) and to executive producer David Corvo (*Dateline*

NBC), along with Joe Delmonico, Keith Morrison, Bette Brady, Luce Villareal, Dawn Fratangelo, and Mike Kosner; at the *New York Times Magazine,* to editor Catherine Saint Louis; at *Salon.com,* to my editor Jennifer Sweeney.

My heartfelt gratitude to the great Alice Mayhew whose vision propelled this book into reality, whose laserlike editing made the book better, and who welcomed me into the pantheon of authors privileged to be published by her. Many, many thanks to associate editor Emily Takoudes and the remarkable Emily Remes, Esq., as well as to publisher David Rosenthal, who gave this book its title and his support. To the best of the best: Victoria Meyer, Aileen Boyle, and Elizabeth Hayes in publicity; Isolde Sauer, copyediting supervisor, and her team—Judith Hoover, Betty Harris, Jane Herman, Suzanne Anderson, Adrian C. James, Joel Van Liew, Christopher Carbone, Chris Carruth, and John Wahler; Jackie Seow, who art-directed the book cover; managing editor Irene Kheradi; and unflappable fact-checker Valerie Wright.

I am grateful to my longtime agent, Mort Janklow, who continues to call me "kiddo," for his wisdom and clarity. Along with the most erudite literary agent anywhere, Tina Bennett, he guided this book to its proper home. Thanks also to Svetlana Katz, Maria Gallagher, Jeff Popish, and Bennett Ashley.

Continuing thanks to the colleagues with whom I covered the Andrea Yates trial: author Suzy Spencer, a woman of personal and professional integrity; Bruce Nichols; Shara Fryer; Jim Yardley; Thom Marshall; Carol Christian; Lisa Teachey; Pam Easton; Tim Roche; Gabrielle Cosgriff; Jenna Jackson; Steven Long; Marilyn Cutler; and Cynthia Hunt.

My "life of crime" might never have materialized without the peerless Ed Kosner and editor Clare McHugh, who sent me to cover my first trial as a contributing editor of *New York* magazine. Thanks are due to writer, lawyer, and producer Michael Chernuchin who, along with Rene Balcer, hired me to write my first script for *Law & Order* on the recommendation of an equally superb writer—David Black. I owe a great deal to three writing partners and producers, Ed Zuckerman, Jeremy Littman, Steve Smith, as well as to *Law & Order* creator, Dick Wolf. Not to be forgotten are *Texas Monthly* publisher Michael Levy and founding editor William Broyles, who published my first piece of investigative journalism, nor Amanda Urban—for when we were both fledglings.

I am indebted emotionally, artistically, and materially to: PEN; The Actors' Fund; The St. Bernard's School; The Yale Club of New York library; Mark Sine; John Waechter; Adam Pattantyus; Justine, Magdalene, and Adrian Pattantyus; Marianna Reges; Sheila White Berry; Marcella Robbins; Meg Bolton; my forty-six first cousins; and to Mary Elizabeth O'Malley and Scott Martin Burnett who were married on September 27, 2003. Also special thanks to Sam Moss of Wheaton College radio station WCCS 96.5 FM, for his musical expertise.

In Texas, I thank particularly: Peter Roussel, who "introduced me to world leaders" and calmed me; Kathi "the vault" Mosbacher; Mimi Swartz; Katherine Miller, Esq.; Bob Loman, Esq.; Betty Osborne, Esq.; Greg Bolton; the law firm of King & Pennington LLP, especially Charles Guy King III, Kris Casey, and Paul Brauer; Craig Muessig, Esq.; Jim "Mac" McIngvale; Leigh Benton-Wells; Nancy Ouzoonian; Olga Pineda; and Starbucks #6360.

I could not have undertaken or persevered in this project without the inspiration, love, and material support of my family. My mother, Irma O'Malley, supplied me with advice, encouragement, and an invaluable sense of the context of this story. She has given me everything she has (including her stubbornness and fierce independence, which I didn't ask for), as well as everything she ever wanted for herself. My late father, Donald L. O'Malley, taught me, by his example, to exceed my fears. He gave me the great gift of telling me that if I never accomplished another thing in life, I had already exceeded his wildest expectations.

Much gratitude is due the indomitable Stiles family, especially Mary Beth Stiles O'Malley, RN, and her husband, my brother James O'Malley, artist and musician—my jester and life witness—and to their children, Bridget Jayne and Neil "Bear" O'Malley. A very large thank-you to my son, Zack O'Malley Greenburg, whose choices and inspiration—editorial and otherwise—help make my writing possible. And thanks to the person who convinced me to write this book—you know who you are.

I couldn't have written *"Are You There Alone?"* without the cooperation of the many people who appear in its pages. I am indebted to the individuals, families, friends, attorneys, spouses, physicians, academics, clergy, seers, health-care givers, and public servants who generously gave their words into my care.

Finally, I offer my deepest gratitude to the memory of Noah Yates, John Yates, Paul Yates, Luke Yates, and Mary Yates, upon whose lives and deaths I have briefly intruded.

INTERVIEW LIST

Asterisked names indicate sources whose testimony author witnessed in court proceedings.

Andrea Pia Kennedy Yates
Russell "Rusty" Edison Yates*
Dora Yates*
Jutta Karin Kennedy*
Brian Kennedy
Andrew Kennedy
Patrick Kennedy*

Honorable Greg Abbott, Attorney General, State of Texas
Terry L. Arnold, Home Education Partnership of Texas*
Deborah Bell
Erlinda Bernal
Greg Bolton, communications director, Service Corporation
    International
Edward Brandt III, Esq.
Steve Brill, Esq.
Harold J. Bursztajn, MD, associate clinical professor of psychiatry at
    Harvard Medical School and law professor
Rich Cebelak, world history teacher
Janice Clemens, RN, former Devereux program director
Ted Cruz, Solicitor General, State of Texas
Dick DeGuerin, Esq.

David de la Isla
Herb Deromedi, football coach
Scott Durfee, General Counsel for Harris County
Lana Dunlap, Andrea Yates's high school swim coach
Lisa Dye, monument maker, Dye Granite Corporation
Sissy Farenthold, Esq.
Jim Faulkner, staff attorney, Harris County Sheriff's Department
Melissa Ferguson, MD, Harris County Jail psychiatrist*
Byron Fike, pastor, Clear Lake Church of Christ
Mary Haisten, Information Officer, Harris County Police Department
Genevieve Hearon, Capacity for Justice
Deborah Holmes*
Robert Holmes*
Stephen Johnson, next-door neighbor
Roy Jordan
Joanne E. Juren, Home Education Partnership of Texas
Kathryn M. Kase, Esq.
Fred King, Harris County Communications Coordinator
Laboris Lacour, competency hearing juror
Steven Long, journalist
Molly Maguire-Stephano*
Robert Malek, swim team member
Edward Mallet, attorney for Russell Yates
Tim Maxey
Marie McAuley, former Eurovan owner
Paul McHugh, MD
Bob Misner, religion teacher
Molly Odom, Esq.
Wendell Odom Jr., Esq.
Burl Osborne, Chairman of the Board, Associated Press
Debra Osterman, MD, Harris County Jail psychiatrist*
John O'Sullivan, Esq.
Joseph Owmby, Assistant District Attorney
George Parnham, Esq.*
John Parry, Esq., Executive Director of the ABA Commission on
　　　Mental Health and Physical Disability Law
Don Peddie, football coach

Michael Perlin, JD, Professor of Law, New York Law School

Jeanine Pirro, District Attorney, Westchester County, New York

Lucy Puryear, MD (for the defense)*

Phillip Resnick, MD (for the defense)*

George Ringholz, MD (for the defense)*

Brian Rose, Assistant General Counsel for Harris County

Charles A. Rosenthal, Jr., District Attorney

Melissa Ryan

Jim Shaack, wrestling coach

Cynthia Schroer, MA

Debra Sichel, MD

Dave Smith, Vice President, Deputy Managing Editor, *The Dallas Morning News*

Studie Smith

Suzy Spencer, author

Margaret Spinelli, MD

Stephen M. Stahl, MD

Eileen Starbranch, MD*

Sergeant David Svahn*

Jill Swinney

Jack Thompson, District Courts Coordinator

James P. Thompson, PhD*

John Treadgold, Houston KPRC, NBC affiliate

Janet Warner, District Courts Coordinator

Kaylynn Williford, Assistant District Attorney

Dick Wolf, producer, *Law & Order*

Abraham Woroniecki

David Woroniecki

Elizabeth Woroniecki

Joshua Woroniecki

Michael Woroniecki

Rachel Woroniecki

Ruth Woroniecki

Sarah Woroniecki

Kimberly Yonkers, MD

Nick Zeckets, student, University of Arizona, *Arizona Daily Wildcat*

Ellen Allbritton, MD
John Bayliss, RN
Beverly C. Bedard
Reverend Fairy Caroland
Deputy John Carrier
Mary Alice Conroy, PhD
Park Dietz, MD
    (for the prosecution)
James Flack, MD
Jean Garcia
Gerald Harris, MD
Gary Johnson
Harold Jordan, investigator
Officer Robert King
Officer David Knapp
Joe Lovelace
Lauren Marangell, MD
Sergeant Eric Mehl

Patricia J. Moore, DO
Sylvia Morris
Harminder S. Narula, MD
Steven Rosenblatt, MD
Steven Rubenzer, MD
Mohammad Saeed, MD
Jesus Sanchez, MD
Deputy Sawyer
Sergeant Boyd Smith[1]
Deputy Michael Stephens
Doreen Stubblefield
Sergeant Frank M. Stumpo
Marlene Burda Wark
Officer Glenn West
Earlene Wilcott
Harry Wilson, MD
Randall "Randy" Yates

---

1. *Sergeant Boyd Smith committed suicide by shooting himself with his service revolver at his desk at Harris County Police Headquarters on the afternoon of October 29, 2001.*

ORGANIZATIONS THAT CAN PROVIDE MORE INFORMATION

For information on, or to make donations to, the Yates Children Memorial Fund for Women's Mental Health Education (YCMF) write to:

YCMF
c/o Mental Health Association of Greater Houston
2211 Norfolk, Suite 810
Houston, TX 77098
Phone: 713-523-8963
Website: http://www.mhahouston.org/
Select "women's health" option.

Postpartum Resource Center of Texas
Toll-free hotline: 877-472-1002
Website: http://www.texaspostpartum.org/

For national and international assistance contact:
Postpartum Support International (PSI)
927 North Kellogg Avenue
Santa Barbara, CA 93111
Website: http://www.postpartum.net/

INDEX

ABOUT THE AUTHOR

Suzanne O'Malley's investigative reports on the Yates trial appeared in the *New York Times Magazine; O, the Oprah Magazine;* and on *Dateline NBC.* She has written for the *New York Times Book Review, Esquire, Harper's Bazaar, Salon.com,* and *Texas Monthly,* and has been a producer and consultant for NBC and MSNBC. She is a Phi Beta Kappa graduate of the University of Texas at Austin. She lives in New York City and Houston.